INTERCEDING FOR THE NATIONS

100 Sermon Outlines on Missional Prayer

DENZIL R. MILLER
EDITOR

A DECADE OF PENTECOST PUBLICATION

Interceding for the Nations: 100 Sermon Outlines on Missional Prayer.
© 2018, AIA Publications. All rights reserved. No part of this book may be reproduced, stored in a retrieval system, or transmitted in any form or by any means—electronic, mechanical, photocopy, recording, or otherwise—without prior written permission of the copyright owner, except brief quotations used in connection with reviews in magazines or newspapers.

All Scripture quotations in this book, unless otherwise indicated, are from the Holy Bible, New International Version. Copyright © 1973, 1978, 1984 by International Bible Society. All rights reserves.

Scripture citations noted ESV are taken from The Holy Bible, English Standard Version®, Copyright © 2001 by Crossway, a publishing ministry of Good News Publishers. All rights reserved.

Scripture citations noted KJV are taken from the Authorized (King James) Version. All rights reserved.

Scripture citations noted NKJV are taken from the New King James Version®. Copyright © 1982 by Thomas Nelson. All rights reserved

Scriptures citations noted NLT are taken from The Holy Bible, New Living Translation, Copyright© 1996, 2004, 2007 by Tyndale House Foundation. Used by permission. All rights reserved.

Scripture citations noted NASB are taken from the NEW AMERICAN STANDARD BIBLE®, copyright© 1960, 1962, 1963, 1968, 1971, 1972, 1973, 1975, 1977, 1995 by The Lockman Foundation. Used by permission

Library of Congress Cataloging-in-Publication Data
Miller, Denzil R., 1946–
Interceding for the Nations: 100 Sermon Outlines on Missional Prayer / Denzil R. Miller

ISBN: 978-0-9997032-2-9

1. Prayer   2. Bible   3. Practical Theology   4. Homiletics   5. Missions

Printed in the United States of America
AIA Publications, Springfield, MO, USA
© 2018

Websites:
   www.DecadeofPentecost.org
   www.ActsinAfrica.org

Table of Contents

Table of Contents 3
Books of the Bible 7
Other Abbreviations Used in Book 8
Contributor Index 9
Introduction 13
How to Use This Book 16

Section 1: Prayer Basics 19
1   Prayer Basics 20
2   When You Pray 22
3   When You Fast 24
4   Praying God's Way 26
5   The Mystery of Prayer 28
6   The Sin of Not Praying 30
7   Our Part in Prayer 32
8   God's Part in Prayer 34
9   Kingdom Praying 36
10 Working with God in Prayer 38
11 Abiding in Jesus 40
12 Five Powerful Prayer Insights 42
13 A Key to Effective Prayer 44
14 When Women Pray 46
15 Turn Aside and Hear the Voice of God 48
16 End-Time Praying 50

Section 2: The Power of Prayer 53
17 Power Praying 54
18 Pray! Pray! Pray! 56
19 Prayer Unlimited 58

20	Mighty Prevailing Prayer	60
21	Hannah's Mighty Prayer	62
22	The Power of United Prayer 1	64
23	The Power of United Prayer 2	66
24	The Power of United Prayer 3	68
25	Prayer That Brings Down the Spirit	70
26	The Cry That Stops God	72
27	How to Pray Effectively	74
28	The Prayer of Elijah	76
29	Expanding Your Prayer Life	78

Section 3: Commitment to Prayer 81

30	They Devoted Themselves to Prayer	82
31	Praying with Jesus for Believers	90
35	A Plan for Action	92
36	Persistence in Prayer	94
37	Devoted to Prayer	96
38	Seven Obstacles to Answered Prayer	98
39	Wrestling with God in Prayer	100

Section 4: Intercessory Prayer Warfare 103

40	Interceding for the Nations	104
41	Elijah Does Spiritual Warfare	106
42	Intercessory Prayer in the Spirit	108
43	Prayer Strategies for Spiritual Warriors	110
44	Intercessory Prayer and Church Growth	112
45	Interceding with Paul	114
46	God's Call to Intercessory Prayer	116
47	This Matter of Intercessory Prayer	118
48	A Serious Battle	120
49	Fighting the Good Fight of Faith	122

Section 5: The Holy Spirit and Prayer 125

50	Asking for the Holy Spirit	126
51	Praying Down Pentecost	128
52	After They Had Prayed	130
53	Praying and Hearing God's Voice	132
54	From Groaning to Glory	134
55	The Spirit Helps Us Pray	136
56	Eight Compelling Reasons	138
57	Prayer and the Baptism in the Holy Spirit	140
58	Acts 1:8 Praying	142
59	The Overlooked Piece of Armor	144
60	Lord, Stretch Out Your Hand!	146
61	Spirit-Anointed Prayer	148

Section 6: Praying for the Church and Revival 151

62	Revival Praying	152
63	Praying Your Church to Its Full Potential	154
64	Praying for Spiritual Leaders	156
65	Prayer That Makes the Mission of God Unstoppable	158
66	Jesus' Missional Prayer for Believers	160
67	Praying for New Believers (Part 1)	162
68	Praying for New Believers (Part 2)	164
69	Overcoming Threats in Mission	166

Section 7: Praying for Missionaries and Missions 169

70	A House of Prayer for All Nations	170
71	Ask the Lord of the Harvest	172
72	Foundations for Missional Prayer	174
73	A Soulwinner's Prayer	176
74	Pray the Lord of the Harvest	178
75	Praying Effectively for God's Mission	180

76	Praying for the Salvation of Souls and Workers in the Harvest	182
77	Prayer and God's Mission	184
78	Praying for the Lost	186
79	Advance God's Kingdom Through Prayer	188
80	Prayer and Mission Connection	190
81	How to Pray for Your Missionaries	192
82	Opening Prayers	194
83	Prayer and the Missionary Task	196
84	The Mercy Prayer	198
85	A Prayer for the Nations	200
86	How to Pray for the Lost	202
87	Pray for the Harvest	204
88	Interceding for Our Hometown	206

Section 8: Prayer Guides 209

89	Three Essential Missionary Prayers	210
90	A Prayer Guide for Africa	212
91	Praying for the Harvest	214
92	Ways to Pray for Missions	216
93	Praying the Nations Out of Darkness	218
94	You Can Be a Prayer Missionary	220
95	Praying with Jesus for Believers	222
96	A Prayer Guide for New Church Plants	224
97	Acts 1:8 Conference Prayer Guide: Day 1	226
98	Acts 1:8 Conference Prayer Guide: Day 2	228
99	Acts 1:8 Conference Prayer Guide: Day 3	230
100	Acts 1:8 Conference Prayer Guide: Day 4	232

Scripture Text Index 235

Other Decade of Pentecost Books 239

Books of the Bible

Old Testament

Genesis	Ge
Exodus	Ex
Leviticus	Le
Numbers	Nu
Deuteronomy	Dt
Joshua	Jos
Judges	Jdg
Ruth	Ru
1 Samuel	1Sa
2 Samuel	2Sa
1 Kings	1Ki
2 Kings	2Ki
1 Chronicles	1Ch
2 Chronicles	2Ch
Ezra	Ezr
Nehemiah	Ne
Esther	Es
Job	Job
Psalms	Ps
Proverbs	Pr
Ecclesiastes	Ec
Song of Solomon	So
Isaiah	Is
Jeremiah	Je
Lamentations	La
Ezekiel	Eze
Daniel	Da
Hosea	Ho
Joel	Jl
Amos	Am
Obadiah	Ob
Jonah	Jnh
Micah	Mic
Nahum	Na
Habakkuk	Hab
Zephaniah	Zep
Haggai	Hg
Zechariah	Zec
Malachi	Mal

New Testament

Matthew	Mt
Mark	Mk
Luke	Lk
John	Jn
Acts	Ac
Romans	Ro
1 Corinthians	1Co
2 Corinthians	2Co
Galatians	Ga
Ephesians	Ep
Philippians	Phi
Colossians	Col
1 Thessalonians	1Th
2 Thessalonians	2Th
1 Timothy	1Ti
2 Timothy	2Ti
Titus	Tit
Philemon	Phm
Hebrews	He
James	Ja
1 Peter	1Pe
2 Peter	2Pe
1 John	1Jn
2 John	2Jn
3 John	3Jn
Jude	Jd
Revelation	Re

Other Abbreviations Used in Book

AG	Assemblies of God
AGWM	Assemblies of God World Missions
cf.	confer or compare
e.g.	for example
etc.	et cetera, and so forth
f	and the verse following
ff	and the verses following
i.e.	in other words
Illus:	Illustration
NT	New Testament
OT	Old Testament
v.	verse
vv.	verses
w/	with

Contributor Index

BALR	Be Arthur Lala Rijamamy	President, Assemblies of God Madagascar (77)
BB	Bob Braswell	AGWM Missionary, Africa (57)
CK	Claver Kabandana	General Superintendent, Pentecostal Assemblies of God, Rwanda (53)
CO	Chidi Okoroafor	General Superintendent, Assemblies of God Nigeria (18, 34)
DB	Dick Brogden	Strategic Leader, Live-Dead Arab World (11, 84)
DM	Daniel Mbiwan	General Superintendent, Full Gospel Mission, Cameroon (65)
DRM	Denzil R. Miller	Director, Acts in Africa Initiative, Springfield, Missouri, USA (1, 2, 3, 6, 10, 16, 17, 19, 21, 51, 52, 55, 56, 57, 58, 60, 62, 70, 71, 73, 85, 86, 88, 89, 90, 94, 96)
DCS	Donald C. Stamps	General Editor, *Full Life Study Bible* (31, 95).
DS	Dan Saglimbeni	AGWM Missionary, Africa (78)
EC	Edward Chitsonga	President, Malawi Assemblies of God (72)
EG	Edwin Gbelly	General Superintendent, Liberia Assemblies of God (93)
EYA	Emile Yaovi Adote	President, Benin Assemblies of God (13)
EKA	Emmanuel Kwasi Amoafo	Attached Clergy, Anglican Church of Kenya, Parish of Christ Church, Nairobi (44)
GB	Greg Beggs	Regional Director, AGWM-Africa (41)

GL	Gordon Lindsay	Revivalist, author, and founder of Christ for the Nations Institute, 1906-1973 (35)
JDE	Jimmy D. Easter	Assemblies of God minister. Texas, USA (12)
JL[(1)]	Jared Lee	Publications Coordinator, Africa's Hope (29)
JL[(2)]	Jimmie Lemons	AIA Team Member; Francophone Coordinator, Pan Africa Theological Seminary (4)
JM	John Maxwell	Author, Founder and Director of EQUIP and the John Maxwell Company (63, 64).
JMT	Jean-Marie Tiacoh	General Secretary, Assemblies of God, Côte d'Ivoire (49, 69)
JN	Jerome Ndayisaba	General Superintendent, Burundi Assemblies of God Fellowship (75)
JSa	Jephté Sawadogo	Treasurer General of the Assemblies of God of Burkina Faso; Director of the Koubri Bible School (26, 38)
JSp	Jerry Spain	AGWM Missionary, Former East Africa Area Director (48)
JVY	John V. York	Founder and Director of Africa's Hope (1990-2005) (33)
LB	LeRoy Bartel	Dean, College of Bible and Church Ministries, Southwestern Assemblies of God University (2004-2016) (54)
LP	Lemuel Perry	Assemblies of God minister, USA (74)
MG	Mark Gardner	AGWM Missionary, Africa (15)
MHA	Moussa Hamani Ali	President, Niger Assemblies of God (27, 28)
MO	Michel Ouedraogo	President, Burkina Faso Assemblies of God (76)

MRT	Mark R. Turney	Associate Director, Acts in Africa Initiative; Principal, West Africa Advanced School of Theology (81)
NS	Nadine Sandoz	Assemblies of God minister, Nebraska, USA (37, 61, 79, 80, 87)
PFM	Paul Frimpong-Manso	General Superintendent, Assemblies of God Ghana (22, 23, 24)
PW	Peter Watt	General Superintendent, Assemblies of God, South Africa (82, 83)
PY	Paul York	National Missions Trainer, Chi Alpha, USA (10)
QMc	Quentin McGhee	Assemblies of God World Missionary, Developer, Faith & Action Series (66, 67, 68)
SD	Sandra Drake	Former AGWM Missionary to Ghana and Tanzania, founding director of the AG National Prayer Center (46. 47)
SM	Sandy Miller	Administrator, Acts in Africa Initiative (14)
SP	Steve Pennington	Assemblies of God World Missions, East Africa Area Team Leader (9, 36, 59)
UA	Uche Ama	Director of Foreign Missions, Assemblies of God, Nigeria (91)
TCA	Timothy C. Anderson	Assemblies of God minister; Faculty, North Texas District AG School of Ministry; Chaplain, US Air Force (Retired) (45)
TL	Tim Lord	AGWM Missionary with Africa's Hope (7, 8)
WD	Wesley Duewel	Author, Missiologist, and President of One Mission Society (1969-1982) (20)

Introduction

"God does nothing except in response to believing prayer."

So said John Wesley, the great founder of Methodism. While a theological hairsplitter might object to Wesley's broad assertion, we must not miss his point. Wesley was championing the importance of prayer, and he was calling Christians to lives of committed prayer. Paul was doing much the same when he exhorted the Thessalonians to "pray continually" (1Th 5:17). In another place, the apostle admonished, "Devote yourselves to prayer" (Col 4:2). My sincere hope is that this book will serve Pentecostal pastors and teachers, helping them to do the same.

This it is a book on prayer. More specifically, it is a book on *missional prayer,* as its subtitle indicates. Missional prayer is prayer for others—for those who do not yet know Christ as Savior. It is prayer that seeks to advance God's mission in the earth. God's mission is to redeem and call to himself a people "from every tribe and language and people and nation" (Re 5:9). Missional prayer is the kind of prayer Jesus advocated when He charged His disciples to "pray earnestly to the Lord of the harvest to send out laborers into his harvest" (Mt 9:38 ESV). Missional prayer is thus intercessory prayer. It is standing in the gap between the lost and God who seeks to save them (Ex 22:30). This book was prepared to aid pastors and other Christian leaders in creating such prayer movements in their churches.

This is the third in a series of sermon outline books published by the Acts in Africa Initiative. The first two books were *Proclaiming Pentecost: 100 Sermon Outlines on the Power of the Holy Spirit* and *Proclaiming Christ to the Nations: 100 Sermon Outlines on Spirit-Empowered Mission.* It was commissioned by the Africa Assemblies of God Alliance led by Dr. Barnabas Mtokambali, General Superintendent of the Tanzania Assemblies of God.

This and the two previous sermon outline books were developed as practical resources for pastors during the Africa Assemblies of God "Decade of Pentecost" emphasis from 2010 to 2020. During these ten years, the fifty national church that make up the Africa Assemblies of God Alliance (AAGA) have committed themselves to achieving the following:

- Seeing 10 million new believers baptized in the Holy Spirit and mobilized as Spirit-empowered witnesses
- Raising up 100,000 intercessors who will pray daily for a Pentecostal outpouring on the African church.
- Planting 50,000+ new Spirit-empowered missionary churches.
- Recruiting, training, and deploying tens of thousands of new Spirit-empowered pastors, church planters, and cross-cultural missionaries.
- Engaging the more than 850 yet-to-be-reached people groups of sub-Sahara Africa.
- Partnering with others to penetrate the 120+ unreached people groups of North Africa.

Fulfilling these ambitious goals will require certain commitments from the leaders, pastors, and lay members of the church. Pastors and teachers must preach often and effectively on the baptism in the Holy Spirit. They must then pray with their members to be filled with the Spirit and empowered as witnesses according to Jesus' promise in Acts 1:8. Our first sermon outline book, *Proclaiming Pentecost,* was developed to help pastors in this endeavor. It is now in the hands of more than 35,000 pastors across Africa.

Secondly, if our Assemblies of God churches are to fulfill their Decade of Pentecost goals of planting thousands of churches and deploying hundreds of Spirit-empowered cross-cultural missionaries, pastors must preach and teach often on the mission of God. Then, they must call on God's people to commit themselves to that mission. Our second book, *Proclaiming Christ to the Nations,* was prepared to help leaders accomplish this task.

Finally, if the Assemblies of God is to fulfill its God-given mission in Africa and beyond, we must become a people of prayer. Each of our local congregations must become, in the words of Jesus, "a house of prayer for all nations" (Mk 11:17). Pastors must call their people to pray and lead them in focused Spirit-anointed missional prayer. This book has been prepared to help pastors in this endeavor.

The 100 sermon outlines in this book were submitted by 45 seasoned Pentecostal preachers. Each one is a missionary, missions leader, or missional pastor. They hail from both Africa and American. I have personally contributed several of the outlines.

You can identify the creator of each sermon by matching the initials at the end of the outline with the "Contributors Index" on pages 9-11. Also, after each contributor's name and particulars you will find in parentheses a list of the sermons he or she contributed. I extend a heartfelt thank you to each of these men and women who allowed us to use their sermon outlines without cost.

With these thoughts in mind, I commend this volume to you. It is my sincere prayer that you use it often as a tool to mobilize Christ's church to pray for the success of God's mission. I would love to hear from you concerning how these outlines have helped you. Please send your testimonies and prayer requests to ActsinAfrica@agmd.org.

Denzil R. Miller
Editor

How to Use This Book

Allow me to suggest how you may best use this book. The process begins with choosing a sermon. If, for instance, you want to preach from a certain text, you can begin your search by checking the "Sermon Text Index" at the back of the book. This search will lead you to any sermon that may have been developed based on your chosen text.

Possibly, you want to preach a sermon on prayer, but you are unsure of exactly what you want to preach about. In such a case, you can browse the book for a sermon. You may want to begin your search in the "Table of Contents" at the beginning of the book. In doing this, you will note how the book is divided into eight sections, including the following:

- Prayer Basics
- The Power of Prayer
- Commitment to Prayer
- Intercessory Prayer Warfare
- The Holy Spirit and Prayer
- Praying for the Church and Revival
- Praying for Missionaries and Missions
- Prayer Guides

One of these categories may appeal to you. You can then begin looking for a message in that section of the book, thus streamlining your search.

The "Sermon in a Sentence" feature at the beginning of each outline can also be helpful. By reading this one-sentence summary of the message, you can get a quick idea of whether or not you want to investigate further. If the subject interests you, you can then look more closely at the outline.

Perhaps you want to achieve a particular goal with your sermon. For instance, you want your listeners to know some of the basics of prayer, or you want them to commit to ongoing intercessory prayer for missions. In such cases, you will want to scan the "Sermon Purpose" feature at the beginning of each outline. In this way, you can choose a sermon that will help you to attain your goal.

Note further that each outline in this book has been formatted to fit onto two pages. In doing this, I have attempted to include enough content in each outline to give the user a clear indication of the substance and flow of the message. At the same time, I have sought to be brief enough to give preachers and teachers ample room to develop and customize the messages to the unique needs of their listeners. As you study, pray over, and preach these outlines, I trust that the Holy Spirit will inspire you with fresh ideas of how to develop your own messages on prayer.

You can use your chosen outline in a number of ways. The first and most obvious way is to preach the sermon exactly as it is written. It is more likely, however, that you will want to adapt the message to your own unique burden and the particular needs of your audience. You will also want to add your own insights to the message.

In addition, as you pray over and meditate on the sermon, the Spirit will speak to you. You will want to incorporate these insights into your message. And, of course, you will want to add your own illustrations and anecdotes to the message. In other words, you should feel free to make the sermon your own.

How to Preach a Great Message

I conclude with some recommendations on how you can take these sermon outlines and preach great messages.

Be filled with the Spirit. First, to preach an effective sermon, you must be full of the Holy Spirit. Often in the Book of Acts, the apostles began their sermons by being filled with the Spirit (Acts 2:4 and 14; 4:8; 4:31). There is no substitute for Spirit-anointed preaching. No amount of personal charm or showmanship can make up for a lack of the Spirit's presence upon the preacher. Let Jesus be your model. As He began His ministry, He announced, "The Spirit of the Lord is on me, because he has anointed me to preach good news..." (Luke 4:18).

Own the sermon. Once you choose an outline, begin to make the sermon your own. Begin to "internalize" the message contained in the outline. Implant the message into your heart and mind by thoughtfully and prayerfully reading through it several times. Mentally preach the sermon to yourself. As you do, respond to its message. Heed what it says. If you need to stop and pray, then do so; if you need to repent, do that.

It is also important to memorize the text and other key scriptures to be used in the sermon. This too will help to imbed the message in your heart. It will also help you as you preach. Because the texts are in your heart and mind, the message will flow more freely. Your listeners will sense your passion and your mastery of the subject, and they will respond better to what you are saying. It will also be helpful to memorize the main points of the sermon. By doing this will be liberated from your notes, and you will speak more directly and more persuasively to the people.

Pray. How foolish it would be to attempt to preach a sermon on prayer without first praying over the message. Before we ever preach with our mouths, we preach with our lives. As our members see us in prayer, they too will want to pray. This is what happened with Jesus' disciples. As they watched Him pray, they asked Him, "Lord, teach us to pray" (Lk 11:1). Prayer moves the hand of God—and God moves the hearts of people.

Deliver your sermon. As you preach your message on prayer, keep two things in mind. First, *be concise.* That means that you should not load your message with unnecessary words and irrelevant thoughts. Stay on point. Remember your goal, and say nothing that will not help you to achieve that goal. Secondly, as you preach, *aim for the altar.* In other words, everything you say must be designed to bring people to a commitment and move them into action. Then, as you conclude your message, "cast the net." As a fisherman casts his net into the water and pulls the fish into his boat, you should cast the net by inviting people to come to the altar. Call them to commit themselves to intercede for God's mission and to be empowered by the Spirit to accomplish that end.

Section 1
Prayer Basics

1 Prayer Basics

Sermon in a Sentence: We should incorporate the "seven facets of effective of prayer" into our daily prayer times.

Sermon Purpose: That Christians would broaden their daily prayer times to include seven facets of effective prayer.

Text: Matthew 6:9-13

Introduction
1. We have just read what is known as "The Lord's Prayer."
2. It could be better called "The Disciples' Prayer" for it is a prayer Jesus gave His disciples to guide their prayers.
3. It is to be used as an outline to guide our prayers today.
4. From this prayer we discover seven facets of effective prayer.
5. We should include each facet in our daily prayer lives.

I. PRAYER IS CONVERSATION
A. Jesus began His prayer by addressing God as "Our Father."
B. Prayer is a conversation with our Heavenly Father.
1. Prayer thus involves not only talking *to* God; it also *listening* to what He has to say.
2. Illus: God talked with Moses as His friend (Ex 33:11).

II. PRAYER IS COMMUNION
A. Look again at Jesus' instruction to pray, "Our Father" (v.9).
B. This phrase further implies that prayer is communion.
1. It is founded on one's relationship with God.
2. We are sons and daughters of God.
3. In prayer we draw near to God and get to know Him better (Je 29:13-14; Ja 4:8a).

III. PRAYER IS WORSHIP
A. Jesus continued by saying, "hallowed be your name…" (v.9)
B. This is an expression of worship.
1. In worship, we acknowledge and affirm God's greatness.
2. David exhorts us revere God's name: "Sing to the Lord, you saints of his; praise his holy name" (Ps 30:4).
3. Sincere worship is a vital part of our prayer times.

IV. PRAYER IS MISSION
A. Next, we are to pray, "Your kingdom come…" (v.10).
B. This is a prayer for God's mission to be accomplished.

1. God's mission is to redeem and call unto Himself a people out of every tribe, tongue, and nation on earth (Re 5:9).
2. God's kingdom comes when people are saved, healed, filled with the Holy Spirit, delivered from demonic bondage—or otherwise touched by the Holy Spirit.
3. God's kingdom will come in fullness when Jesus returns in power and great glory (Re 19:11-16; 22:20).

V. PRAYER IS SUBMISSION
1. We are then to pray, "your will be done on earth as it is in heaven…" (v.10).
2. As we pray, we submit ourselves to God and His will.
   1. This is what Jesus did in Gethsemane (Mt 26:42).
   2. We must do the same today.

VI. PRAYER IS PETITION
A. We then pray, "Give us today our daily bread. Forgive our debts…and lead us not into temptation" (vv.11-13).
B. We ask God to meet our physical and spiritual needs.
   1. This kind of prayer is called petition.
   2. God delights in granting the requests of His children (Mt 7:7-11).

VII. PRAYER IS WARFARE
A. Finally, Jesus said, "…deliver us from the evil one" (v.13).
   1. The "evil one" spoken of here is the devil.
B. Prayer thus involves spiritual warfare.
   1. In prayer we resist, challenge, and defeat the enemy (Lk 18:18-19; Ja 4:7; 1Pe 5:8-9).
   2. Jesus did spiritual battle in the wilderness (Mt 4:1-11).
   3. He taught us to "tie up the strong man" (Mt 12:29).
C. Such warfare prayer can be done only in the power of the Holy Spirit (Zec 4:6; Mt 12:28; Ep 6:18).

Conclusion and Altar Call
1. We must broaden our prayer lives to include these seven facets.
2. Come now, be filled with the Spirit, and commit yourself to expanding your prayer life.

[DRM]

2 When You Pray

Sermon in a Sentence: Jesus teaches us how we should pray.
Sermon Purpose: That believers will commit themselves to praying as Jesus taught.
Text: Matthew 6:5-15
Introduction
1. This teaching of Jesus is found in His Sermon on the Mount.
   a. In this sermon Jesus teaches principles of kingdom living.
2. In chapter 6, He deals with three essential Christian disciplines: giving (vv.1-4), praying (vv.5-15), and fasting (vv.16-18).
3. This message will focus on Jesus' teaching on prayer.
   a. Three times in three verses, Jesus begins with the phrase, *"When you pray..."* (vv.5, 6, and 7).
   b. He tells us two things we *must not do* when we pray, and six things *we must do:*

I. WHEN YOU PRAY, DON'T DO THIS
  • *Jesus tells us two things we must not do when we pray:*
  A. Don't be a hypocrite. (Read v.5)
   1. Don't pray to be seen (and heard) by people.
   2. So much of our public praying is aimed at the ears of people rather than at the ears of God. (Read v.1).
   3. Such prayers receive no answer from God. (Read v.1b, 5b)
  B. Don't be like the pagans. (Read v.7)
   1. Pagans think their gods will hear their constant babbling.
      a. They mindlessly repeat prayers or magical phrases.
      b. Illus: Like the prophets of Baal. (1Ki 18:20-29)
   2. We should talk to God as we would talk to any person:
      a. Knowing He is hearing.
      b. Expecting Him to answer.

II. WHEN YOU PRAY, DO THIS
  • *Note the phrase: "This then is how you should pray..."*
  • *Jesus tells us six things we should do when we pray:*
  A. Get alone with God. (Read v.6)
   1. The only sure way to avoid "praying to be seen of men."
   2. We meet God in the secret place: *"Pray to your Father who is in the secret place"* (NKJV).
   3. God promises to reward such prayers (v.6b).
  B. Submit yourself to God. (Read v.9)

1. We are to come before God in humility and submission.
2. We submit to His Name, that is His sovereign authority.
3. And we humbly acknowledge His awe-inspiring holiness.
4. We must never "command God" as some foolishly teach.

C. Pray for God's Kingdom to come. (Read v.10)
- *To pray for God's kingdom to come means three things:*
1. We are to pray for people *to be saved*.
    a. The kingdom comes to an individual when he or she is born again (Jn 3:3; see Lk 17:21).
2. We are to pray for people *to be filled with the Holy Spirit, healed,* and *delivered* from demonic bondages (Mt 12:28 with Lk 11:20; Lk 10:9).
3. We are to pray for Jesus *to come again* (Re 22:20).

D. Ask God to meet your needs. (Read v.11)
1. By "our daily bread" Jesus meant our daily needs.
2. Jesus teaches us to ask (Mt 7:7, 11).
3. We must ask in faith (Mt 21:22).

E. Forgive others. (Read vv.12, 14)
1. If we expect God to forgive us, we must forgive others.
2. Illus: Jesus's answer to the question, "Lord, how many times shall I forgive by brother when he sins against me?" Tell the Parable of the Unforgiving Servant (Mt 18:21-35)

F. Pray for God guidance and protection. (Read vv.13)
1. We are to ask the Lord to guide us.
    a. "Lead us not *into* temptation…"
    b. We must ask for Jesus' presence and the Spirit's power so that temptation does not *take us in*—that is, overcome us.
2. We are to ask the Lord to protect us for the evil one.
    a. We are protected from the evil one (Satan) when we put on the full armor of God (Ep 6:11).
    b. We must be filled with God's Word and God's Spirit.

Conclusion and Altar Call
1. Remember, Jesus said, "When you pray" not "If you pray."
2. We would do well to follow Jesus' instructions when we pray.
3. Come now to be filled with the Spirit, and to commit yourself to a life of prayer.

[DRM]

3 When You Fast

Sermon in a Sentence: God calls His people to seek Him with prayer and fasting.
Sermon Purpose: To call God's people to a time of prayer and fasting.
Text: Matthew 6:16-18
Introduction
1. In the Sermon on the Mount, Jesus identifies three practices He expects from every disciple. He expects each of us...
    a. ...to give: *"When* you give..." (Mt 6:2-3).
    b. ...to pray: *"When* you pray..." (vv.5-7).
    c. ...to fast: *"When* you fast... (vv.16-17).
    d. Note that Jesus says, "When..." not "If..."
2. In this message, we will focus on Jesus' third expectation— *"When you fast..."*
    a. God calls every disciple to times of fasting.
    b. Let's look at three biblical insights about fasting:

I. THE CALL TO FAST
A. In the Bible, God calls us to times of prayer and fasting:
    1. "Even now, declares the Lord, return to me with all your heart, with fasting and weeping and mourning" (Jl 2:12).
    2. The time to fast is now!
        a. The bridegroom is now away from us (Mt 9:14-15).
        b. We should practice fasting until He returns.
B. The Bible contains many examples of those who fasted.
    1. The Old Testament saints fasted.
        a. For example: Moses (Ex 34:28), Hannah (1Sa 1:7), David (2Sa 12:16). Elijah (1Ki 19:8), Daniel (9:3).
    2. Jesus fasted (Mt 4:1-2).
    3. The early Christians fasted:
        a. Anna fasted (Lk 2:37).
        b. The Christians in Antioch fasted (Ac 13:2).
        c. Paul and Barnabas fasted (Ac 14:23).

II. THE PURPOSE OF FASTING
A. What are some *wrong reasons* for fasting?
    1. To manipulate God: That is, to try to "twist God's arm" and force Him to do what He does not want to do.
    2. To flaunt one's spirituality.
        a. Jesus warned against such fasting (Mt 6:16-18).

B. Some *right reasons* for fasting:
   1. We fast to break strongholds, liberate people, and move into the realm of God's power and presence.
   2. Three biblical reasons we must fast:
      a. To *be heard* in heaven (Ezr 8:23)
      b. To *hear* from heaven (Da 9:2-3, 21-22)
      c. To *free* the captives (Is 58:6; Mt 17:21)
C. With all these benefits, we should all practice fasting.

IV. THE WAY TO FAST
A There are personal and public fasts.
   1. *Personal fasting:* When the Spirit guides an individual, and he or she purposes in their hearts to fast.
      a. Illus: Jesus fasts in the wilderness (Mt 4:1-2).
   2. *Public calls to fast:* When the leadership of the church calls the people to a time of prayer and fasting.
      a. Jeremiah called a public fast (Je 36:6).
      b. Joel called a public fast (Jl 2:15).
      c. The Antioch church called a public fast (Ac 13:2).
      d. True spiritual leaders will call their churches to seasons of prayer and fasting.
B. How not to fast:
   1. We should not practice ritualistic, Spirit-less fasting.
   2. Such fasting is a mere form of godliness, which denies God's power (2Ti 3:5).
C. How to fast:
   1. We should fast unto God (Zec 7:5; Ac 13:2).
   2. We should fast *with* prayer (Ezr 8:23; Ne 1:4).
D. Three kinds of fasting:
   1. The *normal* fast: To abstain from solid food (Mt 4:2).
   2. The *absolute* fast: To abstain from all solid food and liquid (Moses, Ex 34:28; Saul, Ac 9:9).
   3. The *partial* fast: To abstain from certain foods (Da 10:3).

Conclusion and Altar Call
Come let's commit ourselves to a time of prayer and fasting.

[DRM]

4 Praying God's Way

Sermon in a Sentence: We must learn to pray God's way, that is, the way Jesus taught us to pray.

Sermon Purpose: That God's people will know how to pray more effectively.

Text: Luke 11:1-13

Introduction
1. Billy Graham wrote, "A prayerless Christian is a powerless Christian. A prayerless Christian is also a contradiction, because we should yearn for fellowship with the One who redeemed us." He adds, "Throughout both the Bible and the history of the Church, those who made the greatest impact for God were those who prayed the most."
2. In this message, we will learn to pray *God's way,* that is, the way Jesus prayed—and the way He taught us to pray.

I. HOW JESUS MODELED PRAYER
A. In our text, we are given a glimpse of Jesus' prayer life.
   1. Luke 11:1a: "Jesus was praying in a certain place."
   2. His disciples took note of His prayer (v.1b).
   3. We too should take note of Jesus' prayer life.
B. Look what the Bible says about how Jesus prayed:
   1. Jesus prayed often (Lk. 18:1).
   2. Jesus prayed with intensity (He 5:7).
   3. Jesus prayed before and during significant events:
      a. At His baptism (Lk 3:21-22).
      b. Before choosing His disciples (Lk 6:12-13).
      c. On His way to the cross (Lk 22:39-41).
   4. Jesus prayed alone and with His disciples:
      a. Alone (Lk 5:16; Mt 14:23; Mk 1:35).
      b. With His disciples (Jn 6:11;.17:1ff).
   5. Jesus continues to pray today (He 7:25).
C. If we are going to pray God's way, we must imitate the prayer life of Jesus.
   1. We are called to follow Jesus' example (1Jn 2:6).
   2. Illus: In a certain village, the believers' custom was for each one to choose his or her individual prayer place in the bush. After time, the path to each prayer place would become clearly marked, since it was all dirt. Believers

would often encourage each other to pray by saying, "Brother, don't let the grass grow on your path."

II. HOW JESUS INSTRUCTS US TO PRAY
A. When the disciples noticed how Jesus prayed, they asked Him, "Lord, teach us to pray" (Lk 11:1).
  1. Jesus then gave them this teaching on prayer (vv.2-13).
  2. He was teaching His followers to pray God's way.
B. Here, Jesus teaches us five things about how we are to pray:
  1. First, Jesus teaches us to focus our prayers on *glorifying God* and *advancing His kingdom.* (Read v.2)
     a. The primary focus of our prayers should not be on our own problems but on our great God.
     b. And our primary motive for praying should be on the advancement of God's kingdom. (Read Mt 6:33)
  2. Next, He teaches us to *trust God for our daily provision.*
     a. He says, "Give us each day our daily bread" (v.2).
     b. It is okay to ask God to meet our needs; however, we must avoid focusing all our prayers on ourselves.
  3. Third, Jesus teaches us to *seek forgiveness* (Read v.4).
     a. We do this to maintain our relationship with God.
     b. We should not ask God to do something for us that we are unwilling to do for others. (See Mt 18:21-35)
     c. We should also pray that God will help us to avoid temptation (v.4).
  4. Fourth, Jesus teaches us to *persist in prayer.*
     a. He told the story of the persistent friend (vv.5-7).
     b. Then in verses 8-9, He applied the story.
     c. A literal translation of these verses is "keep on asking…keep on seeking…keep on knocking…"
  5. Finally, Jesus teaches us to *keep asking for the Holy Spirit.* (Read v.13)
     a. The disciples obeyed His command and prayed for the Spirit (Ac 1:14).
     b. Then, on the Day of Pentecost, Jesus fulfilled His promise. (Read Ac 2:1-4).
     c. We must seek the Spirit's filling every day.

Conclusion and Altar Call
Come; be filled with the Holy Spirit and commit yourself to prayer.

[JL[(2)]]

5 The Mystery of Prayer

Sermon in a Sentence: God asks us to join Him in His mission through the "mystery of prayer."

Sermon Purpose: That God's people will realize the privilege they have in prayer and that they will commit themselves to praying for the nations.

Text: Matthew 6:10

Introduction
1. Jesus' life on earth was a life of prayer.
2. He taught His disciples to do the same.
3. Our text is taken from the "Lord's Prayer" (Mt 6:9-13).
4. It is a missional prayer:
   a. We are to pray for God's kingdom to come.
   b. We are to pray for God's will to be done.
5. When you think about it, prayer is a mysterious thing.

I. THE MYSTERY OF PRAYER
   A. Let's think for a moment about the nature of God:
      1. He is *omnipotent:* He has the power to do anything He chooses (Je 32:17).
      2. He is *sovereign:* He has the right to do as He pleases (Ps 115:3).
      3. He has a *will* concerning His creation (2Pe 3:9).
   B. In requiring us to pray, God has intentionally chosen to limit himself.
      1. There are things that He will not do unless we pray—even if He wants these things done.
      2. In many cases, if we don't pray, His will *will not* be done.
      4. Illus: He even required the Messiah to ask! (Ps 2:8)
   C. Why doesn't God just cut out the "middlemen" and do what He pleases?
      1. Why would He leave something as important as the salvation of people in our fallible hands?
      2. We don't know all the answers to this question, but we can know from Scripture that God requires that we pray.

II. THE REASON FOR PRAYER
   A. One reason God requires that we ask in prayer is that He desires fellowship with us.
      1. Fellowship requires personal interaction.

      2. God receives pleasure from our asking (Lk 12:29-32).
      3. As we go to Him in prayer our relationship grows.
  B. God graciously invites us to join Him in His mission.
      1. One way we join Him in His mission is in prayer.
      2. What a great privilege!
  C. Our mighty God calls on us to pray mighty prayers (Je 33:3).
      1. Let's look at five powerful missional prayers:

III. FIVE POWERFUL MISSIONAL PRAYERS (taken directly from Scripture)

  A. *"Ask of me."* (Read Ps 2:7-8.)
      1. This is the Father's appeal to the Son.
      2. He promises the Son the nations—if He will ask.
      3. We can join Jesus in asking for the nations.
  B. *"Pray to the Lord of the Harvest."* (Read Lk 10:1-2.).
      1. This command of Jesus reveals God's concern for souls.
      2. This is Jesus' enduring instruction to His church.
  C. *"Here am I, send me."* (Read Is 6:8.)
      1. Isaiah is responding to God's call (vv.1-7).
      2. God is looking for those who will respond like Isaiah.
  D. *"Join me in my struggle."* (Read Ro 15:30.)
      1. Paul describes his missionary work as a "struggle."
      2. He invites the Roman Christians to join him in his ministry by praying for him. (Read vv.31-32.)
      3. We can join our missionaries in their work by praying for them.
  E. *"That they may all be one."* (Read Jn 17:21-22.)
      1. This is part of Jesus' "High Priestly Prayer."
      2. He is praying for those who would choose to follow Him (v.9), the ones He has sent into the world (v.21).
      3. He prays for their unity so that, together, they may effectively fulfill their God-given mission.
      4. We must pray the same way.

Conclusion and Altar Call

1. What a marvelous privilege we have to join God in mission through prayer.
2. Come, commit yourself to intercessory prayer for the nations today.

[BB]

6 The Sin of Not Praying

Sermon in a Sentence: We must not sin against God by failing to pray.
Sermon Purpose: That the people will commit to living prayer-filled lives.
Texts: 1 Samuel 12:23
Introduction
1. Our text comes at the conclusion of Samuel's farewell address.
2. In this address, he solemnly warns the people not to forsake God as their fathers had done in the past (vv.14-15, 21).
3. He shows them God's power (vv.16-18).
4. He promises to pray for them: "Far be it from me that I should sin against the Lord by failing to pray for you" (v.23).
5. In this message, we will examine "The Sin of Not Praying."

I. THE SIN OF PRAYERLESSNESS
- *Three reasons not praying is a sin:*
A. Not praying is an *act of disobedience.*
   1. The Bible commands us to pray (e.g. Col 4:2; 1Th 5:17).
   2. Jesus taught us to pray: *"When* you pray…" (three times in Mt 6:5-7); then "…you *should* pray…" (v.10)
   3. When we fail to pray we sin: "Anyone, then, who knows the good he ought to do and doesn't do it, sins" (Ja 4:17).
B. Not praying is an *expression of distrust.*
   1. When we don't pray, we say to God, "I don't trust you. I don't need your help… I can live my life without you."
   2. Not asking shows that we have little faith.
C. Not praying is a *symptom of a weak relationship.*
   1. Relationships grow through communion.
   2. They decline when there is little or no communication.

II. THE FOLLY OF PRAYERLESSNESS
A. The one who does not pray is foolish indeed:
   1. "The fool says in his heart, 'There is no God'" (Ps 53:1).
      - To not pray is to say, "There is no God."
   2. "The fool folds his hands and ruins himself" (Ec 4:5).
      - To not pray is to sleep in the time of harvest (Pr 10:5).
   3. ""My people are fools; they do not know me" (Je 4:22a).
      - To not pray is to not want to know God.
   4. 'Woe to the foolish prophets who follow their own spirit and have seen nothing!" (Ez 13:3).

- To not pray is to see nothing and follow our own spirits rather than God's Spirit.
B. Four reasons not praying is foolish:
1. Not praying *leaves the gate open* for the enemy.
   a. "The devils prowls around like a…lion…" (1Pe 5:8b).
   b. Prayerlessness leaves our lives open to Satan.
2. Not praying *renders us weak* and ineffective.
   a. As exercise strengthens our bodies, prayer strengthens our spirits (1Ti 4:8a; Ep 3:16).
   b. If we don't pray, we become spiritually weak.
3. Not praying *closes the door* to God's blessings.
   a. John Wesley said, "We receive noting from God but in answer to believing prayer."
   b. James: "You do not have, because you do not ask" (Ja 4:3).
4. Not praying *paralyzes the forward motion* of the church.
   a. "The church marches forward on its knees."
   b. Prayer brings down the Spirit of God (Ac 4:31).
   c. Prayer opens the door for preaching the gospel (Col 4:3).
C. How foolish to neglect the awesome privilege of prayer.

III. A REMEDY TO PRAYERLESSNESS

A. Admit your wrongdoing.
1. If not praying is a sin, then we must repent of our prayerlessness (Re 2:5).
2. Repentance involves realizing, admitting, confessing, and tuning from one's sin. (Read Ac 3:19).
B. Commit yourself to prayer.
1. Choose to pray.
2. "God forbid that I should sin…in ceasing to pray…"
C. Be filled with the Spirit.
1. The Spirit will inspire you to pray.
2. The Spirit will help you pray (Ro 8:26-27).
D. Don't wait! Begin today.

Conclusion and Altar Call

Come, now; repent of your prayerlessness, be filled with the Spirit, and commit yourself to a life of prayer.

[DRM]

7 Our Part in Prayer

Sermon in a Sentence: If we want God to answer our prayers, we must humble ourselves, pray, seek His face, and turn from our sins.
Sermon Purpose: That God's people will begin to pray more effectively.
Text: 2 Chronicles 7:14
Introduction
1. In our text, God appears to Solomon in a night vision.
2. God makes three amazing promises: (1) to hear our prayers, (2) to forgive our sins, and (3) to heal our land.
3. Think what it would be like if that actually happened.
4. This message will discuss 4 conditions for answered prayer.

I. WE MUST HUMBLE OURSELVES BEFORE GOD
- *"If my people...will humble themselves..."*
A. Pride is a great and common sin shared by all people.
   1. Paul describes mankind's condition. (Read Ro 3:10-18).
   2. Prayer forces us to bow before God and acknowledge our need of Someone greater than ourselves.
B. It matters how we come to God.
   1. As shocking as it may seem, there are times when God does not hear (that is, listen to) our prayers.
   2. Because God knows our hearts when we pray (1Sa 16:7).
   3. Illus: When King Uzziah became powerful, His heart was filled with pride and God rejected his prayer (2Ch 26:1-19).
   4. Illus: God also rejected the Pharisee's prayer (Lk 18:9-14).
C. When we pray, we must humble ourselves before God.

II. WE MUST COMMIT OURSELVES TO PRAYER
- *"If my people...will...pray..."*
A. True prayer requires both time and faith.
   1. God answers prayer in His own time.
      a. After time, it seems as if God has not heard our prayer.
   2. Real prayer, however, cannot be compressed so that an hour of praying can be accomplished in 2 minutes.
   3. Illus: We must be like the persistent widow (Lk 18:1-8).
B. True prayer requires focus and commitment.
   1. Often, we do not sense the Spirit's moving because we are not focused—Our minds are on other things.

2. And because we lack commitment, our prayer lives are inconsistent and weak.
   3. We must commit ourselves to focused, persistent prayer.

III. WE MUST SEEK GOD'S FACE
   • *"If my people...will...seek my face..."*
   A. To seek God's face is to seek His presence.
      1. The Hebrew word here translated "face" (*paniym*) is translated "presence" 76 times in the OT.
      2. We are not too seek God's blessings; we are rather to seek His presence.
      3. We are to seek Him with all our hearts (Je 29:13).
      4. Jesus promised, "Seek and you will find..." (Mt 7:7).
   B. God is a constant outside of our immediate surroundings.
      1. Like the sun, He never changes (Ja 1:17).
         a. Illus: When we lose direction, we can look and see the sun and know which way to go.
         b. Remember, God dies bit get lost—we do.
      2. His presence will go with us to guide us (Illus: Ex13:21).
         a. The Holy Spirit will be our internal guide.
         b. Even in the darkest night, He will show us the way.
   C. We must learn to seek God's face.

IV. WE MUST TURN FROM OUR SINS
   • *"If my people...will...turn from the wicked ways..."*
   A. God's demands purity of life.
      1. If we persist in sin, or prayers will be hindered.
      2. Sin separates us from God and His blessing on our lives. (Read Is 59:1-2; Je 7:16-18; Pr 28:9).
   B. This does not mean we have to be perfect for God to hear and answer our prayers.
      1. It does mean that Christ has set us free, and as His followers, we are to be different from the world around us.
      2. E.M. Bounds: "Prayer and sinning cannot keep company with each other. One or the other must of necessity stop."

Conclusion and Altar Call
Come now; humble yourself, repent of your sins, be filled with the Spirit, and commit to seeking God's face.

[TL]

8 God's Part in Prayer

Sermon in a Sentence: We can be confident that God will hear and answer our prayers.
Sermon Purpose: That Christians will begin to pray with confidence.
Text: 2 Chronicles 7:14
Introduction
1. In our last message, we discussed "Our Part in Prayer" (see sermon #6).
2. From our text we learned that we must humble ourselves, pray, seek God's face, and turn from or wicked ways.
3. In this message, we will discuss "God's Part in Prayer," that is, He will hear and answer our believing prayers.
4. We will look at four reasons why we can have confidence that God will hear and answer our prayers:

We can have confidence that God will answer our prayers...
I. BECAUSE IT IS HE WHO CALLS US TO PRAY
A. It is God's will that we pray.
1. In our text, God himself exhorts us to pray.
2. Paul says that prayer and thanksgiving are God's will for us. (Read 1Th 5:17-18)
3. Jesus expects His followers to pray. He said, *"When* you pray" not *"If* you pray…" (Mt 6:5-7).
B. Since God commands us to pray, we can be confident that He is prepared to hear and answer our prayers.
1. We can "approach the throne of grace with confidence" (He 4:15).
2. And we can expect to "find grace to help us in our time of need."

We can have confidence that God will answer our prayers...
II. BECAUSE, IN LOVE, GOD LISTENS TO OUR CRIES
A. God has demonstrated His great love for us.
1. In love He sent His Son (Jn 3:16).
B. Because He loves us, He listens when we cry out to Him.
1. God told rebellious Israel, "With everlasting kindness I will have compassion on you" (Is 54:8).
2. Listen to these two amazing promises…
   a. Read 1Ch 7:14: "If my people, who are called…"

        b. "The prayer of a righteous man is powerful and effective" (Ja 5:15).
   C. We can therefore cry out in confidence to God.
      1. Read 1 Jn 5:14-15: "This is the confidence we have…"
      2. We do not come to a stingy God, but a generous, loving Heavenly Father.

We can have confidence that God will answer our prayers…
III. BECAUSE HE HAS FORGIVEN OUR SINS
   A. How do we know that God answers prayer?
      1. We know because He forgave our sins.
      2. When we asked Him to save us, He answered our cry and washed our sins away in Christ's blood.
      3. Every Christian knows the feeling of the burden of sin being lifted from their shoulders.
   B. If He answered that prayer, we can be confident that he will answer other prayers.
      1. David expressed this very sentiment. (Read Ps 116:1-2)
      2. What sin do you have in your life? Come to Christ in faith and repentance, and He will freely forgive you.

We can have confidence that God will answer our prayers…
IV. BECAUSE HE EMPOWERS US BY HIS SPIRIT
   A. The Spirit comes upon people as they seek Him in prayer.
      1. He empowers us to be Christ's witnesses (Ac 1:8).
      2. Jesus promised, "Ask and it will be given you…" (Read Lk 11:9-10, 13).
      3. Each time we experience God's Spirit, it is evidence that God answers our prayers.
   B. The Spirit will also help us pray (Read Ro 8:26-27).
      1. He will pray through us.
      2. He will pray in accordance with God's will.

Conclusion and Altar Call
1. If we will pray as Scripture directs, we can be confident that God will hear and answer our prayers (Read 2Ch 7:14).
2. Come, "Let's pray that God will pour out His Spirit on us, and that the lost will be saved.

[TL]

9 Kingdom Praying

Sermon in a Sentence: The Lord's prayer is a model of kingdom praying that we should follow.
Sermon Purpose: That believers will understand and practice kingdom praying.
Text: Matthew 6:9-13
Introduction
1. God's kingdom is invading the earth.
   a. God is taking back what the devil has stolen.
   b. Jesus said, "If I drive out demons by the Spirit of God, then the kingdom of God has come upon you" (Mt 12:28).
2. Our part in the invasion is sending, going, and proclaiming.
3. Our part also includes "Kingdom Praying!"
4. Today, we will focus on what is popularly known as the "Lord's Prayer" in Mt 6:9-13. We will discover that…

I. THE LORD'S PRAYER IS A KINGDOM PRAYER
A. It is significant that this prayer is found in the gospel of Matthew—because Matthew is "all about Kingdom."
   1. He mentions God's kingdom 52 times.
   2. He generally calls it the "kingdom of heaven."
   3. He begins and ends his gospel with a kingdom emphasis.
      a. Jesus' first message "The kingdom…is at hand" (4:17).
      b. He links the kingdom to the Great Commission: (24:14).
B. In this context, Jesus teaches us how to pray (Mt 6:9-13).
   1. Note how His prayer begins with the kingdom. (Read v.10)
   2. He also ends it with the kingdom. (Read v.13, KJV).
C. Three times Jesus says, "When you pray…" (vv.5-7)
   1. Then he says, "…you should pray" (v.9).
   2. He thus assumes that His followers will pray.
D. Jesus' Kingdom Prayer has two focuses: *heaven* and *earth*.
   1. That is, on *God* and *God's people*.
   2. Let's look at those two focuses:

II. OUR KINGDOM PRAYING SHOULD FOCUS ON HEAVEN
   • *Read vv.9-10 noting three phrases:*
A. *"Hallowed be your name"*—We must focus on God's name.
   1. The *direction* of our prayer is toward the Father (Ro 8:15).
   2. The *attitude* of prayer is God's holiness (Is 6:3; 1Pe 1:15-16).
   3. The *basis* of prayer is God's reign from heaven. (Ps 103:19).

       4. To sum up, we pray to our Heavenly Father who reigns in holiness from His throne in heaven.
  B. *"Your kingdom come"*—We must focus on God's kingdom.
       1. The heart of praying is for God's kingdom to advance in the earth (Mt 24:14).
       2. Pray that Christ will reign in people's hearts (Jn 3:3).
       3. Pray that Christ will reign among the nations (Re 11:15).
  C. *"Your will be done..."*—We are to submit to God's will.
       1. In heaven God's will is perfectly executed.
       2. From earth we cry out that His will may be perfectly executed in our lives, in our churches, and among all peoples! (Read Ps 67:1-4.)
       3. This prayer of submission must begin with us.

III. OUR KINGDOM PRAYING SHOULD FOCUS ON EARTH
- Read vv.11-13 noting three phrases:

  A. *"Give us today our daily bread"*—We focus on our needs.
       1. "Our daily bread" includes all aspects of our lives.
       2. Another passage in Jesus' Sermon on the Mount that speaks of God's provision: (Read Mt 6:31-33).
  B. *"Forgive us our debts"*—We must address our sins.
       1. We have a continual need for cleansing (1Jn 1:8).
       2. We have continual provision for cleansing (1Jn 1:7, 9).
  C. *"Deliver us from the evil one"*—We must pray for deliverance.
       1. "Lead us not into temptation" can also be translated, "don't let us yield to temptation" (NLT).
       2. "Deliver us from the evil one" could be paraphrased, "Give us power over the devil and his demons" (1Jn 3:8).
       3. This saying of Jesus speaks of kingdom warfare (Ep 6:12; 2Co 10:4; 1Jn 4:4).

Conclusion
1. In the Lord's Prayer, Jesus addresses six kingdom issues: (1) God's name, (2) God's kingdom, (3) God's will, (4) our needs, ((5) our sins, and (5) our deliverance.
2. Can we believe for His kingdom to come in fullness?
3. Let's pray together, "Your kingdom come, your will be done on earth as it is in heaven"

[SP]

10 Working with God in Prayer

Sermon in a Sentence: God wants His people join Him in prayer to fulfill His will in them and in others.

Sermon Purpose: That God's people will pray more effectively by understanding God's purposes in prayer.

Text: Daniel 9:1-7; 16-19

Introduction
1. Three puzzling questions about prayer: (1) *If God all-knowing,* why must we tell Him what we need? (2) *If God is all-powerful,* why must we entreat Him to act? (3) *If God is all-good,* why must we ask Him to meet our needs?
2. This message will explore these questions and more.
3. We will learn that God wants His people to work with Him in prayer to accomplish His will in the earth.

I. DANIEL'S PERPLEXING PRAYER
A. The setting of Daniel's prayer: (Da 9:1-2)
   1. By reading the prophecy of Jeremiah, Daniel discovered that the time of Babylonian captivity would soon end.
   2. But instead of just going on his way, Daniel prayed with intense urgency for God's plan to be fulfilled.
B. The content of Daniel's prayer: (Da 9:3-19)
   1. He prayed for the very thing God already said He would do.
   2. Daniel knew that, even though God had announced what He wanted to do, he still needed to pray.
   3. He began by confessing his sin and the sins of his people.
   4. He prayed for God's glory, for God's people, and for the nations.
C. God answered Daniel's prayer.
   1. God sent an angel to speak to Daniel (Da 9:20-21).
   2. God did indeed bring His people back from captivity.

II. UNRAVELLING THE MYSTERY OF PRAYER
   - *Three reasons we, like Daniel, must pray:*
A. First, we must pray because, although God does not need to be reminded about the needs of humanity—*we do!*
   1. God does not need our help compiling His "to-do list."
   2. In prayer, we listen to God's plans for us and for His world!
   3. As we pray, God helps us to see more clearly the needs of those around us—and the needs of those around the world.

B. Second, we should pray, understanding that God does not immediately meet our every need—because He wants us to grow strong in Him.
  1. He wants us to learn to "abide in Christ" (Jn 15:8, 16).
  2. As we abide in Christ, we become more and more like Him (2Co 3:18).
  3. We become holy as He is holy and loving as He is loving.
C. Third, we should pray because God has chosen to do some things only in answer to His people's prayers.
  1. Some things God will do even if we do not pray.
  2. Other things God will not do, even if we do pray.
  3. However, there are a vast number of things that God wants to do, but He has sovereignly decided that He will do them only *if* His people pray. (Illus: 2Ch 7:14)

III. UNDERSTANDING GOD'S PURPOSES IN PRAYER
A. God's desire for the world is changed people as well as a changed world.
  1. When we pray, God uses our prayers to change the world.
  2. At the same time, He uses them to changes us.
B. There are many things God will do *only if* His people pray.
  1. And a burden to pray is an invitation from God to be changed ourselves.
C. What then should we do?
  1. We should ever remember that God is all-powerful, all-knowing, and all-good.
  2. We should also remember that, in many areas, God has chosen to work *only if* His people pray.
  3. As we pray…
    a. We should read and heed His voice in His Word.
    b. We should listen for the voice of the His Holy Spirit.
    c. And we should pray according to the Father's will with great sincerity, true feeling, and much faith!

Conclusion and Altar Call
  1. Come now; let's commit ourselves to work with God by praying according to His will.
  2. As we pray, let us listen to His heart, not only for ourselves, but for those around us—and for the unreached nations of the world.

[PY]

11 Abiding in Jesus

Sermon in a Sentence: We must learn to abide in Jesus.
Sermon Purpose: That God's people will commit themselves to—and begin to practice—abiding in Christ.
Text: John 15:4-5 (ESV)
Introduction
1. Every true follower of Jesus yearns for greater spiritual depth.
2. However, most of us do not know how to get there.
3. Without a deep relationship with Christ, our lives and ministries produce only wood, hay, and straw (1Co 3:11-13).
   a. Jesus: "Apart from me you can do nothing" (Jn 15:5).
4. We develop a deep relationship with Jesus by abiding in Him.
5. This message: "Abiding in Jesus"
   a. We will discover what such abiding looks like.
   b. We will commit ourselves to do what it takes to abide.

I. ABIDING IN JESUS BEGINS WITH DESPARATION
A. We abide in Jesus out of necessity.
   1. While discipline is necessary (as we shall see), abiding in Jesus begins with desperation.
   2. Desperation comes from our understanding that without Christ we are powerless frauds with wicked and deceitful hearts (Je 17:9).
   3. We must daily draw life, wisdom, guidance, correction, and strength from Jesus (2Co 3:18).
B. Our desperation for Jesus will empower our discipline.
   1. The discipline of abiding in Jesus is not easy.
   2. We must desire it enough to pay the price to get it.
   3. We abide because we know the rewards are great:
      a. Abiding results in intimacy with Jesus.
      b. Abiding results in power for ministry.
      c. Abiding results in joy in serving Jesus.

II. ABIDING IN JESUS CONTINUES WITH DISCIPLINE
A. Fruitful men and women of the past knew how to abide.
   1. They all spent extravagant time in the presence of Jesus.
   2. They all did it in the early morning.
   3. They adjusted their bedtimes so they could get up early.
B. We must do the same.
   1. We must lay aside the things that steal our time (He 12:1).

      2. We must chop away expendable activities.
  B. Adopt the motto, "No Bible, no breakfast."
      1. Wake up with a greeting to Jesus on your lips.
          a. A simple prayer of thanks and a plea for help.
      2. Go immediately to your abiding place.
  C. Then, throughout the day, combine prayer with other activities.
      1. For instance, pray as you walk or ride the bus to work.
      2. And pray as you go about your daily chores and activities.

III. SIX STRATEGIES FOR ABIDING IN JESUS
  A. Create a "distraction-free zone."
      1. Choose a comfortable place away from distractions.
      2. Each morning, go to the abiding place.
      3. Then, settle down to spend time in Jesus' presence.
  B. Get inspiration from others.
      1. Get inspiration from men and women of prayer in the Bible (Illus: Abraham, Moses, David, Jesus, Paul, and others)
      2. Read great books on prayer.
  C. Pray with your Bible in hand.
      1. You can use passages of Scripture as a prayer guide.
      2. Spend time memorizing chosen passages.
      3. Quote the Bible verses you have hidden in your heart.
  D. Use a prayer journal.
      1. Write down lessons learned from your reading.
      2. Record what the Spirit says to you.
      3. By doing this you can better harness what God gives you.
  E. Use the ACTS method to structure your prayer time. (Adoration, Confession, Thanksgiving, and Supplication)
      1. Spend 15 minutes on each part.
      2. During your supplication time, pray for lost people.
      3. Then pray for personal and family needs.
  F. Learn to pray "breath prayers."
      1. A good breath prayer is "Be near me, Lord Jesus."
      2. Another is, "I receive the Holy Spirit" (Jn 20:22)
      2. Pray them many times each day (1Th 5:17).

Conclusion and Altar Call
1. As we abide with Jesus, He will abide with us (John 15:4-5).
2. Come, commit yourself to a life of abiding in Jesus.

                                                          [DB]

12 Five Powerful Prayer Insights

Sermon in a Sentence: We must better understand the practice of prayer and commit ourselves to a life of prayer.
Sermon Purpose: That believers will commit themselves to more effective and consistent prayer lives.
Text: 1 Timothy 2:8
Introduction
1. Our text is one of many texts on prayer I could have chosen.
2. In it, Paul expresses his desire for God's people everywhere to become people of prayer.
3. This message: "Five Powerful Insights on Prayer"

I. PRAYER IS SIMPLE
   A. Sadly, some Christians avoid prayer because they think it to be a difficult and complex task.
      1. They think it requires a special gift or level of holiness.
   B. Prayer however, is simple.
      1. God designed it for every one of His children.
      2. Prayer requires no special gift or special position in life.
      3. It is simply meeting and talking with God.
   C. The simplicity of prayer is illustrated by who can pray:
      1. Both saints and sinners can pray (Re 8:4; Lk 18:13).
      2. Even a child can pray. (Illus: Tell the story of God talking to Samuel in 1Sa 3:1-11.)
      3. Jesus taught us a simple prayer (Mt 6:9-12).

II. PRAYER INVOLVES STRUGGLE
   A. Although prayer is simple, one should not conclude that there is no struggle in prayer.
      1. It sometimes involves confronting spiritual forces (Ep 6:12).
      2. We struggle against the world, flesh, and devil.
      3. Illus: Jesus struggled in Gethsemane (Mk 14:32-42).
   B. The good news is we do not war in our own strength.
      1. The Spirit will enables us to pray (Ro 8:26-27).
      2. Jude exhorted believers to build themselves up by praying in the Holy Spirit (Jude 20).

V. PRAYER SATISFIES
   A. God created humans to commune with Him.

       1. St. Augustine prayed, "You have made us for yourself, O Lord, and our heart is restless until it rests in you."
       2. David: "My soul finds rest in God alone…" (Ps 62:1).
  B. Prayer satisfies the human heart.
       1. It brings us into closer relationship with Christ.
       2. Illus: The old hymn. "Sweet Hour of Prayer" expresses how prayer satisfies the heart: "In seasons of distress and grief, my soul has often found relief, and oft escaped the tempter's snare by thy return, sweet hour of prayer!"
       3. The greatest satisfaction of prayer is the closeness it brings us to our Lord Jesus.

III. PRAYER SANCTIFIES
  A. The ultimate goal of the Christian life is to become like Jesus.
       1. The process of becoming like Jesus is called sanctification.
  B. One essential means of sanctification is prayer.
       1. (Note: Three other means of sanctification are the studying the word of God, fellowshipping with believers, and walking in the Holy Spirit).
       2. Through prayer, we draw close to Jesus.
       3. During those sacred of times of waiting on the Lord, the Spirit molds us into Christ's image (2Co 3:18).
  C. We must dedicate time to waiting on the Lord (Is 40:31).

IV. PRAYER BRINGS SUCCESS
  A. Prayer is one key to a successful Christian life.
       1. Success is not getting what we want from God; success is getting what God wants for us.
       2. He knows what is best for us.
  B. Prayer brings success in three ways:
       1. God sometimes grants the desire of our heart (Ps 21:2).
       2. We receive God's strength (2Co 12:8-10; Ep 3:16).
       3. The greatest success in prayer is that we discover and receive power to do God's will (Ps 40:8).

Conclusion and Altar Call
1. How foolish we would be not to pray; how wise to pray.
2. Come now, and commit yourself to a life of prayer.

[JDE]

13 A Key to Effective Prayer

Sermon in a Sentence: To pray effectively, we must focus on the coming of God's kingdom and the accomplishment of God's will.
Sermon Purpose: That God's people will learn how to pray more effectively.
Text: Matthew 6:10
Introduction
1. In Matthew 6:5-15, Jesus teaches His disciples how pray.
2. This teaching includes what is known as the "Lord's Prayer" (vv.9-13).
3. This message will focus on Jesus' words in v.10: "Your kingdom come, your will be done on earth as it is in heaven."
4. These words are a "Key to Effective Prayer."

I. THE DEFINITION OF PRAYER
A. What prayer *is not:*
 1. Prayer *is not* a set of manmade formulas we are to memorize and then repeat over and over.
   a. Jesus warned against such praying (Mt 6:7).
 2. Prayer *is not* phrases in a prayer book to be read without understanding or feeling.
B. What prayer *is:*
 1. Prayer *is* conversation with God.
 2. God speaks to us by His Word and His Spirit; we speak to Him in prayer.
 3. Being a conversation with God, prayer must be done in all seriousness.
 4. Because we are praying to God, our prayers must be done in humility and faith.

II. THE FOCUS OF OUR PRAYER
▪ *In our text (v.10), Jesus emphasized two important issues we should focus on when we pray:*
A. We should focus on *the reign (or kingdom) of God.*
 1. Jesus directs us to pray, "Your kingdom come" (v.10).
 2. This is a prayer for the coming of Christ's reign on earth.
 3. Advancing God's kingdom involves binding demonic spirits in the power of the Holy Spirit (Mt 12:28-29).
 4. The coming of God's kingdom will result in many people coming to Christ (Ac 2:41).

B. We should focus on *the will of God*
 1. Jesus directs us to pray, "Your will be done..." (v.10)
 2. God's will is for all people hear the gospel and be given an opportunity to be saved (Mt 24:14; 2Pe 3:9).
 3. It is also God's will that peace reign on earth as it is does in heaven (He 12:14).
 4. Let us claim the will of God in our prayers (1Jn 2:6).

III. THE CONTENT OF OUR PRAYER
 • *What should we pray about?*
A. We should pray *for our nation*. (Read 2Ch 7:14.)
 1. We should pray *for the authorities*. (Read 1Ti 2:1-3.)
 2. Our prayers can heal our nation (1Ti 2:3-4).
B. We should pray for people to be saved. (Read 1Ti 2:4.)
 1. Jesus is the only way (Ac 4:12).
C. We should pray *for our missionaries.*
 1. Paul prayed for the churches (1Th 1:2; Phi 1:4.)
 2. He also asked the churches to pray for him:
   a. They were to pray for open doors and the effective proclamation of the gospel. (Read Col 4:2-4.)
 3. Jesus told us to pray for harvest workers. (Read Lk 10:2.)
D. Several other issues we should pray about:
 1. Pray that God will pour out His Spirit (Lk 11:13; Ac 4:31).
 2. Pray that we will not to fall into temptation (Mt 26:41).
 3. Pray for the brothers and sisters (Eph 6:18; Ja 5:16).
 4. Pray for all of God's servants (Eph 6:19).
 5. Pray that God will forgive sinners (Da 9:16).
 6. Pray for personal needs (Phi 4:6).

IV. THE CONDUCT OF OUR PRAYER
 • *How are we to pray?*
A. We should pray with *faith* (He 11:6)
B. We should pray *constantly* (1Th 5:17).
C. We should pray with *perseverance* (Ac 2:42).
D. We should pray in the *name of Jesus* (Jn 14:13-14).

Conclusion and Altar Call
Come, commit yourself to pray that God's kingdom will come and that His will be done on earth as it is in heaven

[EYA]

14   When Women Pray

Sermon in a Sentence: We can learn much about prayer from Hannah, Mary, and the women of Pentecost.
Sermon Purpose: That women of God will be filled with the Spirit and commit themselves to prayer.
Text: 2 Chronicles 7:14
Introduction
1. Our text is a promise given to Solomon by God at the dedication of the temple in Jerusalem (2Ch 7:1-13).
2. It is a promise for both men *and women.*
   a. Note that God does not say "If *my men* will pray..."
   b. He says, "If *my people...*" meaning both men and women.
3. This message: "When Women Pray."
   a. We will look at the prayers of two women (Hannah and Mary) and one group of women (the women of Pentecost).
   b. We will learn some valuable lessons on prayer.

I. *WHEN HANNAH PRAYED*—GOD OPENED HER WOMB AND GAVE HER A SON
   A. Tell Hannah's story (1Samuel 1:10-17):
      1. Hannah's predicament—she was beloved but barren.
      2. She had one consuming desire—to bear a son.
      3. Her desire drove her to her knees in prayer.
      4. She persisted in prayer until God granted her request.
      5. Her prayer blessed a nation and advanced God's kingdom.
         a. Her son, Samuel, became the greatest of all the judges.
   B. We can learn three lessons from Hannah:
      1. Like Hannah, we should *be specific* when we pray.
         a. She knew exactly what she wanted from God.
         b. Therefore, she prayed specifically. (Read v.11)
         c. What do you want from God? Ask specifically!
      2. Like Hannah, we should *pray in earnest.*
         a. She sought God with all her heart (Read vv.10-13).
         b. She would not be deterred. (Read vv.7, 12, 16)
         c. God promises to answer our earnest prayers (Je 29:13).
      3. Like Hannah, we must *pray in faith.*
         a. She believed God would hear and answer her prayer.
         b. We too can be certain that God will hear and answer our faith-filled prayers (Mk 11:24).
         c. But we must pray in His will (1Jn 5:14-15).

II. *WHEN MARY PRAYED*—SHE GAVE GLORY TO GOD
A. Tell Mary's story (Luke 1:46-56):
   1. God revealed His plan to Mary thru Gabriel (vv.26-37).
   2. Mary humbly submitted to God's will (v.38).
   3. Soon after this, she traveled to Judea to see her elder cousin, Elizabeth (39-45).
   4. Meeting Elizabeth, Mary prayed a Spirit-inspired prayer: "My spirit rejoices in God my Savior…" (vv.46-55).
B. Lessons we learn from Mary's prayer:
   1. Submitting to God's will brings blessing and anointing.
   2. The Spirit will anoint us to pray (Ro 8:26-27).
   3. The Spirit will fill and inspire our praise (Jn 4:24).

III. *WHEN THE WOMEN OF PENTECOST PRAYED*—GOD EMPOWERED THEM TO PROCLAIM THE GOSPEL
A. Tell the story of the Women of Pentecost (Acts 1:12-14):
   1. When Jesus was about to ascend into heaven, He left His church with a final message. (Read Acts 1:4-5, 8)
      a. This promise of power was for women as well as men (Read 2:17-18).
      b. The women prayed alongside the men (Ac 1:13-14).
   2. God answered their prayer on the Day of Pentecost (2:1-4).
B. Note the following about the women at Pentecost:
   1. They received the *same command* and the *same promise* as did the men (Lk 24:49; Ac 1:4-5, 8).
   2. They joined in the *same prayer* with the men (Ac 1:14).
   3. They received the *same Spirit* the as men: "They were *all* (men and women) filled with the Holy Spirit…" (Ac 2:4).
   4. They *spoke in tongues* "declaring the wonderful works of God" just like the men (Ac 2:4, 11).
   5. They became *Spirit-empowered witnesses* just like the men.
C. From this story, we learn that…
   1. God wants to fill women with the Spirit.
   2. God wants to use Spirit-empowered women to advance His kingdom.

Conclusion and Altar Call
1. These are but three of the many biblical examples of how God used praying women.
2. Come now; let's commit ourselves to pray. [SJM]

15 Turn Aside and Hear the Voice of God

Sermon in a Sentence: God wants us to turn aside, hear His voice, receive His power, and do His will.
Sermon Purpose: That God's people will commit to spending time in prayer in order to receive God's power and direction.
Text: Exodus 3:1-4; 4:1-4 (KJV)
Introduction
1. God is still looking for people who will "turn aside" in prayer and listen to His voice and receive His power.
2. Picture yourself as Moses in this story: God is appearing to you, calling you into His service.
3. Moses wisely "turned aside" to hear the voice of God (v.3).
4. From this story, we learn three important lessons:

I. TURNING ASIDE IN PRAYER WILL ENABLE US TO HEAR GOD'S VOICE
A. Because Moses chose to turn aside, he heard the voice of God. (Read Ex 3:3-4.)
   1. God wanted Moses to know what was in His heart.
   2. Had Moses not turned aside, He would have never heard.
   3. Illus: Jesus often turned aside to pray.
      1. Read: Mt 14:23; Mk; 1:35; Lk 5:16.
      2. He tells us to do the same (Mt 6:6).
B. God shared with Moses His desire to deliver His people.
   1. Read Ex 3:7-8: "I have seen their affliction…
   2. God sees the needs of the lost souls around us and around the world, and He wants to use us to deliver them.
C. When we turn aside to pray, God will speak to us.
   1. Just as He spoke to Moses.
   2. Just as He spoke to Jesus (Jn 5:19-20).
   3. If you will hear the voice of God, you must make time to turn aside in prayer.

II. TURNING ASIDE IN PRAYER WILL ENABLE GOD TO SHOW US THE KEYS TO SUCCESS
A. God had great plans for Moses; however, Moses doubted his own abilities (vv.10-11; 4:1).
   1. It is often the same with us: when God calls us to do something, we respond by telling Him why we cannot.
B. God answered Moses by showing him His power (4:2-5).

1. God showed Moses the first step He must take:
   a. He asked Moses, "What is in your hand?" (4:2).
   b. Then, "Cast [your rod] to the ground…" (v.3).
   c. The rod turned into a snake and back into a rod again.
2. God would show Moses His power again and again throughout Moses' life (Ex 4:21; Dt 6:22; Ac 17:36).

C. God was showing Moses the key to his future success.
   1. God was, in effect, saying, "If I have power to turn a rod into a snake, I can turn a shepherd like you into a mighty deliverer. I will deliver Israel by My mighty power!"
   2. God is saying the same thing to us today.
      a. If we will turn aside and pray, He will give us the key to success (Je 33:3).
      b. He will empower us with the Holy Spirit (Ac 1:8).
      c. He will direct us and show us what we must do next.
   3. But like Moses, we must turn aside and allow God to work in our lives.

III. TURNING ASIDE IN PRAYER WILL ENABLE GOD TO SHOW US WHAT IS HINDERING OUR SUCCESS

A. Moses' feeling of inadequacy was hindering him from doing God's will.
   1. "Who am I for such a great task?" (Ex 3:11).
   2. "They will not believe me, nor hearken unto my voice" (4:1).
   3. We often ask the same question, "Who am I?"
B. God, however, showed Moses that He was greater than Moses' feelings of inadequacy.
   1. Moses could accomplish the impossible—if he would depend on God.
   2. The same is true for us today, God can use us to accomplish the seemingly impossible—if we will depend on Him.

Conclusion and Altar Call
1. To be used by God, we must learn to "turn aside" and get alone with God to receive His power and hear His voice.
2. Come now, be filled with the Spirit, and commit yourself to spending time with God and listening to His voice.

[MG]

16 End-Time Praying

Sermon in a Sentence: We should pray in light of Jesus' coming.
Sermon Purpose: That Christians understand how the soon coming of Jesus should affect their prayers.
Text: Revelation 22:17-20 (emphasize v.20)
Introduction
1. We have just read the closing words of the Bible.
2. They include a declaration and a prayer.
   a. The *declaration* is from Jesus: "Yes, I am coming soon."
   b. The *prayer* is from John: "Amen, Come Lord Jesus."
3. This message will focus on John's prayer.
   a. It can serve as an inspiration for our prayers today.
   b. It is an example of "End-Time Praying."
4. This prayer of John informs our praying today in three ways:

John's prayer helps us to know that...
I. **WE MUST PRAY IN KEEN ANTICIPATION OF CHRIST'S SOON COMING** (v.20)
   A. We must keep in mind, that we are living in the Last Days.
      1. The "Last Days" began with Jesus' first coming, and will continue until His second coming.
      2. We are an "eschatological people"—that is, a "last days" people (1Co 10:11).
      3. Jesus is coming soon: "Yes, I am coming soon! (Re 22:20; See also Mt 24:27; 1Co 15:51-52).
      4. We are living at the "end of the end times."
   B. This fact should affect how we pray.
      1. We should pray with a sense of *urgency*.
      2. We should pray with a sense of *anticipation*.

John's prayer helps us to know that...
II. **WE MUST PRAY WITH AN UNDERSTANDING OF—AND STRONG COMMITMENT TO—GOD'S MISSION** (v.17)
   A. John prayed in response to Christ's call to lost people to "Come."
      1. Read Re 22:17: "The Spirit and the bride say, *'Come...'*"
      2. Jesus often called on people to "Come!"
         a. Mt 4:19: "*Come*, follow me..."
         b. Mt 12:28: "*Come* to me, all you who are weary..."
         c. Mt 22:4: "Everything is ready. *Come* to the...banquet."

3. Now, in our text, the Spirit and the Bride (the Church) join Jesus in calling people to come to Him.
   a. It is a universal call: *"Whoever* is thirsty..."
   b. It is a gracious call: "Let him take the *free gift* of eternal life" (Re 22:17).
B. In this context, John prays, "Amen. *Come,* Lord Jesus!"
   1. The lesson is this: When we pray, "Come Lord Jesus," we should pray with an understanding of God's mission to redeem the nations.
   2. Jesus taught us to pray, "Your kingdom come," but He also taught us to pray "Your will be done on earth as it is in heaven" (Mt 6:10).
   3. Pray that God's mission will advance in the earth (Mt 24:14).

John's prayer helps us to know that...
III. WE MUST PRAY WITH THE HELP OF THE HOLY SPIRIT
A. In our text, the Spirit encourages prayer (v.17).
   1. John began Revelation with the words, "On the Lord's Day, I was in the *Spirit...*" (Re 1:10).
   2. Now, he ends the book by saying *"The Spirit* and bride say, 'Come!'"
   3. The Spirit is guiding him in his prophecy—and his prayer.
B. Paul knew we need the Spirit's help when we pray.
   1. He wrote, "I will pray with the spirit, and I will pray with the understanding also" (1Co 14:15).
   2. In Ro 8:26-27 he explains how the Spirit helps us pray:
      a. He says, "We don't know what we ought to pray for."
      b. Then he says, "The Spirit himself intercedes for us with groanings too deep for words" (v.26 ESV).
      c. Then he says, "The Spirit intercedes...in accordance with the will of God" (v.27).
C. If we are going to pray as God wants us to pray, we must allow the Spirit to help us.

Conclusion and Altar Call
1. We are living in the end-times.
2. This fact should affect the way we pray. (Recap the 3 main points.)
3. Come, let's commit ourselves to End time Praying.

[DRM]

Section 2
The Power of Prayer

17 Power Praying

Sermon in a Sentence: We should pattern our prayer meetings after the one found in Acts 4.
Sermon Purpose: That believers will be filled with the Spirit and begin to pray powerful prayers like the believers in Acts.
Text: Acts 4:23-31
Introduction
1. Acts has much to say about the prayer life of the New Testament church.
    a. Prayer is mentioned at least 35 times in Acts.
    b. The NT church was constant in prayer.
2. In this message, we go into one of their prayer meetings.
    a. An example of what could be called "Power Praying."
    b. Briefly tell the background of the prayer meeting (Ac 3-4).
3. Three lessons we can learn about how we should pray today:

I. WE LEARN HOW WE SHOULD PRAY
  ▪ *Like theirs, our prayer meetings today should be characterized by two things:*
  A. First, our praying should be *fervent*.
    1. v.23: "They *raised* their voices…"
    2. It was Spirit inspired praying.
  B. Next, our praying should be *unified*.
    1. v.23: They raised their voices *together…"*
    2. There is tremendous power in unified prayer!
        a. Jesus' promise: (Read Mt 18:19-20)
        b. Dt 32:30 (One will chase 1,000; two 10,000)

II. WE LEARN WHAT WE SHOULD PRAY FOR
  ▪ *Like them, we should pray for the following:*
  A. We should pray *God-centered* prayers.
    1. Read vv.24-30 emphasizing the words *You* and *Your.*
    2. This is much different from the problem-centered prayers we often hear today.
    3. Jesus taught us to begin our prayers by focusing on God:
        a. Read Mt 6:9: "Our father in heaven, hallowed…"
  B. We should pray *Christ-exalting* prayers.
    1. Notice how their prayer exalted Jesus (Read vv.27, 30).
    2. Jesus must be at the center of our prayers (Jn 14:13-14).

C. We should pray *faith-filled* prayers (vv.29-30).
1. They prayed as if they expected God to answer their prayer.
2. We too must pray as if we expect God to answer.
D. We should pray *mission-oriented* prayers
1. They did not ask to be delivered from the problems, but that God use them to advance His mission.
2. v.29: "Lord…enable your servants to speak your word with great boldness."
3. This prayer must often be on our lips.
E. We should pray *Spirit-invoking* prayers.
1. They asked God to move by His Spirit:
    a. v.29: Lord, "enable your servants to speak your word with great boldness" (Echoes the promise of Ac 1:8)
    b. v.30: *"Stretch out your hand* to heal and perform miraculous signs…"
    c. Note: For God to "stretch out His hand" is for Him to move by His Spirit (Ez 37:1; Lk 11:20 w/ Mt 12:28; Ac 11:21).

III. WE LEARN WHAT WE CAN WE CAN EXPECT TO HAPPEN WHEN WE PRAY
- *Like them, we can expect these results:*
A. We can expect *God to make His presence known.*
1. v. 31: "the place where they were meeting was shaken..."
2. We can expect God to manifest His presence through miracles, wonders, conviction of sin, and changed lives.
B. We can expect our churches to be *filled with the Holy Spirit.*
1. v.31: "And they were all filled with the Holy Spirit…"
2. Like on the Day of Pentecost (Ac 2:4).
C. We can expect powerful *proclamation of the gospel.*
1. v. 31 "…and spoke the word of God boldly…"
2. What was the result of their Spirit-empowered proclamation? (Read vv.32-33; Ac 5:14).

Conclusion and Altar Call:
1. Come, let's commit ourselves to pray like the believers in the book of Acts.
2. Come, let's ask God to fill us with the Holy Spirit.

[DRM]

18 Pray! Pray! Pray!

Sermon in a Sentence: The Bible encourages us to pray! pray! pray!
Sermon Purpose: That God's people will commit themselves to ongoing and effective prayer.
Texts: Exodus 17:8-13; Nehemiah 1:1-4; Ezekiel 22:29-31; Isaiah 62:6-7

Introduction
1. In each of our four texts, we are encouraged to pray:
   a. As long as *Moses'* hands were lifted, Israel prevailed.
   b. *Nehemiah* prayed day and night for God's intervention.
   c. In *Ezekiel,* God sought for a man to stand in the gap.
   d. In *Isaiah,* God challenged His people to give Him no rest until He answers their prayers and establishes Jerusalem.
2. These prophets are telling God's people to "Pray, pray, pray!"
3. At the close of this message, we will commit ourselves to ongoing and effective prayer.

I. **A DEFINITION OF PRAYER** (What is prayer?)
   A. Prayer is…the pulse of life.
      1. …the secret of success in our walk with God.
      2. …spiritual oxygen giving life to our souls.
      3. …fuel for the engine of God's mission.
      4. …spiritual breathing—exhaling the spirit of man and inhaling the Spirit of God.
      5. …spiritual disinfectant—purifying the space of demonic activity.
   B. Through prayer, we…draw near to God.
      1. …satisfy our hunger for God.
      2. …enter into the presence of God.
      3. …give the devil a flogging.
      4. …set our hearts aflame for God and His mission.
      5. …acquire the anointing to do God's work.

II. **THE PROBLEM OF PRAYERLESSNESS**
   A. Rather than pray, it is easier to plan, preach, sing, or hold a committee meeting.
   B. However, a prayerless Christian is…a powerless Christian.
      1. …a fruitless Christian.
      2. …a crooked Christian.
      3. …a backsliding Christian.

C. Because, when we stop praying...we start sinning.
   1. ...we forfeit the continuous presence of God.
   2. ...we have no manifestation of spiritual gifts.
   4. ...we bury people rather than seeing them healed.
   5. ...our testimonies are filled with what the devil is doing rather than how God is answering our prayers.
D. However, when we do pray...
   1. ...more sick people are healed.
   2. ...the church grows both numerically and spiritually.

III. THE POWER OF PRAYER
A. Prayer has the power to...
   1. ...demolish strong barriers and melt hard hearts.
   2. ...cause earthquakes in the kingdom of darkness.
   3. ...spark a true Pentecostal revival.
   4. ...open doors of effective ministry.
   5. ...empower us to accomplish much for God.
B. Prayer has no substitute, because it alone can...
   1. ...bring persuasive power into the pulpit.
   2. ...turn dead theology into flaming "kneeology,"
   3. ...transform head knowledge into heart passion.
   4. ...release the supernatural into our lives and ministries.
   5. ...change our dead services into encounters with God.
C. If we want to pray more powerfully...
   1. We must overcome an undisciplined life, including...
      a. ...laziness, late sleeping, sit sleeping, "knee sleeping"
      b. ...overeating.
      c. ...wandering thoughts.
   2. We must depart from sin (Pr 28:9; Ps 66:18), including...
      a. ...the careless use of the tongue.
      b. ...unfaithfulness to God and His work.
   4. We must forsake of wrong attitudes, including...
      a. ...an unforgiving spirit and malice towards others.
      b. ...lack of burden for lost souls.

Conclusion and Altar Call
1. First, we must repent of our prayerlessness.
2. Then, we must commit ourselves to "Pray, pray, pray!"
3. Come now, let's do business with God.

[CO]

19 Prayer Unlimited

Sermon in a Sentence: Since God is unlimited in by space, time, or degree, our prayers to Him are also unlimited

Sermon Purpose: That God's people will have confidence to *ask largely of the Lord!*

Texts: Jeremiah 32:17; Luke 1:37

Introduction
1. We often speak of the *power of prayer*.
    a. However, in reality, it is not prayer that is powerful; it is our God who answers prayer who is powerful.
    b. Prayer is unlimited because God is unlimited.
2. Both of our texts speak about the unlimited ability of God.
    a. Je 32:17: "Ah, Lord God…nothing is too hard for you…"
    b. Lk 1:37: "Nothing is impossible with God."
3. Prayer is thus unlimited in three ways:

I. PRAYER IS UNLIMITED BY SPACE
A. Prayer is as vast as the God who hears us when we pray.
   1. God is omniscient—that is, He is everywhere present.
   2. David spoke about this. (Read Ps 139:7-10).
B. Because God is everywhere, prayer is not limited by space.
   1. Through prayer, you can go anywhere.
   2. Wesley Duewel: "Prayer can give us instant entrance into any home, any hospital, any government office, and any courtroom in any part of the world. Just as distance cannot hinder your reach in prayer, neither can walls or 'no entry' signs halt our presence or stay our hand in prayer."
   3. Because when you pray *here*—God is always *there*.
C. Through prayer, you can become a missionary anywhere in the world without ever leaving your home.

II. PRAYER IS UNLIMITED BY TIME
A. Because God dwells in eternity, He is not limited by time.
   1. Moses prayed, "From everlasting to everlasting you are God" (Ps 90:2).
   2. He added, "For a thousand years in your sight are like a day that has just gone, or like a watch in the night" (v.4).
   3. Peter wrote, "With the Lord a day is like a thousand years, and a thousand years are like a day" (2Pe 3:8).

       4. Isaiah added that God is "the high and lofty One…who lives forever…" (Isa 57:15).
   B. Because God lives forever, our prayers live forever.
       1. Sometimes, the answer to prayer comes after we have died.
       2. The prayers of a mother or father for their children live on—even after they are placed in the grave.
       3. The prayers for unreached peoples and places live on—even after the intercessors have gone to be with the Lord.
   C. So, keep praying—you prayers will never die.

III. PRAYER IS UNLIMITED BY DEGREE
   A. Because we serve and all-powerful God, our prayers are unlimited as to what they can accomplish.
       1. Remember our texts:
           a. "Ah, Sovereign LORD, you have made the heavens and the earth by your great power and outstretched arm. Nothing is too hard for you" (Je 32:17).
           b. "Nothing is impossible with God" (Lk 1:37).
       2. Paul adds that God "is able to do immeasurably more than all we ask or imagine" (Ep 3:20).
   B. Because God is all-powerful, there is no prayer He cannot answer.
       1. Jesus told His disciples, "I tell you the truth, if you have faith as small as a mustard seed, you can say to this mountain, 'Move from here to there' and it will move. Nothing will be impossible for you" (Mt 17:20).
   C. We should therefore pray with great confidence.
       1. We should *ask largely of the Lord!*
       2. Song: Got any rivers you think are uncrossable?
                 Got any mountains, you cannot tunnel through?
                 God specializes in things thought impossible.
                 And He can do what no other power can do.

Conclusion and Altar Call
   1. Believing prayer is unlimited by space, time, or degree.
   2. Let's come and ask God to work miracles.

[DRM]

20 Mighty Prevailing Prayer

Sermon in a Sentence: If we will, we can prevail in prayer.
Sermon Purpose: That God's people will commit to unified, fervent, audacious, faith-filled, Spirit-anointed intercessory prayer.
Texts: Mark 11:22-24
Introduction
1. Are you longing for more power in prayer?
   a. Do you crave the ability to get answers from God?
   b. Would you like to be able to prevail in prayer?
2. In our text, Jesus says that through believing prayer we can move mountains.
   a. He is calling us to mighty prevailing prayer.
   b. Prevailing prayer is prayer that obtains the answer sought.

I. **THE NATURE OF MIGHTY PREVAILING PRAYER**
   A. Prevailing prayer is God's ordained means…
      1. …for defeating Satan and his empire of darkness.
      2. …of accomplishing His will among the nations.
      3. …of extending His kingdom to the ends of the earth.
      4. Prevailing prayer is a mighty force in the hands of the committed follower of Christ.
   B. What does prevailing prayer look like?
      1. It looks like the afflicted woman pushing through the crowd to touch the hem of Jesus' garment (Lk 8:43-48).
      2. It looks like the Syrophoenician woman entreating Jesus to deliver her demon possessed daughter (Mk 7:25-30).
      3. It looks like Jacob, when he wrestled with the angel: "I will not let you go unless you bless me" (Ge 32:22-26).
   C. Any Christian can prevail in prayer.
      1. Such mighty prayer is not reserved for the spiritual elite.
      2. God stands ready to answer our prayers; however, we must commit ourselves to pray.

II. **SIX DYNAMICS OF MIGHTY PREVAILING PRAYER**
   A. The dynamic of *desire:*
      1. Desire for God is at the heart of all prayer (Ps 42:1).
      2. Like Jesus, we must desire what God desires (He 10:7).
      3. The deeper our desire, the more powerful our prayer.
   B. The dynamic of *fervency:*
      1. "Fervent prayer…avails much" (Ja 5:16 KJV).

2. God has no use for lukewarm prayers (Re 3:16).
   3. We can approach God's throne with boldness (He 4:16).
C. The dynamic of *persistence:*
   1. We must pray like the persistent friend (Lk 11:5-7).
   2. "Persistence" (NKJV) or "shameless audacity" (NIV).
   3. God calls us to bold, audacious prayer.
D. The dynamic of *faith:*
   1. Faithless prayer is powerless prayer (Ja 1:5-7).
   2. However, faith-filled prayer moves the hand of God (Mk 11:24).
   3. We can choose to pray in faith,
E. The dynamic of *the Spirit:*
   1. When we do not know how to pray, the Spirit will come and help us (Ro 8:26).
   2. Spirit-anointed prayer is powerful prayer (Ep 6:18).
   3. The Bible commands, "Be filled with the Spirit (Ep 5:18).
F. The dynamic of *unity:*
   1. There is great power in unity (Ec 4:12).
   2. Unified prayer brings the Spirit:
      a. Illus: At Pentecost (Ac 1:14 then 2:1-4).
      b. Illus: After Pentecost (Ac 4:22-23 then 31).
   3. Let us join together in prayer for the Spirit.

III. OUR COMMITMENT TO MIGHTY PREVAILING PRAYER
A. If we will pray, God will answer.
   1. God promises, "Call to me and I will answer you and tell you great and unsearchable things you do not know" (Je 33:3).
   2. Jesus promised, "Whatever you ask for in prayer, believe that you have received it, and it will be yours" (Mk 11:24).
B. We must commit ourselves to unified, fervent, audacious, faith-filled, Spirit-anointed prayer.

Conclusion and Altar Call
Come; let's commit ourselves to "Mighty Prevailing Prayer."

[WD]

This sermon was inspired and adapted from Wesley Duewel's book, *Mighty Prevailing Prayer,* Zondervan, 1990

21 Hannah's Mighty Prayer

Sermon in a Sentence: Hannah is an example of how women can become powerful in prayer.
Sermon Purpose: That women will be encouraged to dedicate their lives to intercessory prayer.
Text: 1 Samuel 1:1-28
Introduction
1. Hannah was a woman mighty in prayer.
2. Her prayer changed the course of a nation.
3. Note three things about Hannah's prayer:

I. **NOTE THE OCCASION OF HANNAH'S PRAYER**
   A. Hannah was *favored*—yet she was *barren*.
      1. Her husband favored her over Peninnah (vv.4-5, 8).
      2. However, God had closed her womb (vv.2, 6).
      3. Her condition describes many Christians and churches:
         a. They are blessed but barren.
         b. They have "God's favor" but they are spiritually barren; they are not winning the lost to Christ.
   B. Hannah was living in shame (vv.6-7).
      1. Peninnah mocked her because she was barren (vv.6-7).
      2. Many churches today are living in similar shame.
         a. They seek God's blessing while ignoring those for whom Christ died.
         b. Satan laughs are their shameful behavior.
   C. Hannah's shame drove her to pray (vv.9-10).
      1. She did more than fret—she went to God in prayer.
      2. Our spiritual barrenness should drive us to prayer.

II. **NOTE THE NATURE OF HANNAH'S PRAYER**
   A. She began by *committing herself* (and her child) to God (v.11).
      1. She gave herself to God.
      2. She vowed to give her son to God (v.11).
   B. She prayed *from her heart:*
      1. She knew exactly what she wanted—a son (v.10).
      2. She poured out her soul to God (v.10, 15-16).
   C. She *persisted* in prayer:
      1. "She kept on praying" (v.12).
   D. We would do well to follow Hannah's example:
      1. We must commit ourselves to God and to His mission.

2. We must commit ourselves to reaching the lost.
3. We must seek God from the depths of our hearts: "Oh Lord, give us souls! gives us spiritual sons and daughters."
4. We must persist in prayer God answers.

III. NOTE THE EFFECTS OF HANNAH'S PRAYER
A. Hannah's prayer changed the course of a nation.
1. Her prayer is memorialized in Scripture.
2. God answered Hannah's prayer and gave her Samuel (20).
3. In turn, Hannah fulfilled her vow to God (vv.24-28).
4. Her child then pointed the nation to God.
B. Listen to what the Bible says about Hannah's son, Samuel:
1. He is mentioned 121 times in the Bible.
2. His name means "name of God."
3. God called him while he was still a boy (1Sa 3:1-21).
4. He was both a prophet and priest (1Sa 3:20; 1Sa 7:9).
5. The was the last and greatest of the Hebrew Judges.
6. He anointed the first two kings of Israel (Saul and David).
7. He then challenged them and called the nation back to God
8. He was mighty in prayer: He was "among those who called upon [God's] name…and He answered them" (Is 99:6).
C. Only God knows the far-reaching effects of women's prayers.
1. Prayer moves the hand of God, and the hand of God moves the hearts of kings and other powerful leaders.
2. Through prayer, any woman can…
   a. ….overpower the devil and cancel his plans.
   b. …call down revival fire from heaven.
   c. …enter the halls of government and influence the decisions of powerful men and women.
   d. …open the doors of peoples and nations to the proclamation of the gospel.
   d. …go with missionaries to the foreign field and stand beside them as they preach the gospel.

Conclusion and Altar Call
Come, join me in the front, and let's dedicate ourselves to prayer.

[DRM]

22 The Power of United Prayer 1
~ Praying for an Outpouring of the Spirit ~

Sermon in a Sentence: We must come together in united prayer for an outpouring of the Holy Spirit.
Sermon Purpose: That God's people will unite in prayer for an outpouring of God's Spirit
Texts: Luke 24:51-53; Acts 1:12-14, 24-26, 2:1-4
Introduction
1. In his gospel, Luke wrote much about prayer (see: 6:12-13, 11:1-10, 18:1-17).
2. Then, in the book of Acts, he showed us on how the early church prayed.
   a. One remarkable characteristic of their prayer was how they prayed in unity.
   b. In our texts, this unified prayer prepared their hearts for the outpouring of the Spirit on the Day of Pentecost.
3. Let's look at three ways united prayer helped the disciples receive the Holy Spirit:

I. **UNITED PRAYER PREPARED THEM FOR THE COMING OF THE HOLY SPIRIT** (Lk 24:51-53)
   A. Just as we prepare to receive visitors into our homes, the early church prepared for the coming of the Holy Spirit.
   B. They prepared in two ways:
      1. They prepared *with praise and worship* (Lk 24:51-53).
         a Praise and worship drew them into the presence of the Giver of the Holy Spirit.
         b. Worship brings the presence of God (Ps 22:3; 100:4).
      2. They prepared *with prayer and supplication* (Ac 1:14).
         a. As they waited together for the coming of the Spirit, they offered their requests to God (Ac 1:14).
         b. For ten days they waited in one accord (Ac 2:1 KJV).
      3. God answered their prayer by sending the Holy Spirit (2:4).
   C. We too must prepare ourselves for the Spirit' coming through united prayer.

II. **UNITED PRAYER HELPED THEM TO CHOOSE SOMEBODY TO REPLACE JUDAS** (Ac 1:24-26)
   A. God needs men and women He can use to spread the gospel.
      1. Every person is important in the ministry.

      2. The absence of even one person can affect the work.
- B. Their prayer for Judas' replacement shows us two things:
  1. It shows that *God uses people with pure hearts* (v.24).
     a. Only those with pure hearts will see God (Mt 5:8).
     b. The Spirit uses those whose hearts are prepared.
     c. He looks into the heart before He chooses workers for His vineyard (1Sa 16:7).
  2. It shows that *we need God to choose for us* (v.24).
     a. We must beware of using human methods in choosing leaders.
     b. We must rather seek God for His guidance (Lk 6:12-13; Ac 13:1-4).
     c. Since the work belongs to God, He knows what each of us can do best.

III. UNITED PRAYER BRINGS THE POWER OF GOD
- A. As they waited in unified prayer and worship, God poured out the Holy Spirit on them all (Ac 2:1-4).
- B. Note these two things about their receiving the Spirit:
  1. They waited *with one accord* (Ac 2:1 KJV).
     a. They we in unity of mind and purpose.
     b. The Holy Spirit fell on them (vv.3-4).
     c. They began to work in unity (Ac 2:44-47).
  2. They were *all* filled with the Holy Spirit (Ac 2:4).
     a. Every one of them received the Holy Spirit—men, women, and all.
     b. This was as Joel had prophesied (Ac 2:16-18).
     c. Everybody has a role to play in building the kingdom of God; therefore...
     d. Everybody must be filled with the Holy Spirit.
- C. We too must pray in one accord until God pours out His Spirit.

Conclusion and Altar Call
1. When the church prays with one accord, great things happen.
2. Come now, let's join hearts and ask God to pour out His Spirit on our church.

[PFM]

23. The Power of United Prayer 2
~ Praying for God's Empowering ~

Sermon in a Sentence: When we face opposition, we must unify in prayer asking God to empower us with the Holy Spirit.

Sermon Purpose: That God's people will unify in prayer for the Spirit when facing opposition to the gospel.

Text: Acts 4:23-31

Introduction
1. How should we respond when we face opposition to the preaching of the gospel?
2. In this passage, we will learn how the early church responded.
3. They responded with unified, faith-filled prayer.
    a. Tell the background story of their prayer (Acts 3-4).
    b. Reread their prayer (4:23-31).
4. What lessons can we learn from this account?

I. THE APOSTLES' OMINOUS REPORT (v.23)
A. When Peter and John were released, they reported to the church all that had happened (v.23).
   1. It was an ominous report.
   2. The Jewish leaders had been commanded to stop preaching in Jesus' name—or suffer the consequences (vv.17-18).
B. Peter and John made the only choice they could make…
   1. They refused to stop preaching (vv.19-20).
   2. The Jewish leaders threatened them, then let them go.
C. We too face a choice today.
   1. Satan opposes our witness for Christ
   2. He attacks us both spiritually and physically.
   3. None of these should stop us from preaching the gospel.

II. THE CHURCH'S UNIFIED RESPONSE (v.24)
A. The church responded with unified, faith-filled prayer.
   1. They did not overlook the report; they rather treated it with all the seriousness it deserved.
   2. Then, they gathered the church for prayer.
B. Note these four ways they responded in unified prayer:
   1. *They acted promptly* (v.24a).
      a. This shows how united the church was.
      b. Thus unified, nothing could stop them (Ge 11:6).
   2. *They prayed to God* (v.24b).

           a. They did not make their appeal to the authorities, or begin commanding demons, they directed their pray to God.
        3. *They mentioned what God had done in the past.*
           a. He "made the heaven and the earth…" (v.24c)
        4. *They mentioned what God had said* (v.25; ref Ps 2:1-6)
           a. Such praying strengthened their faith and resolve.
    C. When we face opposition today, we must come together in unified, faith-filled, God-honoring prayer.

III. THE DISCIPLES' FAITH-FILLED REQUEST (v.29)
    A. They did not pray for safety, but for boldness to fulfill their God-given mission (v.29).
    B. They specifically asked for three things:
        1. They asked for *boldness to speak* (v.29).
           a. That is, divine enablement to preach the gospel.
        2. They asked God to *stretch out His hand* (v.30).
           a. This is a prayer for the Holy Spirit.
        3. They asked for *miraculous signs* to confirm the message of the gospel (v.30).
           a. This is what Jesus had promised (Mk 16:15-20).
    C. We too must be unified in our commitment to preach the gospel and to pray often for the Spirit's empowering.

IV. GOD'S POWERFUL RESPONSE (v.31)
    A. God heard and powerfully answered their prayer (v.31).
        1. He "stretched out His hand" by sending the Holy Spirit.
    B. Two specific ways God responded to their prayer:
        1. God *manifested* His powerful presence—the place shook.
        2. God *filled* them with the Holy Spirit (v.31b).
           a. They *all* prayed—and they were *all* filled.
           b. They were *all* empowered to preach the gospel.
           c. They *all* spoke the word with boldness (vv.31, 33).
    C. We can expect God to respond the same way today.

Conclusion and Altar Call
    1. When we face opposition, we should together turn to God in in unified, faith-filled prayer.
    2. Come, let's ask God to fill us again with His Holy Spirit and energize us to preach the gospel in the face of opposition

[PFM]

24 The Power of United Prayer 3
~ Praying for Deliverance ~

Sermon in a Sentence: If we will unite in prayer, God will deliver those in physical and spiritual bondage.

Sermon Purpose: That God's people will commit themselves to praying for those in physical and spiritual bondage.

Text: Acts 12:4-17

Introduction
1. Like Peter in prison, many in the church and in the world today are in bondage, both physical and spiritual.
2. United prayer can break these shackles.
3. Today's Scripture reading illustrates this truth.
   a. Tell the story of Peter's arrest and imprisonment (12:1-5).
   b. Tell how the church responded with unified prayer (v.5).
4. From this story, we can learn three powerful lessons concerning united prayer:

I. **UNITED PRAYER BREAKS CHAINS** (v.7)
   A. As a result of the church's prayer, Peter's chains fell off (v.7).
      1. Tell of how the angel freed Peter (v.7-8).
      2. In Acts God often answered people's prayer by sending angels to minister to them (5:9; 10:4; 12:8; 27:23).
      3. Angels are God's messengers sent to minister to God's children (He 1:14).
      4. In another place in Acts, God chose to use other means (an earthquake) to deliver His servants (Ac 16:26).
         a. This deliverance also came as a result of prayer (v.25).
   B. If we will pray, God will deliver those in chains:
      1. He will deliver *Christians from physical chains.*
         a. We must unite in prayer for our brothers and sisters in prison for preaching of the gospel.
         b. Even if they should die in the persecution, God will give them courage to endure (Re 2:10).
      2. He will deliver *sinners from spiritual chains.*
         a. We should pray that God will deliver sinners from spiritual bondage.
         b. Then, we must go out and proclaim the good news in the power of the Holy Spirit (Ac 1:8).

II. **UNITED PRAYER BREAKS BARRIERS** (v.8-10)

A. Tell how the angel led Peter to the iron gate (vv.8-10).
  1. Although the chains were gone, Peter was still in prison.
  2. (Remember, the church was still praying for Peter.)
  3. When he came to the iron gate, it miraculously opened.
B. God is able to do the same today.
  1. As we preach the gospel, and do kingdom work, we will encounter roadblocks and barriers:
     a. Barriers such as governmental restrictions and religious bigotry.
     b. Barriers such as lack of workers and lack of funding.
  2. At such times, we must not allow anything to threaten us (Ps 57:4-7).
  3. We must rather unite in prayer, believing that God will break every barrier.

III. UNITED PRAYER CAUSES SURPRISES (vv.9-15)
A. The miracle of Peter's deliverance caused two surprises:
  1. First, Peter himself was surprised to find himself on the street outside of the prison (Ac 12:9-11).
  2. Second, the praying church was surprised to see Peter at the door of their house of prayer (vv.12-16).
  3. When we unite in prayer, we can expect such wonderful surprises from God (Eph 3:20).
B. However, like the church in Acts, our united prayer must be earnest and constant (v.5, NKJV, NIV; Ja 5:16).
  1. It continued through the night until the answer came (v.12).
  2. They prevailed and God answered (Lk 18:6-8).
C. Also, like the early church, our prayer must be selfless.
  1. Their prayer was focused on Peter's deliverance not on their own concerns and blessing.
  2. James warns of praying such selfish prayers (Ja 4:1-3).
  3. While there is nothing wrong with asking God to meet our needs, it becomes alarming when that becomes our focus.

Conclusion and Altar Call
  1. If we will unite in prayer, God will deliver those in bondage.
  2. This understanding gives us confidence to preach the gospel, even in dangerous places.
  3. Let's all come and commit ourselves to united prayer.

[PFM]

25 Prayer That Brings Down the Spirit

Sermon in a Sentence: We can pray in a way that will bring down the Spirit into our lives and into our church services resulting in powerful Spirit-inspired witness.

Sermon Purpose: That believers would pray to God and experience the power of His Spirit giving them boldness to witness for Christ.

Text: Acts 4:23-31

Introduction
1. In Acts, prayer is intimately connected with receiving the Spirit. (Examples: Ac 1:14; 8:17; 9:11; 10:2, 9; 19:6)
2. Our text is the only recorded instance in Acts where we are given the content of their prayer.
3. It was a prayer that brought down a mighty outpouring of the Spirit on the people, resulting in the church being empowered and multitudes coming to the Lord.
4. Let's look more closely at this mighty prayer:

I. IT WAS A "EVERYONE-PARTICIPATING" PRAYER
A. The prayer was not lead by one person while everyone else gave their silent consent.
B. Every person was an active participant in the prayer (v. 24).
C. If we are to see the Spirit poured out powerfully in our midst we must all be involved in prayer.

II. IT WAS A GOD-CENTERED PRAYER
A. Unlike much of our praying today that focuses on our own personal wants and problems, their prayer focused on the power and sovereignty of God. (Read vv. 24b-25)
B. Prayer that brings down the power of the Spirit is God-centered prayer.

III. IT WAS A CHRIST-HONORING PRAYER
A. At the heart of their prayer was the will and work of Christ. (Read vv.26-28)
B. Prayer that brings down the Spirit focuses on the will and work of Christ.

IV. IT WAS A MISSION-ORIENTED PRAYER
A. They did not ask for deliverance but for boldness to fulfill the mission of God. (Read v. 29).

B. Prayer that brings God's Spirit into our lives and into our church services is mission-oriented prayer.

V. IT WAS A SPIRIT-INVOKING PRAYER
A. Their prayer was that the Spirit would manifest His presence through signs and wonders and confirm the gospel they were boldly proclaiming. (Read v. 30)
   1. (Note: The "hand of God" is a reference to the Holy Spirit. See: Ez 31:1; Lk 11:20; Ac 13:11).
B. We should boldly ask the Spirit of God to fill us and manifest His power in our midst.

VI. IT WAS A FAITH-FILLED PRAYER
A. They fully expected that God would hear and answer their prayer.
B. Prayer that brings down the Spirit of God is faith-filled prayer.

VII. IT WAS A GOD-ANSWERED PRAYER
A. God answered their prayer by manifesting His power and presence. (Read v.31a).
   1. And by filling them with His Spirit
   2. This resulted in bold, Spirit-empowered witness (vv. 31b, 33).
B. We, too, can expect God to answer our prayer:
   1. He will send His Spirit
   2. He will empower us as His witnesses.

Conclusion and Altar Call
1. Come, let's pray that the Spirit will manifest His power and presence.
2. Let's pray that He will fill each one with His Spirit.

[DRM]

26 The Cry That Stops God

Sermon in a Sentence: If we will cry out to God in faith, He will stop and listen to our prayer.
Sermon Purpose: The Christians will cry out to God, asking Him to fulfill His mission.
Text: Mark 10:46-52
Introduction
1. Tell the story of Bartimaeus' healing.
2. His cry stopped the Son of God: "Jesus stopped" (v.49)
3. This story illustrates the kind of prayer that gets God's attention—the kind of prayer that God "stops" and listens to.
4. Six ways we can describe Bartimaeus' cry:

I. **IT WAS A TIMELY CRY**
   A. Bartimaeus made the most of his opportunity.
      1. Jesus was about to leave the village (v.49).
      2. Bartimaeus was about to miss the opportunity of a lifetime.
      3. If he had missed this opportunity, he would have remained blind until he died.
   B. We are living in a time of great missionary opportunity.
      1. The Spirit is being poured out on all flesh (Ac 2:17).
      2. The fields are "ripe for harvest" (Jn 4:32).
   C. We must seize the opportunity.
      1, We must cry out to God for the nations.
      2. We must quickly put in the sickle and reap (Mk 4:29).
      3. Illus: It is like the banana tree that produces only one flower in its lifetime. If the conditions are right, it produces a large harvest. If not, it dies without producing any fruit.

II. **IT WAS A FOCUSED CRY**
   A. Bartimaeus knew exactly what he wanted from Jesus.
      1. When Jesus asked Him, "What do you want me to do for you?" Bartimaeus answered, "I want to see" (v.51).
   B. We must know what we want from God.
      1. Be specific with your prayer.
      2. We need an outpouring of the Spirit: "Ask ye of the Lord rain in the time of the latter rain" (Ze 10:1, KJV).
      3. We need workers for the harvest. (Read Mt 9:37-38).

III. IT WAS A DETERMINED CRY
A. Bartimaeus did not allow either the rebukes of the crowd nor the silence of Jesus to stop his cry (vv.48).
B. Like Bartimaeus, we must persevere until the answer comes.
 1. When we pray in the will of God, we must understand that delay does not means denial (1Jn 5:14-15).
 2. Tell the Parable of the Late-night Visitor (Lk 11:5-9).
 3. Tell the Parable of the Persistent Widow (Lk 18:1-8).

IV. IT WAS A FAITH-FILLED CRY
A. Bartimaeus called out in faith (v.52).
 1. Jesus told him, "Your faith has healed you" (Mk 10:52).
 2. Illus: Like the woman with the issue blood: She believed, "If I touch His clothes, I will be healed" (Mk 5:28).
B. We must cry out to God in faith.
 1. God will answer our faith-filled request. (Read Mk 11:24)

V. IT WAS AN EFFECTIVE CRY
A. Bartimaeus received from Jesus what He desired.
 1. Jesus was "moved with compassion" (Mt 20:34).
 2. Jesus then touched him and "immediately, he received his sight" (Mk 10:52).
B. If we will cry out to Jesus, we can expect the same result.
 1. God will hear our prayer—and He will answer.
 2. He will heal our backsliding (Je 3:22).
 3. He will heal our nation (2Ch 7:14).

VI. IT WAS A CONSECRATED CRY
A. Once Bartimaeus received his answer, he left everything and followed Jesus.
 1. Bartimaeus wanted more than healing, He wanted a relationship with Jesus.
B. When we pray we must be prepared to follow Jesus.
 1. Jesus is looking for disciples (Mk 8:34).
 2. He wants to make us "fishers of men" (Mk 1:17).

Conclusion and Altar Call
1. When we cry out to God in faith, He stops and listens.
2. Join me in the altars and let's cry out to Jesus to save the lost.

[JSa]

27 How to Pray Effectively

Sermon in a Sentence: We can learn to pray more effectively.
Sermon Purpose: That Christians will pray more effectively.
Text: Acts 12:1-5
Introduction
1. We all want our prayers to be effective.
2. We must therefore learn to pray in the right way.
3. In our text, we see the New Testament church going to prayer.
   1. Tell the story of Peter's capture (Ac 12:1-4).
4. Note what the church *did not* do:
   a. They *did not* organize a commando raid to free Peter.
   b. They *did not* arrange a petition signing.
   c. They *did not* receive a big offering to pay a bribe.
4. Note what they *did* do:
   a. The *did* pray.
   b. They *did* understand that prayer is the Christian's most powerful weapon. (Read 2Co 10:4)
5. God answered their prayer by sending an angel to deliver Peter (vv.6-11).
   a. We too can pray effective prayers.
6. This message: Three insights into how to pray more effectively:

If we would pray effectively...
I. WE SHOULD DIRECT OUR PRAYERS TO GOD
   A. This is what the church did in our story:
      1. "Peter was kept in prison, but the church was earnestly praying *to God* for him" (v.5)
   B. This advice may surprise you, because we believe that all prayers are addressed to God.
      a. However, thousands of prayers that are prayed every day where the focus is not on God.
      b. Rather, people's focus is on themselves and their problems — their health, their child, their financial situation, etc.
   C. Our focus must be on God and His greatness.
      1. On His ability to answer our prayers (Je 32:17).
      2. Illus: Notice how the early Christians focused on God when they prayed: (Read Acts 4:23-28)

If we would pray effectively...
II. WE SHOULD ENTER INTO GOD'S PRESENCE
   A. God invites us into His presence.
      1. Ja 4:8: "Draw near to God, and he will come near to you."
      2. Jesus's instructions on prayer: (Read Mt 6:6)
      3. First, enter His presence, and then make your petitions.
   B. Three ways we enter into God's presence:
      1. We enter His presence by the *blood of Jesus* (He 10:19).
         a. His blood cleanses us and makes us fit (v.22).
         b. We can then approach God with confidence (4:16).
      2. We enter His presence by *faith* (Ep 3:12).
         a. Through faith we acknowledge His presence.
      3. We enter His presence by the *Holy Spirit* (Ep 2:18).
         a. When we worship in the Spirit, God manifests His presence (Jn 4:23; Ps 22:3, KJV).
   C. Once in His presence, we can present our petitions to God.

If we would pray effectively...
III. WE SHOULD PRAY IN THE HOLY SPIRIT
   A. It often happens that when we want to pray, we feel empty.
      1. At such times, we should not be discouraged.
      2. We should ask the Spirit to come, fill us, and help us.
      3. The Holy Spirit will anoint us and help us pray.
   B. Paul tells us how this works:
      1. "In the same way, the Spirit helps us in our weakness. We do not know what we ought to pray for, but the Spirit himself intercedes for us with groans that words cannot express. And he who searches our hearts knows the mind of the Spirit, because the Spirit intercedes for the saints in accordance with God's will" (Ro 8:26-27).
      2. As we yield to the Holy Spirit, He prays through us (1Co 14:14-15).
   C. As the Spirit prays through us, we pray effectively.

Conclusion and Altar Call
   1. You can pray more effectively.
   2. Remember these three principles: (Recap major points.)
   3. Come, be filled with the Spirit, and commit yourself to prayer.

[MHA]

28 The Prayer of Elijah

Sermon in a Sentence: Although Elijah was a mere man like us, he prevailed in prayer—and so can we.

Sermon Purpose: That God's people will learn to pray and trust Him for answers.

Text: James 5:17-18

Introduction
1. Many believe that the prophets and apostles in the Bible were super-saints and that it was normal for God hear them.
   a. This is not biblical thinking.
   b. On the contrary, God's word teaches that there is only one perfect man—Jesus.
   c. Everyone else is a fallen human being, and we all need God's mercy and grace (Ro 3:10-12; 23).
2. In this message we will look at one of those fallen people—the prophet, Elijah.
3. From him we will learn some important lessons on prayer.

I. **ELIJAH WAS A HUMAN BEING—JUST AS WE ARE**
   A. James writes, "Elijah was a man just like us…"
      1. We think of Elijah as a "super-prophet."
      2. But he just like you and me.
   B. From the Bible, we learn the following about Elijah:
      1. He sometimes made *wrong judgments*.
         a. For instance, during the persecution of Ahab, Elijah totally misjudged the situation (1Ki 19:14-18).
         b. He bragged about his own zealousness (v.14).
         c. He claimed he was the only one serving God, but God told him there were 7,000 others (vv.14-18).
      2. On one occasion, he *acted like a coward.*
         a. He defeated the prophets of Baal, but when threatened by Jezebel, He ran in fear (1Ki 19:3).
      3. He struggled with *discouragement.*
         a. After receiving the message from Jezebel, he prayed, "'Take my life; I am no better than my ancestors" (v.3)
   C. We can identify with Elijah.
      1. We make wrong judgments; we act cowardly; and we get discouraged when things do not go our way.
      2. But that's not the end of the story…

II. ELIJAH PRAYED—JUST AS WE CAN
A. James writes, "Elijah was a man just like us. [But] *he prayed earnestly* that it would not rain, and it did not rain on the land for three and a half years" (Ja 5:17).
   1. Despite all of Elijah's problems, He prayed a powerful history-making prayer.
   2. He prayed that it would not rain, and God shut up the heavens for 3½ years.
   3. Then, he prayed a second time, and the rains came (v.18).
B. We too can be mighty in prayer—just like Elijah.
   1. Like Elijah, our prayers do not depend on our perfection but on God's faithfulness and power.
   2. Illus: John Knox prayed "Give me Scotland or I die."
   3. Let's ask God for spiritual rain.
      a. For a mighty outpouring of the Holy Spirit.
      b. Ask ye of the LORD rain in the time of the latter rain" (Zec 10:1, KJV).
   4. God has promised to pour out his Spirit in our day (Ac 2:17-18).
C. Note also how Elijah persevered in prayer.
   1. James wrote, "And [Elijah] *prayed again,* and the heaven gave rain, and the earth brought forth her fruit" (5:18).
      a. In fact, he prayed seven times before he received an answer from God (1Ki 18:42-46).
   2. We too can claim the promises of God through persevering prayer.
      a. Illus: The Parable of the Persistent Widow (Lk 18-1-8).
      b. Illus: Abraham's perseverance (Ge 18:22-33)

Conclusion and Altar Call
1. We can be encouraged by Elijah's example; though he was a mere human, God answered his prayer.
2. Come, commit yourself to persevering prayer.

[MHA]

29 Expanding Your Prayer Life

Sermon in a Sentence: Following Paul's instructions to Timothy, we must expand our prayer lives to include the needs of others.

Sermon Purpose: To help believers expand their prayer life to include prayers for all people to come to Christ.

Text: 1Timothy 2:1-7

Introduction
1. If you were about to compete in a sporting event, would you pray for your own team or would you pray for both teams?
2. Most of us would pray for our own team to win.
3. This illustrates a problem in our prayer lives—our prayers are too narrow. They need to be expanded.
4. In our text, Paul urges Timothy to expand his prayer life.

I. THERE IS A PROBLEM TODAY WITH MOST OF OUR PRAYER LIVES: WE TEND TO PRAY FOR OUR OWN PROBLEMS AND CONCERNS

A. Because we live lives controlled by the sinful nature, we live self-centered lives—and we pray self-centered prayers (Ro 8.5-8).
B. The Bible calls us from self-centeredness (Read: Phi 2:3).
C. This others-centeredness should include our prayer lives.

II. THE SOLUTION TO OUR PROBLEM IS THAT WE MUST EXPAND OUR PRAYER LIVES

A. This is what Paul urged Timothy to do: "I urge, then, first of all, that requests, prayers, intercession and thanksgiving be made *for everyone*" (1Ti 2:1).
   1. *Everyone* includes those individuals and tribes we dislike.
   2. Jesus says that we should intercede for them and ask God to help them. (Read: Mt 5:43-45)
B. What then should we pray for?
   1. According to Paul, we should pray "to lead a peaceful quiet life of godliness and dignity" (v.2).
   2. We should also pray for everyone to "to be saved and to come to a knowledge of the truth" (v.4).
C. Paul tells us *why* we should expand our prayer lives: "For there is one God and one mediator…Christ Jesus" (v.5).
   1. Because God loves all people and wants to have a living relationship with them.
   2. This is why Jesus came (v.5b-6).

3. Jesus is the only way: "For there is one God and one mediator between God and men, the man Christ Jesus" (v.5; see also Jn 14:16; Ac 4:12).
4. This is what Paul dedicated his life to (v.7).
5. This is what we must pray for (Mt 9:37-38).

III. LET'S NOW DISCUSS SOME OTHER WAYS WE MAY EXPAND OUR PRAYER LIVES
A. We must expand your *understanding* of prayer.
   1. We must understand that prayer is more than reciting a list of everything we want from God.
   2. Prayer should be a relationship with God where we openly express our full selves to our Creator.
   3. We must understand the different kinds of prayer.
      a. Paul spoke of "prayers, intercession, and thanksgiving" (v.1).
B. We must expand *who* we pray for.
   1. Paul: "for kings and all those in authority" (v.2).
   2. Some more suggestions: Family, friends, church leaders, political leaders, community, country, world, people who agree with you, people who disagree with you, people who are like you, people who are different from you, you enemies, and much more.
   3. In other words, we must pray for "everyone"! (v.1).
B. We must expand *what* you pray for.
   1. Do not make your own personal health, wealth, and wellbeing the main focus of your prayers.
   2. Pray for God's kingdom to come and for God will to be done on earth (Mt 6:10).
   3. That is, pray for God's mission to be accomplished.
   3. Allow the Holy Spirit to guide you and pray through you (Ro 8:26-27).

Conclusion and Altar Call
Come now, be filled with the Spirit, and commit expanding your prayer life.

[JL[(1)]]

Section 3
Commitment to Prayer

30 They Devoted Themselves to Prayer
~ Lessons from the Book of Acts ~

Sermon in a Sentence: We would do well to imitate the prayer habits of the early Christians in Acts.
Sermon Purpose: That Christians will devote themselves to prayer.
Text: Acts 2:42

Introduction
1. Look at the phrase in our text, "They devoted themselves…to prayer."
2. As we shall see in this message, that devotion to prayer continued throughout the book of Acts.
3. It equipped and sustained believers in their missionary work.
4. This devotion to prayer can serve as an example to us today.
5. Note these three things about their prayers:

I. NOTE WHEN THE PRAYED
- *They prayed in at least five circumstances:*
- A. They prayed *when choosing leaders:*
    1. When choosing Judas' replacement (1:24).
    2. When choosing the seven "deacons" (6:4, 6).
    3. When appointing leaders in the Galatian churches (14:23).
- B. They prayed *at the appointed times* of prayer.
    1. In the temple in Jerusalem (3:1).
    2. Peter prayed "about noon" in Caesarea (10:9).
    3. Paul went to prayer on the Sabbath Day (16:13, 16).
- C. They prayed *in times or persecution* and danger.
    1. When they were threatened in Jerusalem (4:18-21; 23-24).
    2. Stephen prayed as he was being stoned (7:59).
    3. Paul and Silas in the Roman prison (16:25).
    4. Paul and his companions in the storm at sea (27:29).
- D. They prayed *when doing ministry.*
    1. Peter before he raised Tabitha (9:40).
    2. Paul before healing Publius' father (28:8).
- E. They prayed *when parting company.*
    1. Paul, when bidding farewell to the Ephesians (20:36).
    2. And when bidding farewell of the disciples in Tyre (21:5).
- F. *Summary:* The early Christians were devoted to prayer.
    1. Before Pentecost they were "constantly in prayer" (1:14).
    2. After Pentecost "the devoted themselves to prayer" (2:42).
    3. Cornelius "prayed to God regularly" (10:2).

4. Paul exhorts us to "pray continually" (1Th 5:17).
   a. And to "pray in the Spirit on all occasions" (Ep 6:18).
   b. He adds "be alert and always keep on praying" (v.18).

II. NOTE HOW THE PRAYED
- *They prayed in at least three ways:*
A. They prayed *when together and when alone.*
   1. When together (1:14; 4:24; 6:6; 12:5; 20:36).
   2. When alone (Peter in 9:4; 10:9).
B. They prayed *with fervor.*
   1. In Jerusalem "they lifted up their voices in prayer" (4:24).
   2. In Philippi, Paul and Silas prayed and sang praises (v.25).
C. They prayed *with expectation.*
   1. They expected God to answer their prayer (4:31).
D. They prayed *with fasting.*
   1. In Antioch before sending out Saul and Barnabas (13:3).
   2. In Galatia before appointing church leaders (14:23).
E. We should do the same.
   1. We must pray when together and when alone.
   2. We must pray with expectation and fasting.

III. NOTE WHAT THEY PRAYED FOR
- *The prayed specifically for at least four things:*
A. They prayed *to be empowered* by the Holy Spirit.
   1. Before Pentecost (1:14).
   2. Before the Second Jerusalem Outpouring (vv.24, 31).
B. They prayed *for others to be empowered* by the Spirit.
   1. Peter and John prayed for the Samaritans (8:15).
   2. Ananias prayed for Paul (9:14-17).
   3. Paul prayed for the Ephesian disciples (19:7).
C. They prayed *for boldness* to preach the gospel (4:29-30).
D. They prayed *for insight and direction.*
   1. The Eleven, before choosing Judas' replacement (1:24f).
   2. Peter before raising Tabitha (9:40).

Conclusion and Altar Call
Come now. Let's commit ourselves to praying as the early church prayed.

[DRM]

31 Praying with Jesus for Believers

Sermon in a Sentence: Jesus' "High Priestly Prayer" in John 17 can serve as a pattern for leaders' prayers today.
Sermon Purpose: That pastors and other spiritual leaders will learn from Jesus how to pray more effectively for their people.
Text: John 17:1-26 (Read the entire chapter.)
Introduction:
1. Our text is Jesus' final prayer for believers.
2. It has been called Jesus' "High Priestly Prayer."
3. It shows our Lord's deepest longings for His followers.
4. It is further a Spirit-inspired example of how spiritual leaders should pray for their people.
5. Eight ways we can praying for those under our care:

I. PRAY THAT THEY MAY COME TO KNOW JESUS CHRIST INTIMATELY (Read vv.2-3)
A. God wants His people to know Him intimately.
   1. Earlier, Jesus had spoken of that intimacy (Jn 15:9-13)
   2. He prayed that His people may know God (17:3).
   3. We know Christ by knowing His Word (17:17) and by living in the Spirit (Jn 16:13-15).
B. Let's pray that God's people will come to know Christ better by reading the Word and walking in the Spirit.

II. PRAY THAT GOD MAY KEEP THEM SAFE
A. All of God's children face at least four spiritual threats:
   1. Becoming conformed to the world (v.11; Ro 12:2).
   2. Attacks from Satan (v.15; 1Pe 5:8).
   3. Yielding to false teaching (vv.14, 17; Ac 20:29).
   4. Falling away from Christ (v.12).
B. Let's pray that God will keep His people safe from these spiritual threats.

III. PRAY THAT THEY MAY CONSTANTLY POSSESS THE FULL JOY OF CHRIST (v.13)
A. God wants His people to live joy-filled lives (v.13).
   1. Joy is hallmark of the Christian walk.
   2. With joy comes strength for the journey (Ne 8:19).
B. Let's pray that God will flood His people with the joy of the Holy Spirit (Ac 13:52; Ro 14:17).

IV. PRAY THAT THEY MAY BE HOLY IN THOUGHT, DEED, AND CHARACTER (v.17)
A. We are called to walk as Jesus walked (1Jn 2:6).
1. Jesus was holy in thought, deed, and character (1Pe:2:22).
2. Jesus prayed that God would sanctify His people (v.17).
B. Let's pray that God's people will walk in holiness.

V. PRAY THAT THEY MAY BE UNIFIED IN PURPOSE
A. Such unity of purpose is exemplified by Jesus and His relationship with the Father (vv.11, 21-22).
1. The Father and Son walked in complete harmony.
2. Jesus prayed for His church to be the same (vv.21-23).
3. Such unity will enable us to accomplish God's mission.
B. Let's pray that the church will be unified in fellowship, purpose, and mission.

VI. PRAY THAT THEY MAY LEAD OTHERS TO CHRIST
(Read vv.21, 23 noting "that the world may believe...know")
A. God's people are to live as witnesses (Lk 24:46-48; Ac 1:8).
1. They are to shine as lights in a dark world (Phi 2:15).
2. Our unity will serve as a witness to the world (v.23).
B. Pray that Christians will lead others to Christ

VII. PRAY THAT THEY MAY CONSTANTLY LIVE IN GOD'S LOVE AND PRESENCE (v.26)
A. Christ has promised to be with us and in us—and to make God known to us (v.26; Mt 28:20)
B. Let's pray that God's people will live in God presence.

VIII. PRAY THAT THEY MAY PERSEVERE IN THE FAITH AND FINALLY BE WITH CHRIST IN HEAVEN (v.24)
A. God wants His people to make it all the way to heaven.
1. Jesus prayed that we would be with Him in heaven to witness His eternal glory (v.24).
B. Let's pray that God people will remain faithful to the end, and will finally be with Christ in heaven (Mt 10:22).

[DCS]

Adapted from the author's notes on John 17:1 in the
Full Life Study Bible, Zondervan, 1990

32 Never Give Up Praying

Sermon in a Sentence: We should never give up praying for God's will to be done.

Sermon Purpose: That Christians will commit to persist in prayer until the answer comes.

Text: Luke 18:1-8 (then reread v.1)

Introduction
1. On October 29, 1941, soon after the Nazi Blitz on Britain, Prime Minister Winston Churchill visited Harrow School in London to hear the youth choir sing and to encourage the students.
   a. The visit occurred soon after the Nazi attempt to bomb London into submission during the Battle of Britain.
   b. When he stood to speak, Churchill exhorted the students, "Never give in, never give in, never, never, never, never—in nothing, great or small, large or petty—never give in except to convictions of honor and good sense."
2. In our Bible story today, Jesus is saying much the same thing.
   a. He is saying, "Never give up praying! For, if you will persist in faith, the answer will surely come."
   b. Lk 18:1: "Jesus told his disciples a parable to show them that they should always pray and not give up."
   c. This message is to encourage you to never give up praying.
3. Consider the following:

I. IN THIS PARABLE, JESUS ENCOURAGES US TO NEVER GIVE UP PRAYING

A. To make His point, Jesus uses both comparison and contrast.
   1. He *compares* the wise Christian to a persistent widow.
   2. He *contrasts* God with an unjust judge.
B. Jesus encourages us to pray like the persistent widow.
   1. She knew that her cause was right and good.
   2. She therefore refused to give up—even when it seemed the judge was ignoring her request.
C. Jesus also warns us not view God as an unjust judge.
   1. While the judge in the story was unjust, the God we pray too is holy and just.
   2. He is gracious and ready to answer our prayers (Read vv.7-8a; Ex 34:6).

II. ALLOW ME TO SUGGEST A PLAN FOR PERSISTENT PRAYER (Three elements:)
  A. First, ensure that you are praying in *God's will*.
    1. Read: 1Jn 5:14-15
    2. God's will is found in God's word, the Bible.
  B. Second, doggedly *persist* in prayer, knowing that God's is indeed hearing, and will soon answer your prayer.
    1. Read v.8b
    2. Such persistence in prayer is an act of faith rather than an act of doubt as some wrongly teach.
  C. Finally, pray in *faith,* knowing that God will surely answer your prayer.
    1. "Let us not become weary in doing good, for at the proper time we will reap a harvest if we do not give up" (Ga 6:9).
    2. Never, never, never give up praying.

III. FIVE FOR WHICH WE MUST NEVER GIVE UP PRAYING
  A. We must never give up praying *for our lost loved ones.*
  B. We must never give up praying *for God's kingdom to come.*
  C. We must never give up praying *for an outpouring of the Holy Spirit.*
  D. We must never give up praying *for the unreached peoples of Africa and beyond.*
  E. We must never give up praying *to the Lord of the Harvest* to send laborers into the harvest fields.

Conclusion and Altar Call
  1. In his speech at Harrow School, Churchill concluded, "We must learn to be equally good at what is short and sharp and what is long and tough….we have only to persevere to conquer."
  2. The same is true for us today; if we will pesevere in prayer, the answer will come.
  3. Come now and commit yourself to "never give up praying."

[DRM]

33 The Devotional Habit

Sermon in a Sentence: Anyone who wants to minister effectively must develop a strong devotional habit.
Sermon Purpose: That Christians will commit to developing a consistent devotional habit.
Text: Luke 5:15-16; Acts 6:1-4
Introduction:
1. Our two texts reveal Jesus and the apostles' firm commitment to prayer and the Word of God.
   a. These practices were at the heart of all they did.
   b. The same must be true for our ministries today.
2. A number of factors contribute to a successful ministry (such as leadership skills and ministry development).
   a. However, nothing is more important than strengthening our relationship with God.
   b. Succeeding at this point is the key to everything else the Christian worker hopes to accomplish.
3. Our relationship with God is developed and maintained through a healthy devotional life.
   a. We call this practice the "devotional habit."
   b. In this message, we will learn about this vital practice.

I. **UNDERSTANDING THE DEVOTIONAL HABIT**
   A. Devotion is time spent daily with God in His presence.
      1. The apostles valued consistent prayer and study.
         a. Three examples: Acts 3:1; Acts 6:1; Acts 16:13
      2. Jesus valued time spent with His Father (Mk 1:35; Lk 5:16).
   B. Two essential elements of the devotional habit are personal prayer and Bible study.
      a. Our time with God can also include singing, reading devotional books, and personal reflection.
   C. It can be done alone or with someone else (such as one's spouse, children, or ministry colleagues).

II. **BENEFITS OF A DEVOTIONAL HABIT**
   A. It will help us to develop a biblical worldview.
      1. It will help us to see the world through God's eyes.
      2. And it will shield us from a worldly outlook on life.
   B. It will serve as a spiritual anchor against the pressures of life.
      1. We will stay calm when circumstances threaten (He 6:19).

      2. It will deepen our conviction that God's Word is true.
      3. We can thus confidently face the impossible and unknown.
  C. It will help strengthen important relationships:
      1. Our relationship *with God* will be strengthened.
      2. Our relationship *with our families* will be strengthened.
      3. Our relationship w*ith our colleagues* will be strengthened.
  D. It will provide amble time for supplication and intercession.
  E. It will be a constant source of inspired insights for effective preaching and teaching.

III. INSIGHTS INTO THE DEVOTIONAL HABIT
  A. Set objectives for your daily times of devotion, such as…
      1. To learn to love God more and draw nearer to Him.
      2. To gain added confidence and strength from God.
      3. To achieve personal and corporate spiritual growth.
      4. To receive daily direction from God.
  B. Divide your time between prayer and Bible reading.
      1. During your prayer time, include moments of worship, submission, supplication, and intercession for others.
      2. Read the Bible slowly and prayerfully, asking to God speak to you through His Word.
  C. Learn to manage distractions.
      1. Approach your devotional time as a spiritual discipline.
      2. It should be protected and joyously anticipated.
      3. Commit to a daily schedule.
  D. Keep a spiritual journal.
      1. Write down impressions you receive from the Spirit.
      2. Record important prayers and answers to your prayers.
      3. Note spiritual milestones.
      4. Review your journal often.

Conclusion and Altar Call
Come now, and commit yourself to developing a daily devotional habit.

                                                                  [JVY]

Adapted from John York's book, *Missions in the Age of the Spirit,* "Chapter 12: Devotional Habit" (189-214)

34 Prayer Challenge

Sermon in a Sentence: We must not neglect the powerful force of prayer.
Sermon Purpose: That God's people will commit themselves to prayer.
Texts: Nehemiah 1:3-4; Isaiah 59:16; 62:6-7; Ezekiel 22:29-31
Introduction
1. Our texts talk about three men of prayer.
    a. *Nehemiah* prayed and fasted for success.
    b. *Isaiah* spoke of the importance of prayer.
    c. God told *Ezekiel* that He was seeking intercessors.
2. This message will look at this important subject.
    a. It is a prayer challenge.
    b. Four powerful prayer insights:

I. PRAYER IS A POWERFUL FORCE
A. Prayer is...
   1. ...spiritual *oxygen* giving life to God's people.
   2. ...spiritual *fertilizer* causing spiritual and numerical growth in the church.
   4. ...a *shield* that protects us against the attacks of the devil.
   5. ...a *whip* with which we can flog the devil.
   6. ...the *mother* of true Pentecostal revival.
B. When the church begins to pray, anything can happen.
   1. Prayer has no geographical limitations.
   2. Through prayer, the supernatural becomes natural.
   3. Through prayer, spiritual gifts are manifested.
   4. Prayer is the powerhouse for evangelism and missions.

II. THE SAINTS OF OLD WERE PEOPLE OF PRAYER
A. *Abraham* was a man of prayer (Ge 19:27).
   1. In Genesis, we read of his frequent conversations with God.
   2. For example, he interceded for Sodom (Ge 18:22-33).
B. *Moses* was powerful in prayer.
   1. Like Abraham, he often talked with God.
   2. His prayer brought victory (Ex 17:8-16).
   3. Twice he interceded for Israel (Ex 32:7-14; Nu 14:11-19).
   4. Once, after he talked with God, his face reflected God's glory (Ex 34:29-30).

C. *Elijah's* prayer shut up, then opened, the heavens (Ja 5:17-18)
E. *David* prayed in the night watches (Ps 63:6).
F. *Jesus* often withdrew to pray (Lk 5:16).
   a. He spent the night in prayer (Lk 6:12).
   b. He prayed in the early mornings (Mk 1:35).

III. THE BIBLE CONDEMNS PRAYERLESSNESS
A. Prayerlessness is the hallmark of backsliding.
   1. To not pray is a sin (1Sa 12:23).
   2. Any individual, family, or church that does not *pray* becomes open *prey* for the devil (1Pe 5:6-8).
B. Prayerlessness produces a barren life.
   1. Illus: We must overcome our "microwave mentality" in prayer. God does not always give quick answers.

IV. WE MUST COMMIT OURSELVES TO PRAYER
A. During these last days, God wants to tear open the heavens and let loose His power on the church.
   1. Isaiah prayed, "Oh, that you would rend the heavens and come down, that the mountains would tremble before you!" (Is 64:1).
   2. He then calls on God, "Come down to make your name known to your enemies and cause the nations to quake before you!" (v.2).
B. We can actualize God's power through prayer.
   1. We cannot defeat the devil with technology.
   2. True vision is birthed in prayer.
   3. Although prayer is the hardest ministry, it is the most productive.
C. God is looking for intercessors (Ez 22:30).
   1. If we will make an impact in our world, we must set aside time for prayer.
   2. When you cannot *find* time to pray, you must *make* time to pray.

Conclusion and Altar Call
1. If we want to see God move, we must pray.
2. Come now, and commit yourself to prayer.

[CO]

35 A Plan for Action

Sermon in a Sentence: We must commit ourselves to daily prayer.
Sermon Purpose: That Christians develop a daily, effective prayer life.
Text: Hebrews 11:32-35
Introduction:
1. In Hebrews 11, the author tells us of people who changed the world through faith.
2. We, too, have the power to change our world through Spirit-empowered, faith-filled prayer.
3. Seven steps for putting a prayer plan into action:

I. INITIATE A REGULAR PRAYER HOUR
A. The early church had a regular hour of prayer (Ac 3:1).
   1. Peter and John went to the temple at the "hour of prayer."
   2. Jesus taught that we "should always pray…" (Lk 18:1).
B. We must have a regular set time of prayer.
   1. The ideal time for prayer is early in the morning.
   2. Other times are also acceptable.
   3. We must observe our prayer time with determination.

II. DEDICATE YOURSELF TO THE WILL OF GOD
A. Our prayer lives must be oriented to the will of God.
   1. Jesus taught us to pray, "Your will be done…" (Mt 6:10).
   2. John wrote, "If we ask anything according to his will, he hears us" (1Jn 5:14).
B. We learn God's will by reading God's book—the Bible.
   1. Jesus said, "If…my words remain in you, ask whatever you wish, and it will be given you" (Jn 15:7).
   2. Begin your prayer time by praying, "Not my will but yours be done" (Lk 22:42).

III. PRACTICE THE PRESENCE OF GOD
A. As you begin, learn to recognize the presence of God.
   1. True prayer is communion with God.
   2. We must not be like Jacob (Ge 28:16).
B. Recognizing God's presence will give us boldness in prayer.
   1. Illus: When the crowds realized that Jesus was present, they were embolden to come to Him for help.
   2. Jesus promised, "For where two or three come together in my name, there am I with them" (Mt 18:20).

IV. BEGIN YOUR PRAYER HOUR WITH WORSHIP
A. Before you present your petitions, take time to worship God.
1. The Psalmist exhorts, "Enter his gates with thanksgiving and his courts with praise" (Ps 100:4).
2. God is looking for true worshipers (Jn 4:23).

B. Worship produces an atmosphere conductive to prayer:
1. It brings the presence of the Lord.
2. It puts the enemy to flight (2Chr 20:21-25).

V. BRING YOUR PROBLEMS BEFORE GOD
A. Jesus encourages us to pray, "Give us today our daily bread" (Mt 6:11)
B. We can confidently present our needs to God. (Read Phi 4:6)
1. This includes the affairs of our home, our families, our children, our business, and anything else that concerns us.

VI. PRAY FOR GOD'S KINGDOM TO COME
A. Jesus taught us to pray "Your kingdom come" (Mt 6:10)
1. This is a prayer for the evangelization of the lost.
2. It is a prayer for the outpouring of the Spirit.

B. It is also a prayer for Jesus to return (Mt 24:14; Re 22:20).

VII. LET THE SPIRIT OF GOD PRAY THROUGH YOU
A. At times, we sense that our prayers are weak and ineffective.
B. Paul said that the Spirit helps our weakness in prayer.
1. He will come, fill us, and pray through us (Ro 8:26-27).
2. Paul calls this kind of prayer "prayer in the Spirit" or prayer in tongues (1Co 14:14-15).
3. The Spirit prays according to the will of God (Ro 8:27).

Conclusion and Altar Call
1. It is not enough that we know about prayer, we must practice prayer.
2. Come, commit yourself to regular prayer.

[GL]

Adapted from Gordon Lindsay's book, *Praying to Change the World,* Voice of Healing, (122-128)

36 Persistence in Prayer

Sermon in a Sentence: We must persist in prayer until the answer comes.

Sermon Purpose: That God's people will be encouraged to never give up praying until God answers their prayer.

Text: Luke 11:1-13

Introduction
1. Luke mentions prayer more than any other gospel writer.
   a. For example, He speaks of prayer in Lk 18:1-8; 22:40,46
   b. He highlights of prayer in the life of Jesus (Lk 3:21; 5:16; 6:12; 9:18, 28f; 10:21; 11:1; 22:31f, 41ff; 23:46.)
2. Note especially the following verses:
   a. 4:42: "At daybreak Jesus went out to a solitary place..."
   b. 5:16: "Jesus often withdrew...and prayed."
   c. 6:12: "Jesus went out to a mountainside to pray, and spent the night praying to God."
3. In our text, Jesus is again praying (Lk 11:1).
   a. The disciples ask Him, "Lord, teach us to pray."
   b. Jesus responds by teaching them to do as they had often seen Him do.
4. Three lessons we can learn from Jesus' teaching:

I. WE ARE TO PRAY FOR GOD'S KINGDOM TO COME
   A. Verses 2-4 are a shorter version of the "Lord's Prayer" also found in Mt 6:9-13. (Read both)
   1. Both include the phrase "Your kingdom come."
   2. The Lord's Prayer is a "Kingdom Prayer" focusing on the Father and His kingdom.
   3. The prayer has two primary focuses:
      a. God's kingdom and will
      b. Our provision, forgiveness, and protection
   B. To pray for God's kingdom to come is...
   1. ...to pray that God's kingdom will advance.
   2. ...to pray that God's Spirit will be poured out.
   3. ...to pray that Jesus will come again.

II. WE ARE TO PRAY WITH PERSISTENCE
   A. Jesus emphasizes how we must pray by telling a story.
   1. Tell the story of the persistent neighbor (vv.5-8).
   2. The neighbor pleaded with boldness and persistence.

B. Jesus then applies the story to how we should pray.
1. Read vv. 9-10, noting: *"So I say to you…"*
2. Jesus He paints a progressive picture of someone diligently seeking something: "Ask… Seek… Knock…"
3. Grammatically, Jesus' words are in the "present, active, imperative voice." This means He is literally saying, "Keep on asking… Keep on seeking… Keep on knocking…"

C. Jesus' is not so much emphasizing the form of prayer as He is emphasizing the nature of our praying.
1. Jesus is not telling us to be disrespectful to God.
2. However, He is telling us to be tenacious and unrelenting.
3. If we know we are praying in God's will, we must persist until the answer comes.

III. WE ARE TO TENACIOUSLY ASK FOR THE HOLY SPIRIT

A. Jesus is teaching us how to ask for the Holy Spirit.
1. v.13: "Your Father in heaven [will] give the Holy Spirit to those who ask."
2. The disciples ask Jesus to teach them how to pray; He responds by teaching them how to be filled with the Spirit.

B. Note the following about receiving the Spirit:
1. God's response is tied to continuous action: "Keep on asking… Keep on seeking…" (v.9)
2. The promise is for everyone: "Everyone who asks receives…" (v.10).
3. Tenacious prayer refuses to give up until God answers!

Conclusion and Altar Call
1. Jesus calls us to passionate, incessant, powerful, continuous, and unrelenting prayer.
2. Come now, and be filled with the Spirit, and commit yourself to persistent prayer.

[SP]

37 Devoted to Prayer

Sermon in a Sentence: We must devote ourselves to prayer for God's mission.

Sermon Purpose: That God's people commit themselves to prayer for God's Spirit and God's work.

Text: Acts 2:42; then 1:14; 6:4

Introduction:
1. In Acts, because of the work of the Spirit, prayer increased
   a. And because of prayer, the work of the Spirit increased.
2. Our three texts demonstrate how the early believers were devoted to prayer for God's mission.
   a. They depended on prayer.
   b. They persisted in prayer.
3. We too must devote ourselves to prayer for God's mission.

I. JESUS CALLS US TO A LIFE OF DEVOTED PRAYER
A. While here on earth, Jesus devoted Himself to prayer.
   1. He often withdrew to pray (Mt 14:23; Mk 1:35).
   2. He prayed in difficulties, when making decisions, when facing trials, and on many other occasions.
   3. Illus: He prayed when facing the cross (Mk 14:35).
   4. Illus: He prayed while on the cross (Lk 23:34).
   5. He still prays for us today (He 7:25).
B. Jesus taught His followers to devote themselves to prayer.
   1. He taught that we should "always pray" (Lk 18:1).
   2. He taught that we should pray in faith (Mk 11:24).
   3. He taught that we should pray in His name (Jn 14:13-14).
   4. He said that His house should be "a house of prayer for all nations" (Mk 11:17).

II. WE MUST DEVOTE OURSELVES TO PRAYER WHILE WAITING FOR THE HOLY SPIRIT (Acts 1:14)
A. Jesus taught that, when we are seeking for the Spirit, we must "keep on asking, keep on seeking, and keep on knocking" (literal translation of Lk 11:9).
B. Before the Day of Pentecost, the disciples "all joined together constantly in prayer" (Ac 1:14).
   1. They waited in prayer for "the promise of the Father" (1:4-8).
   2. They were "with one accord in one place" (2:4 KJV).

        3. God answered their prayer and poured out His Spirit on them (2:1-4).
  C. God will do the same for us today.
        1. He will empower us as Christ's witnesses.
        2. We must, however, devote ourselves to prayer until the Spirit comes.

III. AFTER BEING FILLED WITH THE SPIRIT, WE MUST CONTINUE TO DEVOTE OURSELVES TO PRAYER (Acts 2:42, 46)

  A. After Pentecost, the disciples continued to pray (Ac 2:42, 46).
        1. The missional life is more than a single experience; we must learn to walk and minister in the Spirit.
        2. The Spirit-empowered life is maintained through prayer.
        3. Illus: When the day-to-day work began to threaten their prayer lives, the apostles took action.
           a. They chose seven men to help them (Ac 6:1-3).
           b. They explained why: "We will give ourselves continually to prayer, and to the ministry of the word" (v.4).
        4. To remain full of the Spirit, we must remain "faithful in prayer" (Ro 12:12 with Col 4:2).
  B. Throughout Acts, the disciples continued in prayer:
        1. Illus: They prayed when threatened (4:23-24, 31).
        2. Illus: The prayed with new believers to receive the Holy Spirit (8:14-15).
        3. They prayed for Peter in prison (12:5, 12).
        4. They prayed for and received guidance (10:9ff; 13:2-3).
        5. They prayed on many other occasions.
  C. Because they prayed and obeyed, the gospel continued to progress from nation to nation.
  D. We can expect the same today—if we will devote ourselves to prayer.

Conclusion and Altar Call
1. Come now, let's be filled with the Spirit.
2. Let's commit to lives of devotion and prayer.

[NS]

38   Seven Obstacles to Answered Prayer

Sermon in a Sentence: If we want our prayers to be answered, we must avoid the "seven obstacles to prayer."
Sermon Purpose: That believers will repent of and forsake those practices causing their prayers to be ineffective.
Text: James 1:6-7; 4:3; 5:14-16
Introduction
1. True prayer made in the name of Jesus is the most powerful force on earth.
    a. Such prayer opens the windows of heaven, takes away our illusions, and makes us alive and powerful in Christ.
    b. We must all commit ourselves to lives of prayer.
2. However, the Bible teaches that there are certain practices that hinder our prayers.
    a. In our text, James gives a wonderful promise of how God answers prayer. (Read James 5:17-18)
    b. He also warns of practices that keep our prayers from being answered. (Read James 1:6-7; 4:3)
3. This message: "Seven Obstacles to Answered Prayer":

I. SELFISHNESS IS AN OBSTACLE TO ANSWERED PRAYER
A. James teaches that selfish motives deprive our prayers of power. (Read James 4:2-3)
   1. Many times, while our requests may be legitimate, the motive behind the prayers is self-centered.
   2. For instance, a pastor prays for an awakening (which is good); however, he secretly wants to increase the number of members to have a more money and prestige.
   3. Such selfish prayers fall helpless to the ground.
B. When we pray, we must examine our motives.

II. SIN IS AN OBSTACLE TO ANSWERED PRAYER
A. Isaiah warned Israel that their sinful practices were keeping God from answering their prayers. (Read Isaiah 19:1-2)
B. Sin is appalling in the sight of God.
   1. Even more appalling is the way sin obstructs prayer by cutting off communication between man and God.
C. If we would see our prayers answered, we must repent (Ac 3:19).

III. IDOLATRY IS AN OBSTACLE TO ANSWERED PRAYER
  A. Ezekiel counselled Israel that their idols were stumbling blocks to God answering their prayers. (Read Ezekiel 14:3)
    1. In the same way, the idols in our hearts compel God to ignore our requests.
    2. An idol is anything that takes the place of God in our lives.
  B. If we want power in prayer, we must forsake our idols.

IV. GREED IS AN OBSTACLE TO ANSWERED PRAYER
  A. Solomon warned, "If a man shuts his ears to the cry of the poor, he too will cry out and not be answered" (Pr 21:13).
    1. Greed causes us to withhold blessing from those in need.
  B. However, God will reward the generous (Pr 19:17; Lk 6:38).

V. WITHHOLDING OF FORGIVENESS IS AN OBSTACLE TO ANSWERED PRAYER
  A. Jesus taught that, while faith results in answered prayer, withholding forgiveness results in unanswered prayer.
    1. Read Mark 11:24-26.
    2. How many cry to out God and wonder why their prayer is not answered—while they hold a secret grudge against someone they feel has wronged them.
  B. Go and be reconciled to your brother, then pray (Mt 5:21-23).

VI. A BAD RELATIONSHIP BETWEEN HUSBAND AND WIFE IS AN OBSTACLE TO ANSWERED PRAYER
  A. Peter instructs husbands to treat their wives with respect "so that nothing will hinder [their] prayers" (1Pe 3:7).
  B. If we want God to answer our prayers, we must mend our relationship with our husband or wife.

VII. DOUBT IS AN OBSTACLE TO ANSWERED PRAYER
  A. James warned that the one who prays and doubts "should not think he will receive anything from the Lord" (James 1:5-7).
  B. When we pray, we must believe (Mk 11:24).

Conclusion and Altar Call
  1. Have you wondered why your prayers are not being answered?
  2. Possibly one of these things is blocking the answer.
  3. Come, get right with God, the go and pray.   [JSa]

39   Wrestling with God in Prayer

Sermon in a Sentence: Like Epaphras, we must learn to wrestle in prayer for the needs of others.
Sermon Purpose: That God's people will commit themselves to passionate intercessory prayer.
Texts: Colossians 4:12
Introduction
1. Paul wrote Colossians from a Roman prison cell.
2. At the end of the letter, Paul mentions several colleagues who were with him in Rome, including Onesimus, Mark, Luke the doctor, and Demas, among others (Col 4:7-11).
3. One in particular was a man named *Epaphras* (vv.11-12).
    a. Paul said, "He is always wrestling in prayer for you."
    b. This message will focus on Epaphras and His powerful ministry of intercessory prayer.
4. We will answer three questions:

I. **WHO WAS EPAPHRAS?**
   A. From the epistles of Colossians and Philemon, we learn that...
      1. Epaphras was Paul's "fellow servant" and "fellow prisoner" in Rome (Phm 23; Col 1:7-8; 4:12-13).
      2. He introduced the Colossians to Christ (Col 1:6-7).
         a. He could have been one of the 12 disciples in Ac 19:1-2.
         b. He was possibly sent out from Paul's training school in the Lecture Hall of Tyranus (Ac 19:9-10).
      3. He carried a message of encouragement from the Colossian church to Paul in prison in Rome (Col 1:8).
         a. This message spurred the writing of Colossians.
   B. Epaphras is primarily distinguished by his prayer ministry.
      1. Col 4:12: "He is always wrestling in prayer for you."
      2. In prison, Paul had prayed with him and watched him pray.
      3. He is an example for all Christians (Ro 15:30).

II. **HOW DID EPAPHRAS DISTINGUISH HIMSELF IN PRAYER?**
   A. Epaphras "wrestled" in prayer for the Colossians (v.12a).
      1. The word "wrestling" is from the Greek word *agōnizomai* from which we get the English word "agonize."
      2. NLT: "I can assure you that *he prays hard for you...*"
      3. This describes Epaphras' ministry of intercessory prayer.

4. Illus: Like the pangs of a mother giving birth.
B. His wrestling in prayer reminds us of two others who wrestled with God in prayer:
   1. *Jacob* wrestled with God in prayer at Jabbok (Ge 32:22-32).
      a. "Jacob was left alone, and a man wrestled with him till daybreak" (v.24).
      b. He was, in fact, wrestling with God. (Read Ho 12:4-5)
      c. He prayed, "I will not let you go unless you bless me."
      d. He named the place *Penuel,* meaning "face of God."
   2. *Jesus* wrestled in prayer in Gethsemane (Mt 26:36-45).
      a. In His hour of greatest trail, He agonized in prayer.
      c. He was tempted to turn from His mission (v.39).
      d. Yet, He prayed, "Not my will, but yours be done" (42).
C. At times, God may call us to wrestle in prayer.

III. WHAT DID EPAPHRAS PRAY FOR?

- Read v.12: *"He is always wrestling in prayer for you, that you may stand firm in all the will of God, mature and fully assured."*

A. Before we discuss what Epaphras prayed for, let's think about what he *did not* pray for:
   1. He *did not* focus his prayers on himself, but on others.
   2. He *did not* pray for personal blessing, health, or wealth.
B. According to Paul, Epaphras prayed for two things:
   1. That the Colossian believers would "stand firm in the will of God" (v.12).
      a. That they would faithfully follow Christ.
   2. That the Colossians would become "mature and fully assured" in Christ.
      a. That they would become like Christ.
   3. These two things were so important in Epaphras' mind that he agonized in prayer for them.
C. Three lessons we can learn from Epaphras' prayer ministry:
   1. We must learn to focus our prayers on others.
   2. When we pray for others, we must focus our prayers on those things that are most important.
   3. At times, God call, on us to intercede for others with great passion and intensity.

Conclusion and Altar Call
Come, commit yourself to wrestling in prayer for others.

[DRM]

Section 4
Intercessory Prayer Warfare

40 Interceding for the Nations

Sermon in a Sentence: God calls us to intercede for the nations.
Sermon Purpose: That God's people will begin to intercede for their homes, for the unreached tribes of Africa, and the nations beyond.
Texts: Ezekiel 22:29-30
Introduction
1. Have you ever lost something you valued very much?
   a. You sought and sought for it, but never found it.
   b. Can you recall the anguish that you felt?
2. This is how God must have felt in our text.
   a. He looked for an intercessor, one who would "stand in the gap" between God and His people (and thus, between God's people and God's judgment), but He found no one.
3. God is still looks for intercessors—those who will "stand in the gap" between God and lost humanity.
   a. Will He find any here today?
   b. This message: "Interceding for the Nations"

II. WHAT IS INTERCESSORY PRAYER? (Four answers:)
A. Intercessory prayer is *"Building up the wall"* and *"standing in the gap"* (Eze 22:30).
   1. The image the prophet is painting: The enemy surrounds the city, and there is a wide opening in the wall where enemy soldiers can enter.
   2. The intercessor stands in the breach fighting back the enemy.
   3. He also repairs the wall, saving the city from destruction.
B. Intercessory prayer is *mediation.*
   1, Mediation is intervening between conflicting parties to bring about reconciliation.
   2. Illus: The story of Moses and Aaron stopping the plague is a picture of the work of mediation (Nu 16:41-48).
C. Intercessory prayer is *spiritual warfare.*
   1. Paul says that we battle against spiritual forces (Ep 6:12).
   2. The intercessor enters the "strong man's house," binds him, and prepares the way for effective evangelism (Mt 12:29).
D. Intercessory prayer is *persevering prayer.*
   1. True intercessors pray until the answer comes.
   2. Tell the Parable of the Persistent Friend (Lk 11:5-8).

II. GOD IS LOOKING FOR INTERCESSORS
A. He is looking for "someone who might rebuild the wall of righteousness that guards the land... for someone to stand in the gap in the wall" and halt God's judgment (NLT).
B. God is calling you and me to intercede for the nations.
1. To intercede for our families.
2. To intercede for our church.
3. To intercede for our people and tribe.
4. To intercede for our nation.
5. To intercede for unreached peoples and places.
6. To intercede for other nations.
C. Will you answer the call?
1. Be like Isaiah who cried out: "Here am I Lord. Send me" (Is 6:8).

III. HOW TO INTERCEDE FOR THE NATIONS (Five actions:)
A. Lift up your eyes and look on the fields (Jn 4:35).
1. Become informed about the lost peoples around you and around the world.
2. Get a map of the world and post it on your wall.
B. Arm yourself for battle (Ep 6:10-18).
1. We fight with spiritual weapons (2Co 10:4).
2. Be filled with the Spirit (Ep 8:16; Ac 1:8).
3. Learn how to pray in the Spirit (Ro 8:26-27).
C. Enter into God's presence.
1. Come boldly before God's throne (He 4:16).
2. Allow the Spirit to move on you and in you (Ro 8:26-27).
D. Pray in Jesus' name (Jn 14:13-14).
1. There is power in the name of Jesus (Mk 16:17)
E. Persevere until the answer comes.

Conclusion and Altar Call
1. God is looking for people to intercede for the nations.
2. Will you be one of those people?
3. Come now, and be filled with the Spirit, committing yourself to be one of God's intercessors.

[DRM]

41 Elijah Does Spiritual Warfare

Sermon in a Sentence: If we, like Elijah, will persevere in prayer, we can have victory over the enemies of God.
Sermon Purpose: That God's people will commit themselves to fervent, believing prayer in anticipation of the coming victory.
Text: 1Kings 18:20-40; James 5:17-18
Introduction
1. James describes Elijah as "a man just like us [and] he prayed earnestly…" (Ja 5:17).
2. In our Scripture reading, we see Elijah doing spiritual warfare.
    a. He gained victory over the enemies of God.
    b. He provides an example for us today.
3. How did Elijah gain victory over the prophets of Baal?

I. ELIJAH RECOGNIZED THE NATURAL ISSUES CAUSING A SPIRITUAL PROBLEM (Read vv.1-2, 15)
A. Elijah was not "passively unaware" of what was going on around him—he clearly understood what was happening.
   1. There was a famine in the land of Israel.
   2. Because of the wickedness of King Ahab, God had shut up the heavens for more than 3 years (1Ki 16:29-33; 17:1).
   3. There was also a spiritual famine like in the days of Amos (Am 8:11).
B. Note Elijah's twofold response to the problem:
   1. The prophet boldly confronted those causing the problem.
      a. The word of the Lord came to him (18:1).
      b. He confronted King Ahab (18:2, 15-19).
      c. He challenged the prophets of Baal (vv.20-21, 25).
   2. He also confronted the problem hindering the work of God.
      a. The people had forsaken God.
      b. Elijah challenged them, "How long will you waver between two opinions?" (v.21).
C. We must respond like Elijah:
   1. We must recognize the problem and its causes.
   2. We must boldly confront the issues in Jesus' name.
   3. How then did Elijah address the issue?

II. ELIJAH PRAYED UNTIL GOD ANSWERED HIS PRAYER (Read vv. 36-37)

A. He challenged the prophets of Baal to a power encounter (vv.20-39).
     1. We too are in a contest with demonic forces (Ep 6:12).
     2. Like Elijah, we must confront them with spiritual weapons (2Co 10:4).
  B. Elijah persevered until God answered his prayer:
     1. He prayed until the *fire* fell! (v.38).
        a. Fire is a type of the power of the Holy Spirit.
        b. The fire of the Spirit cleanses and empowers.
     2. He prayed until the *people* fell! (v.39).
        a. They fell on their faces in submission to God.
        b. A similar thing happened when the fire fell at Pentecost (Ac 2:1-4, 41).
     3. He prayed until *evil* fell!
        a. The prophets of Baal were shamed, routed, and destroyed (v.40).
        b. We too must pray until demons are bound, people are delivered, and the church is established.

III. ELIJAH PREPARED FOR THE COMING VICTORY
  A. Elijah knew that God was ready to break the drought and send rain.
     1. In faith, he told Ahab to get ready for the rain.
  B. Look at how Elijah prepared for the coming victory:
     1. He expected that God would give the victory (v.41).
     2. He again went to God in fervent, believing prayer (v.42).
     3. He persevered in prayer until the answer came (vv.43-44).
        a. Read James 5:14, 17-18
     4. God again answered his prayer.
  C. We too must pray in anticipation of the coming victory!

Conclusion and Altar Call
   1. If we will persevere in prayer, like Elijah, we can have victory over the enemies of God.
   2. Come now, be filled with the Spirit, and commit yourself to fervent, believing prayer.

[GB]

42 Intercessory Prayer in the Spirit

Sermon in a Sentence: Be filled with the Spirit, and then practice daily intercession in the Spirit.
Sermon Purpose: That believers will be filled with the Spirit and commit themselves to daily prayer in the Spirit.
Texts: Romans 8:26-27; 1 Corinthians 14:14; Jude 20-21
Introduction
1. One benefit of living the Spirit-controlled life is the privilege and responsibility of intercessory prayer in the Holy Spirit.
2. Our texts speak of such prayer.
3. In this message, we will look closely at this kind of prayer.

I. **WHAT IS MEANT BY THE TERM "PRAYER IN THE SPIRIT"?** (The Bible uses the term in two ways:)
   A. Generally speaking, prayer in the Spirit is *any prayer* that is prompted and directed by the Holy Spirit.
      1. Paul speaks of such prayer in Ro 8:26-27.
      2. It is a "team effort" between a Spirit-filled individual and the Spirit of God.
      3. It can be in a Spirit-inspired language you know or in a language that the Spirit gives you.
   B. More specifically, prayer in the Spirit is *prayer in tongues.*
      1. The "groans that words cannot express," spoken of by Paul, are likely prayer in tongues.
      2. It is praying "as the Spirit gives utterance" (Ac 2:4).
      3. According to 1Co 14:2, prayer in tongues and prayer in the Spirit are the same thing (see also vv. 14-15.).

II. **HOW INTERCESSORY PRAYER IN THE SPIRIT BLESSES THE ONE PRAYING** (Three ways:)
   A. Paul teaches that, as the intercessor prays in the Spirit, his or her spiritual life is edified or built up (1Co 14:4a).
   B. Jude teaches that, as the intercessor prays in the Holy Spirit, his or her faith is increased (Jude 20).
   C. Jude further teaches that, as the intercessor prays in the Holy Spirit, he or she is kept in the love of God (vv. 20-21a; see also Ro 5:5).

III. **HOW PRAYER IN THE SPIRIT BLESSES OTHERS**
   A. While prayer in the Spirit blesses the one praying, we should

not forget that its main purpose is to bless others—that is, the ones being prayed for.
    1. Let's look at how this intercession for others works.
  B. In Ro 8:26 Paul taught that we all have a weakness in our prayer lives:
    1. He said, "We do not know what we ought to pray for."
    2. How many urgent needs do we fail to pray for simply because we are unaware of them?
    3. And, even when we do know what to pray for, we don't know God's will in the matter.
    4. At such times, "the Spirit himself intercedes for us…with groans that words cannot express."
    5. And He prays through us "in accordance with God's will" (vv. 26-27).
  C. Paul tells of five powerful ways the Spirit helps us in prayer:
    1. He "makes intercession for us."
    2. He does this "with groans which words cannot express."
    3. He "searches our hearts."
    4. He "knows the mind of the Spirit."
    5. He "intercedes for the saints according to the will of God."

IV. THE PATHWAY TO INTERCESSORY PRAYING IN THE SPIRIT (How can we become "Holy Spirit intercessors"?)
  A. Be filled with—and remain full of—the Holy Spirit (Ac 2:4; Ep 5:18). (Here's how:)
    1. Ask God to give you the Holy Spirit (Lk 11:9-13).
    2. Receive Him by faith (Mk 11:24).
    3. Speak (pray) as the Spirit gives utterance (Ac 2:4).
  B. Then, as you pray…
    1. … be sensitive to the prompting of the Spirit.
    2. … yield to the Spirit and allow Him to pray through you.

Conclusion:
  1. We should not neglect this powerful means of intercessory prayer.
  2. Come now to be filled with the Spirit.

[DRM]

43 Prayer Strategies for Spiritual Warriors

Sermon in a Sentence: God is calling us to be spiritual prayer warriors.
Sermon Purpose: That believers will be filled with the Spirit and commit themselves to be spiritual prayer warriors.
Text: Ephesians 6:18-20
Introduction
1. In Ep 6:10-17 Paul describes the believer's spiritual warfare
   a. He urges, "Be strong in the Lord and his...power" (v.10).
   b. He informs them, "Our struggle is not against..." (v.12).
2. He tells them to "put on the full armor of God" (v.13-17).
   a. Defensive weapons: belt of truth, breastplate of righteousness, shield of faith, helmet of salvation.
   b. Offensive weapons: the readiness of the gospel, the sword of the Spirit...
3. Moves to a third powerful offensive weapon—prayer (v.18).
   a. *Seven directives* concerning prayer.
   b. Can serve as a prayer guide for spiritual warriors.

I. WE SHOULD PRAY IN THE SPIRIT
- *v.18: "Pray in the Spirit..."*

A. Paul talks about prayer in the Spirit in another passage (Read Ro 8:26-27).
B. Prayer in the Spirit is Spirit-anointed, Spirit-directed prayer.
   1. It includes prayer in tongues (1Cor 14:15).
C. To pray in the Spirit, one must be full of the Spirit (Ep 5:18).

II. WE SHOULD PRAY ON ALL OCCASIONS
- *v.18: "Pray in the Spirit on all occasions..."*

A. In another place, Paul put it like this: "Pray continually; give thanks in all circumstances..." (1Th 5:17-18).
B. We must pray extensively before making any major decision.
   1. As we pray, the Spirit will direct us.
   2. Illus: The Spirit directs Peter (Ac 11:9-20; cf. 11:12)

III. WE SHOULD PRAY WITH ALL KINDS OF PRAYERS
- *v.18: "Pray...with all kinds of prayers..."*

A. The Bible speaks of several kinds of prayer, including prayers of repentance, petition, submission, intercession, and others.
B. The prayer should fit the need and occasion.

IV. WE SHOULD PRAY FOR ALL KINDS OF REQUESTS
- v.18: "Pray...with all kinds of requests..."
A. Here, Paul is expanding on the prayer of petition (or asking).
B. Jesus taught us to ask in prayer:
   1. Read Mt 7:7 "Ask and it will be given to you..."
   2. Read Mk 11:24 "Whatever you ask for in prayer, believe..."
C. We should pray for spiritual, physical, financial, church, and family needs.

V. WE SHOULD REMAIN ALERT WHEN WE PRAY
- v.18 "...be alert and always keep on praying..."
A. When the disciples went to sleep in Gethsemane...
   1. Jesus told them to "Watch and pray..." (Mk 14:38).
   2. He asked them, "Could you not watch for one hour?" (37).
   3. They slept during Jesus' and their greatest hour of trial.
B. We must not sleep during the time of harvest: "He who sleeps during harvest is a disgraceful son" (Pr 10:5).

VI. WE SHOULD PRAY FOR ALL THE SAINTS
- v.18: "...keep on praying for all the saints."
A. Paul speaks here of intercessory prayer.
B. We must faithfully pray for one another (1Ti 2:1).
C. We must pray for those in chains (Col 4:18).

VII. WE SHOULD PRAY FOR MISSIONARIES
- Read vv.19-20: "And [pray] for me..."
A. Paul, the missionary, requests prayer from the Ephesians
   a. That he would fearlessly preach the gospel (v.19).
   b. Another time: for open doors (Col 4:3).
B. We must pray for our missionaries and church planters.
   1. For spiritual, physical, and emotional needs.
   2. For family and financial needs

Conclusion and Altar Call
1. God calls us to "be strong in the Lord and in his mighty power" and to challenge the enemy in prayer (Ep 6:10, 18-19).
2. Come, be filled with the Spirit, and commit yourself to be a spiritual prayer warrior.

[DRM]

44 Intercessory Prayer and Church Growth

Sermon in a Sentence: The book of Acts shows how intercessory prayer is a key to church growth.
Sermon Purpose: That God's people will commit to intercession for the lost and for the church.
Texts: Acts 6:1-7; 13:1-3; 16:6-10
Introduction
1. These passages from the book of Acts demonstrate how intercessory prayer is essential for church growth.
2. They show how intercessory prayer helps keep the church united, guided, and protected by God—resulting in church growth.

I. NOTE HOW THE APOSTLES WERE COMMITTED TO INTERCESSORY PRAYER
A. Tell the story of the choosing of the seven (Ac 6:1-7).
  1. Note the apostles' commitment: "We…will give our attention to prayer and the ministry of the word" (v.4).
B. The apostles were committed to intercessory prayer for at least two important reasons:
  1. Because Jesus had taught them to pray (Mt 9:37-38).
  2. Because intercessory prayer had enabled them to be powerful proclaimers of God's Word (Ac 4:31).
C. Intercessory prayer further kept the church united and protected from divisions (Ac 6:5-6):
  1. Prayer resulted in a Spirit-inspired solution to the issue of the widows' food distribution.
  2. This prevented what could have been a disastrous church split that would have stalled the church's progress.
D. Paul's missionary journeys were initiated and guided by intercessory prayer.
  1. During a time of prayer and fasting, the Holy Spirit initiated Paul's missionary journey (Ac 13:1-3).
  2. Later, during a time of prayer, the Holy Spirit guided Paul and his missionary colleagues to Macedonia to preach the gospel there (Ac 16:6-10).

II. NOTE HOW INTERCESSORY PRAYER CONTRIBUTED TO THE GROWTH OF THE NEW TESTAMENT CHURCH

A. The apostles' commitment to intercessory prayer resulted in the growth of the church in Jerusalem.
   1. Prayer resulted in the empowering of the church at Pentecost (Ac 1:8, 14; 2:1-4).
   2. Prayer caused the church to continue to grow in Jerusalem (Ac 2:41-42, 47; 3:1; 4:24).
   3. In Acts 6, prayer kept the church unified, thus fueling church growth: "So the word of God spread and the number of the disciples multiplied greatly in Jerusalem" (6:7).

B. Paul's commitment to intercessory prayer resulted in church growth in Europe (Ac 16:11-40).
   1. It resulted in Paul being guided into Europe (vv.6-10)
   2. It led to his winning Lydia to Christ (Ac 16:11-15).
   3. It strengthened the apostles to overcome hardship and persecution (vv.16-25, note v.25).
   4. It resulted in God's miraculous intervention (v.26).
   5. It resulted in the jailer's household coming Christ (vv.27-33).
   6. It resulted in the church being planted in Philippi.

C. If we will commit ourselves to intercessory prayer, we can expect the same things to happen today.
   1. The Spirit will be poured out.
   2. The church will remain unified and on track.
   3. The church will grow and reach the lost.

Conclusion and Altar Call

1. If we want to see the lost reached and the church grow, we must commit ourselves to intercessory prayer.
2. Come now, and commit yourself to intercessory prayer for the lost and for the church.

[EKA]

45 Interceding with Paul

Sermon in a Sentence: Every Christian can have an intercessory prayer life like the apostle Paul.

Sermon Purpose: That God's people commit themselves to follow Paul's example of intercessory prayer.

Texts: Romans 1:9-10a; Ephesians 1:15-16

Introduction
1. In these two texts (and others) Paul demonstrates his commitment to intercessory prayer.
2. Every follower of Jesus should be involved in intercessory prayer.
3. Let us consider five lessons on intercessory prayer we can learn from Paul:

I. **LIKE PAUL, WE SHOULD PRAY WITHOUT CEASING FOR ONE ANOTHER** (Read Ro 1:9-10)
   A. Paul assured the Christians in Rome, "[I] constantly... remember you in my prayers at all times" (Ro 1:9-10).
      1. Paul never ceased to pray for his Christian friends.
      2. He was never without something to pray about.
   B. We too should persist in prayer for our Christian friends.
      1. We must remember them in our prayers at all times.
      2. We should also pray for our missionaries.
      Illus: Paul, the missionary, requested prayer (Ep 6:19).

II. **LIKE PAUL, OUR HEART'S DESIRE MUST BE FOR OUR OWN PEOPLE TO BE SAVED** (Read Ro 10:1)
   A. Paul confessed, "Brethren, my heart's desire and prayer to God for Israel is, that they might be saved" (Ro 10:1).
      1. Paul loved his own people and prayed for them.
      2. Paul chief desire was for them to be saved.
   B. Like Paul, we must pray for our people.
      1. Our love for them must motivate us to pray.
      2. God's Spirit will give us a love for them (Ro 5:5).
      3. We should also pay for specific unreached people groups in our country and beyond.

III. **LIKE PAUL, WE MUST PRAY FOR PEOPLE TO BE RECONCILED TO GOD** (Read 2Co 5:20 KJV)

A. Paul urged the Corinthians, "we pray you in Christ's stead, be ye reconciled to God" (2Co 5:20 KJV).
      1. Paul considered his ministry to be a ministry of reconciliation (2Co 5:18).
      2. Paul thus interceded for people to be reconciled to God.
   B. Like Paul, we too have a ministry of reconciliation.
      1. We have been called out of darkness (1Pe 2:9),
      2. Now, through prayer, we call others into the light of Christ.

IV. LIKE PAUL, WE SHOULD ENCOURAGE BELIEVERS TO PRAY FOR ONE ANOTHER (Read Ep 6:18)
   A. Paul urged the Ephesian believers to "pray in the Spirit on all occasions…and always keep on praying for all the saints."
      1. He also encouraged believers to "pray with all kinds of prayers and requests."
      2. He further encouraged them to "pray in the Spirit."
   B. We too should encourage one another to pray.
      1. Not only should we pray ourselves, we must teach and inspire others to pray.
      2. Illus: Like Paul who exhorted his son in the faith, Timothy, to pray (1Ti 2:1).

V. LIKE PAUL, WE SHOULD MAKE OUR REQUESTS TO GOD WITH JOY (Read Phi 1:4)
   A. Paul told the believers in Philippi, "In all my prayers for all of you, I always pray with joy."
      1. Similarly, he told the Colossians, "We always thank God…when we pray for you" (Col 1:3).
      2. Paul did not consider praying to be a burden.
      3. He rather considered praying to be a joy.
   B. This should be our attitude when we pray for others.
      1. Like Paul, we must discover the joy of interceding for others

Conclusion and Altar Call
Come and commit to have an intercessory prayer life like the apostle Paul.

[TCA]

46 God's Call to Intercessory Prayer

Sermon in a Sentence: We must covenant with God in intercessory prayer.

Sermon Purpose: That God's people commit themselves to a lifestyle of intercessory prayer,

Text: 2 Chronicles 7:14; Jeremiah 33:3

Introduction
1. In both of our texts, God is speaking to His covenant people.
2. He is calling them to committed, believing prayer.
3. He is saying, *"If you will…then I will…"*
4. This message will focus on a certain kind of prayer—intercessory prayer—or prayer for the needs of others.
5. Let's look at four important issues concerning intercessory prayer:

I. GOD'S CALL TO INTERCESSORY PRAYER
A. God calls His people to intercessory prayer.
 1. God is issuing a summons, a battle cry to His people.
 2. He seeks those who will "stand in the gap" (Ez 22:30).
 3. Those who will pray: *"If my people will pray"* (2Ch 7:14).
B. God calls us in three ways:
 1. He calls us to *face the challenge* of intercessory prayer.
  a. The challenge of hundreds of unreached tribes
  b. The challenge of thousands of unreached places
  c. The challenge of millions of unreached people
 2. He calls us to *accept the charge* of intercessory prayer.
  a. The charge to lift up our eyes (Jn 4:35)
  b. The charge to pray (Mt 9:37-38)
  c. The charge to go (Mk 16:15)
 3. He calls us to *make the choice* to pray.
  a. Choose today to become an intercessory prayer warrior.

II. THE COVENANT OF INTERCESSORY PRAYER
A. In our texts, God calls on His people to covenant with Him.
 a. This is seen in the "if-then" wording God uses.
B. Two ways we must covenant with God in prayer:
 1. We must covenant with God *to act obediently.*
  a. God's part of the covenant is to answer our prayers.
  b. Our part is to *obey* Him and pray.
 2. We must covenant with God *to trust completely.*

       a. We must believe His promise:
          1) "I will hear from heaven...forgive..."
       b. We must act on that belief:
          1) "Humble yourselves...pray...seek...".
    3. We can be sure that God will keep His promise.

III. OUR COMMITMENT TO INTERCESSORY PRAYER
  A. Intercessory prayer requires commitment.
    1. Prayer is *hard work,* which requires dedication.
    2. Prayer is *spiritual work,* which requires crucifying the flesh.
  B. Make these two commitments:
    1. Commit yourself to *sense the needs of others.*
       a. As Jesus did (Mk 9:36; Phi 2:5).
    2. Commit yourself to *a lifestyle of intercessory prayer.*
       a. As Jesus did (Lk 6:12)
       b. As Paul did (Ro 1:9)
       c. We must "never stop praying" (1Th 5:17, NLT).

IV. OUR CONFIDENCE IN INTERCESSORY PRAYER
  A. We can be confident that God will answer our prayers.
    1. He has committed himself to answer (Je 33:3).
    2. Jesus, "Ask and it will be given you..." (Mt 7:7).
    3. In prayer we can move mountains (Mt 21:21).
  B. We can have confidence in three ways:
    1. Confidence in *God's word.*
       a. His word is full of promises to answer prayer.
    2. Confidence in *God's character.*
       a. God cannot lie (Nu 23:19).
       b. What He promises He will perform (Ro. 4:21).
    3. Have confidence in *God's power.*
       a. Nothing is too hard for God (Je 32:27).

Conclusion and Altar Call
Come now; let's commit ourselves in a lifestyle of intercessory prayer for the nations.

[SD]

47 This Matter of Intercessory Prayer

Sermon in a Sentence: We should intercede for those around us and for those in distant places.
Sermon Purpose: That the people commit themselves to intercessory prayer for the lost.
Texts: 1 Timothy 2:1-3, 8
Introduction
1. In our texts, Paul urged his son in the faith, Timothy, to "make intercessions for all people."
2. In verses 3-4 he states his reason for his exhortation: "This… pleases God…who wants all people to be saved…"
3. The term *intercessions* suggests a close communion with God.
4. It further involves stepping into someone else's shoes, closely identifying with them, and praying for their needs.
5. Three important issues concerning intercessory prayer:

I. INTERCESSORY PRAYER IS A MATTER OF FACT
A. The fact is, *the Bible commands* us to pray.
   1. In our text, Paul urged Timothy to intercede for all people.
   2. In 1Th 5:17, he urged, "Pray without ceasing" (KJV).
   3. Jesus also commands us to pray (for example):
      a. Mt 26:41: "Watch and pray…"
      b. Mt 9:38: "Pray to the Lord of the harvest…"
B. The fact is, *Jesus modeled* how we should pray.
   1. He spent the first 40 days of His ministry in prayer and fasting (Mt 4:1-2).
   2. He prayed in the "lonely places" (Lk 5:16).
   3. He prayed on the mountain (Lk 9:28).
   4. He prayed during His last hours on earth:
      a. He interceded in the upper room (Jn 17:1ff).
      b. He prayed in the Garden of Gethsemane (Mt 26:36ff).
   5. He now intercedes for us in heaven (He 7:25).
   6. We must learn to intercede like Jesus.
C. The fact is, *God answers* our prayers.
   1. He is ready to answer when we call on Him (Je 33:3).
   2. However, He does not always answer our prayers *when* we want or *how* we want.
   3. Sometimes, the greatest answer to prayer is that God gives us grace and peace to endure our trials.

II. INTERCESSORY PRAYER IS A MATTER OF FAITH
A. We must pray with *faith in God's will*.
1. We must pray in accordance with God's will (1Jn 5:14).
    a. It is God's will that all people be saved (2Pe 3:9).
2. Our faith should be accompanied by action (Ja 2:17).
    a. We must not only pray for the lost, we must go out and seek to win them to Christ (Lk 14:23)
    b. We must believe that some will respond (Lk 5:10).
3. Illus: Robert Savage said, "Prayer is asking for rain; faith is carrying the umbrella."

B. We must pray with *faith in God's word*.
1. We must let Scripture guide our prayers.
2. For example, you can read a passage, and then pray what is in the passage.
3. Illus: Pray using with Great Commission as your guide (Mk 16:15-20).

C. We must pray with *faith in God's way*.
1. His ways are higher than ours (Is 55:9).
2. We can trust Him to do what is best.

III. INTERCESSORY PRAYER IS A MATTER OF FOCUS
A. When we pray, we should *focus on the Lord*.
1. The focus of our prayers is not on ourselves and our own personal needs, but on God and His mission.
2. This is how Jesus prayed (Mt 26:42).
3. This is how the believers in Acts prayed (i.e. Ac 4:23-30).

B. When we pray, we should *focus on the land*.
1. That is, we must focus on our country and people.
2. This is the essence of intercessory prayer, focus on others.
3. We must also focus our prayers on other places (Jn 10:16).

C. When we pray, we should *focus on the lost*.
1. Pray for the lost around you.
2. Pray for the lost in distant places.
3. Pray for unreached peoples in Africa and beyond.
4. Pray for laborers to go into the harvest (Mt 9:35ff).

Conclusion and Altar Call
Come now and commit yourself to the powerful ministry of intercessory prayer.

[SD]

48 A Serious Battle

Sermon in a Sentence: We must engage in spiritual warfare through intercessory prayer.
Sermon Purpose: That God's people commit to challenging demonic forces through Spirit-empowered intercessory prayer.
Text: Ephesians 6:10-20
Introduction
1. Satan seeks to destroy the church in Africa.
   a. He is the Prince of Darkness and has mobilized his powerful demonic forces to capture the hearts of people.
   b. His forces are highly trained and well organized.
   c. Our text describes that battle. (Read vv.12-13)
2. In this message, we will examine the spiritual warfare in which the church is involved.
   a. We will discuss the armor of God which we must wear.
   b. We will especially emphasize the role of prayer in combatting the devil and his evil forces.

I. **LET'S FIRST LOOK AT SATAN'S ARMY**
   A. Paul says that our battle is against demonic forces (Ep 6:12).
      1. Satan has his generals, captains, and lieutenants.
      2. They serve him and direct his forces.
   B. Satan's tactics are many; here are a few:
      1. *Moral subversion.* Satan tells people, "Do as you please." He says, "Your personal freedom should not be hindered by God's moral restrictions."
      2. *Destruction of the family.*
         a. Satan uses pornography to destroy our families.
         b. He also uses the abuse of women and children.
      3. *Racial hatred:* He disguises racism as tribal superiority.
      4. *Political corruption*
         a. Satan fills our government offices with corrupt people.
         b. He seeks to do the same in the church.
      5. He uses many other means to destroy people.
   C. The conflict is intense and difficult.
      1. It is a life and death struggle—a war for time and eternity.
      2. Our chief adversary is not men but the devil (1Pe 5:8).
      3. And God has called each of us to be involved.

II. WE MUST ALL BECOME PRAYER WARRIORS
A. Christian are soldiers by birth—the new birth (Jn 3:3).
B. To fight the battle, we must be empowered by the Holy Spirit (Ac 1:8, 2:1-4, Ep 5:18; 6:18).
C. We must not be entangled with the affairs of this life (2Ti 2:4).
D. We must never give up the fight. (Read Ep 6:13-14)
1. The best defense is a powerful offense.
2. We go on the offensive through intercessory prayer.
3. We defeat the spirits of darkness in the power of the Spirit.

III. WE MUST PUT ON THE FULL ARMOR OF GOD
(Read Ep 6:14-18)
A. We must make *doubly sure* we put on God's armor.
1. Note how Paul repeats this admonition two times (11, 13).
B. Our spiritual armor includes...
1. The *belt of truth:* We must be strong in the Word. Prayer and the Word are two sides to the same sword.
2. The *breastplate of righteousness.* This protects the heart. Christ is made unto us righteousness.
3. The *readiness* that comes from the gospel: Our feet are ready to go, preach, and suffer for Christ.
4. The *shield of faith.* Faith can conquer every enemy.
6. The *helmet of salvation:* The prayer warrior puts heaven in his head and heart.
7. The *sword of the Spirit:* Two powerful weapons are the Word of God and the Spirit-empowered life.
C. Most of all, we must pray. (Read vv.18-19)
1. We must "pray in the Spirit."
2. We must pray "on all occasions."
3. We must pray "with all kinds of prayers and requests."
4. We must "be alert" in prayer.
5. We must "always keep praying for all the saints."
6. We must pray that God will "open [our] mouths" so that we will "fearlessly make known the...gospel."

Conclusion and Altar Call
1. We must recognize our enemy, protect ourselves against attack, be filled with the Spirit, and go on the offensive in prayer.
2. Come, commit yourself to be a prayer warrior.

[JSp]

49 Fighting the Good Fight of Faith

Sermon in a Sentence: We must fight the good fight of faith by putting on the full armor of God and praying in the Spirit.
Sermon Purpose: That God's people will become strong missionary prayer warriors.
Text: Ephesians 6:10-18
Introduction:
1. Every Christian—whether he or she knows it or not—is involved in spiritual warfare.
2. Paul told Timothy, his son in the faith, to "fight the good fight of faith' (1Ti 6:12).
    a. Paul describes that fight. (Rer ead Ep 6:12).
    b. We too are involved in a struggle with spiritual powers.
3. Paul further tells how the Spirit-filled believer can be victorious in spiritual battle and how his or her prayers can contribute to the winning of lost souls.
4. Let us look at three combat strategies Paul discusses in this passage:

I. PAUL DISCUSSES THE SPIRITUAL WARRIOR'S MORALE (vv.10-14a)
A. The Christian warrior's morale must be high.
   1. We should "be strong in the Lord and in his mighty power" (v.10).
B. The Christian warrior's stance must be resolute.
   1. We must "put on the full armor of God" (v.11).
   2. We should always be ready to "take [our] stand against the devil's schemes" (v. 11).
   3. We must "stand [our] ground, and after [we] have done everything, to stand" (v.13).

II. PAUL DESCRIBES THE SPIRITUAL WARRIOR'S ARMOR (Reread vv.14-17)
A. We must put on our defensive armor. (This includes...)
   1. ...the belt of *truth* (v.14).
   2. ...the breastplate of *righteousness* (v.14).
   3. ...the *readiness* that comes from the gospel of peace (15).
   4. ...the shield of *faith,* with which [we] can extinguish all the flaming arrows of the evil one (v.16).
   5. ...the helmet of *salvation* (v.17).

B. We must also take up or offensive weapons. (These spiritual weapons include…)
   1. …the sword of the Spirit, which is the *word of God* (v.17).
   2. …*prayer in the Spirit* (v.18).

III. PAUL EXPLAINS THE SPIRITUAL WARRIOR'S PRAYER LIFE (Read vv.18-20)
A. We must "pray in the Spirit…" (v.18).
   1. Prayer in the Spirit is Spirit-anointed, Spirit-directed prayer.
   2. Paul described such prayer in Ro 8:26-27 and 1 Co 14:14-15.
B. We must pray "on all occasions with all kinds of prayers and requests" (v.18). (Three ways we must pray:)
   1. We must pray on all occasions.
   2. We must pray with all kinds of prayers.
   3. We must pray for all kinds of requests.
C. We must intercede for the advance of the gospel (vv.19-20).
   1. Paul wrote the Ephesians from his prison cell in Rome.
      a. He was there for preaching the gospel.
      b. He called himself "an ambassador in chains" (v.20).
   2. Paul asked them to pray for three things:
      a. That he would preach the gospel fearlessly.
      b. That God would give him the words to speak.
      c. That he would clearly make the gospel known.
D. We must "be alert and always keep on praying" (v.18).
   1. We must be aware of what is going on in the world and in the work of missions.
   2. We must persevere in prayer until the answer come.

Conclusion and Altar Call
1. Such praying opens the door to missionary outreach resulting in the salvation of lost.
2. Come; let's commit ourselves to be strong missionary prayer warriors.

[JMT]

Section 5
The Holy Spirit and Prayer

50 Asking for the Holy Spirit

Sermon in a Sentence: We must persistently ask for the Holy Spirit.
Sermon Purpose: That God's people will ask for and receive the Holy Spirit, and then begin to walk "in step with the Spirit."
Texts: Luke 11:9-13; Galatians 3:14
Introduction
1. In first our text, Jesus is teaching His disciples how to receive the Holy Spirit.
2. He says, "Your Father in heaven [will] give the Holy Spirit to those who ask him!" (Lk 11:13).
3. In our second text, Paul adds, "By faith…we receive the promise of the Spirit" (Ga 3:14).
4. This message: "Asking for the Holy Spirit."

I. WHY JESUS TELLS US TO ASK FOR THE HOLY SPIRIT
  ▪ *Two compelling reasons we must ask:*
  A. We have been given have *a life to live* that is beyond our ability.
    1. We are commanded to be holy as God is holy (1Pe 1:15-16).
    2. We are commanded to walk as Jesus walked (1Jn 2:6).
    3. We can do this only in the Spirit's power (Ro 8:7-9).
  B. We have been given *a job to do* that is beyond our resources.
    1. Christ has commissioned us to take the gospel to all nations before He returns (Mk 16:15; Mt 24:14).
    2. We can do this only in the Spirit's power (Ac 1:8).
  C. We must therefore ask for, and receive, the Holy Spirit.

II. HOW WE CAN ASK FOR AND RECEIVE THE HOLY SPIRIT
  ▪ *Jesus tells us how in Luke 11:9-13:*
  A. First, we must, in faith, consciously *ask for the Spirit*.
    1. Jesus: *"Ask* and it will be given to you…" (Lk 11:9).
    2. We pray, "Father, I ask you now, give me the Holy Spirit."
    3. We must, however, ask in faith, believing that God is hearing and answering our prayer (Ga 3:14).
    4. God will answer your prayer, and give you the Holy Spirit.
    5. You will sense the Holy Spirit coming on you.
  B. Second, we must, by faith, *receive the Spirit*.
    1. Once Jesus offers the gift, we must actively receive it.
    2. Jesus: "Everyone who asks *receives*" (Lk 11:10).

3. Note: In this verse, the Greek word for "ask" (*lambano*) is in the active voice, meaning "to reach out and take."
4. We reach out and take by "believing that that we have received" (Read Mk 11:24).
5. You will sense the Spirit's presence inside.

C. Finally, we must, in faith, *speak by the Spirit*.
   1. This is what happened at Pentecost: "All of them were filled with the Holy Spirit and *began to speak* in other tongues as the Spirit enabled them" (Ac 2:4).
   2. You speak from where you sense the Spirit within.
   3. Note: Speaking in tongues is God's sign that you have been empowered to speak for Him as His Spirit-empowered witness (Ac 1:8).

III. WHAT WE MUST DO ONCE WE HAVE ASKED FOR AND RECEIVED THE HOLY SPIRIT

A. We must immediately begin to *witness in the Spirit*.
   1. In the Spirit's power, we must go and tell others about Jesus (Ac 1:8; 4:31).
   2. This is what happened at Pentecost (Ac 2:14ff).

B. We must daily *pray in the Spirit* (Ro 8:26-27).
   1. Pray in the Spirit for edification (1Co 14:4).
   2. Pray in the Spirit for empowerment (Ac 1:8; 2:4).

C. We must learn to *walk in the Spirit*.
   1. Paul: "Since we live by the Spirit, let us keep in step with the Spirit" (Ga 5:16, 25: Ro 8:1).
   2. We must keep being filled with the Spirit (Ep 5:18; 6:18).

D. We must learn to *minister in the Spirit*.
   1. We must become "competent ministers of the Spirit" (2Co 3:6).
   2. This competency includes…
      a. Anointed preaching (Ac 2:14ff).
      b. Ministering spiritual gifts (1Co 12:8-10).
      c. Challenging and defeating demons (Mt 12:28).
      d. Helping others receive the Spirit (Ac 8:14-17).

Conclusion and Altar Call
1. God's will is for every Christian to live a Spirit-empowered life.
2. Come now, let's ask God to fill us with the Holy Spirit.

[DRM]

51 Praying Down Pentecost

Sermon in a Sentence: We must pray until God pours out His Spirit on us as He did on the Day of Pentecost.
Sermon Purpose: That God's people will commit themselves to praying until revival comes.
Texts: Luke 11:9-10; 24:53: Acts 1:12-14
Introduction
1. The disciples prayed before Pentecost (Read Ac 1:14).
    a. Their prayer resulted in a mighty outpouring of the Spirit. (Read Ac 2:1-4).
    b. Later, they prayed again, and again God poured out His Spirit on them. (Read Ac 4:31)
2. We can learn from their prayer.
    a. Like them, we too can "pray down Pentecost."
    b. That is, we can pray down a mighty Pentecostal revival on our church—and on our beloved continent, Africa.
3. This message will answer three questions about the disciples' prayer before Pentecost:

I. **WHY DID THEY PRAY?** (Three reasons:)
   A. They prayed because Jesus commanded them to wait (Ac 1:4).
      1. He did not mean for them to sit idly and do nothing.
      2. The command to wait implies waiting in prayer (Mic 7:7).
   B. They prayed because *Jesus had taught them to pray,* "Your kingdom come..." (Mt 6:10).
      1. This is, in part, a prayer for the Spirit to come.
      2. Jesus further taught them that the kingdom of God must be forcefully pursued. (Read Mt 11:12, NIV).
         a. One way this is done is through prayer.
      3. The kingdom of God came in power at Pentecost (Mk 9:1).
   C. They prayed because *they understood their own powerlessnesss* to do what Jesus had commanded.
      1. He had commanded them to preach the gospel to all nations (Mk 16:15-18).
      2. They could do this only in God's power (Ac 1:8).
   D. We must pray for Pentecost for the same three reasons.

II. **HOW DID THEY PRAY?**
   A. In two passages, Luke tells us how they prayed:
      1. Ac 1:4: "They all joined together constantly in prayer..."

2. Lk 24:53: "And they stayed continually at the temple, praising God."
3. These 2 passages give us 3 insights into how they prayed:
   a. They prayed *together* (Ac 1:4; cf. 2:1).
   b. The prayed *constantly* (Ac 1:4; Lk 24:53).
   c. Their pray included times of *praise* (Lk 24:53).
B. Further, it is fair to assume that they prayed in accordance with Jesus' final command and promise. (Read Acts 1:4-8)
   1. They remained in Jerusalem (v.4).
   2. They waited for "the promise of the Father" (v.4).
   3. They anticipated being "baptized in the Holy Spirit" (v.5).
   4. They expected to be empowered by the Spirit (v.8).
C. It is further fair to assume that they prayed according to Jesus' instructions in Luke 11, where He taught them how to receive the Holy Spirit. (Read Luke 11:9-13)
   1. They kept on asking, seeking, and knocking (v.9).
   2. They expected to "receive the Holy Spirit" (vv.10, 13).
   3. As they prayed, they believed (Mk 11:24).
D. We must do the same today.
   1. We must join together in constant prayer.
   2. We must pray in expectation.
   3. We must continue in prayer until the answer comes.

III. HOW DID GOD RESPOND TO THEIR PRAYERS?
A. God kept His promise, answered their prayer, and poured out His Spirit (Ac 2:1-4).
   1. This happened again in Acts 4:31.
   2. This pattern continued throughout the book of Acts.
B. God empowered them for witness.
   1. At Pentecost 3,000 were saved (v.41).
   2. And day by day, more were being saved (v.47).
   3. This was according to Jesus' promise in Acts 1:8.
C. We can expect God to do the same for us today.

Conclusion and Altar Call
1. Someone asked, "Since it was the Day of Pentecost, would not God have poured out the Spirit even if they had not prayed?"
2. The answer is, "Yes, He would have poured out His Spirit, but He would not have poured out His Spirit on them."
3. Let's ask God to pour out His Spirit on us today.

[DRM]

52 After They Had Prayed

Sermon in a Sentence: If we will pray, God's Spirit will empower us and enable us to proclaim the gospel with great effectiveness.
Sermon Purpose: That God's people will seek God for the empowering of the Spirit.
Text: Acts 4:23-33
Introduction:
1. John Wesley once wrote, "'God does nothing but in answer to believing prayer."
2. The ministry of the church in Acts was driven by prayer.
3. In our text, Luke takes us into one of their prayer meetings.
   a. Looks much different from many modern prayer meetings.
   b. Possibly thousands were present (Ac 4:4).
   c. They prayed with boldness, fervor, and expectancy.
3. Today, we will focus on the immediate results of their prayer.
   a. Note the phrase, "After they had prayed…" (v.31).

I. **AFTER THE HAD PRAYED, FOUR THINGS OCCURRED:**
   A. First, God made His presence known to them.
      1. After they prayed, "the place…was shaken" (v.31).
      2. This is a *theophany,* that is, a visible manifestation of God's presence.
         a. Illus: Like on the Day of Pentecost (Ac 2:2-3).
         b. Throughout Acts, God manifested His presence through healings, deliverances, and gifts of the Spirit.
   B. Second, "they were all filled with the Holy Spirit" (v.31).
      1. Just as the 120 had been at Pentecost (Ac 2:4).
   C. Third, they "spoke the world of God boldly" (v.31).
      1. Like Peter did on the Day of Pentecost (Ac 2:14ff).
      2. This is what Jesus said would happen (Ac 1:8).
   D. Fourth, "…much grace was upon them" (v.33).
      1. This speaks of the abiding presence of the Spirit.
      2. It resulted in ongoing witness: "the apostles *continued* to testify to the resurrection of the Lord Jesus" (v.33).
      3. Their witness was accompanied by powerful signs and wonders (Ac 5:12).

II. **IF WE WILL PRAY, WE CAN EXPECT THE SAME FOUR THINGS TO OCCUR:**
   A. First, we can expect God to make His presence known.

1. God will come into our meetings and manifest His awesome presence.
2. He will perform signs and wonders (Ac 5:12; Mk 16:17).
B. Second, we can expect God to fill us with His Spirit.
1. As He did in Acts (2:4; 4:8; 4:31)
2. This was Jesus final promise and our greatest need (Ac 1:8).
C. Third, we can expect to boldly proclaim the gospel.
1. We must never forget, the primary purpose of being baptized in the Holy Spirit is power for witness (Ac 1:8).
2. In Acts, every time the Spirit was poured out the result was Spirit-empowered witness.
D. Fourth, we can expect God's grace to remain on us.
1. As we continue in prayer, the Spirit's anointing will continue to rest on us.
   a. Illus: Like it did on Stephen who was "full of the Holy Spirit" (Ac 6:5; 7:55).
   b. Being *"filled* with the Spirit" speaks of the experience; being *"full* of the Spirit" describes His abiding presence.
2. As the Spirit remains on us, we will continue to testify about Jesus (Ac 4:33), and many will believe on the Lord and be saved (Ac 5:12-14).

III. HOW THEN MUST WE RESPOND TO THESE TRUTHS?
A. We must commit ourselves to enthusiastic, believing prayer.
1. Like them, we must lift up our voices in prayer (v.24).
2. Like them, we must ask for the Spirit (vv.29-30).
   a. Note: they were asking for the Spirit when the prayed, "Enable your servants to speak your word with great boldness. *Stretch out your hand...*"
3. Like them, we can expect God to answer our prayer.
B. We must act in faith.
1. We must *ask* in faith.
2. We must *receive* the Spirit by faith (Mk 11:24).
3. We must *preach* the gospel with faith.
4. If we will pray, we can expect God's grace to be upon us.

Conclusion and Altar Call
Come, now. Pray, be filled with the Spirit, and then go out and speak the word of God with boldness.

[DRM]

53 Praying and Hearing God's Voice

Sermon in a Sentence: When sending out missionaries, the church should pray, fast, and listen to the voice of the Spirit.
Sermon Purpose: That the people will commit themselves to praying for missions and listening for the Spirit's direction.
Text: Acts 13:1-4
Introduction
1. In our Scripture reading, Luke takes us into a worship service of the church in Antioch.
2. It was a Spirit-empowered church.
    a. The "hand of the Lord" (that is, the power of the Holy Spirit) was with the church (Acts 11:21).
    b. In the church were prophets and teachers (13:1).
3. As they worshiped and fasted, the Spirit moved.
    a. A prophetic message was given. (Read v.2.)
    b. This message launches a great missionary movement.
4. The church of Antioch is a good model for the churches today wanting to choose and send missionaries.
5. From this story, we learn three important missionary principles:

I. MISSIONS IS A WORK OF THE HOLY SPIRIT
A. The missionary activity of the Antioch church was not launched by human beings but by the Holy Spirit.
   1. Before sending out missionaries, the Christians in Antioch sought the Lord with prayer and fasting (vv.2-3).
   2. The Spirit spoke through spiritual leaders who were deeply devoted to the Lord and His kingdom (v.2).
   3. Barnabas and Saul were thus "sent on the way by the Holy Spirit" (v.4)
B. Like the Antioch church, we too must look to the Holy Spirit to direct us in choosing and sending out workers.
   1. He is the "Spirit of Missions."
   2. He is the "Director of the Harvest."

II. WHEN SENDING OUT MISSIONARIES, THE CHURCH SHOULD PRAY, FAST, AND LISTEN TO THE VOICE OF THE SPIRIT
A. The Holy Spirit spoke to the Christians in Antioch during a time of worship, prayer, and fasting.

1. *Worship* brought the presence of the Lord.
2. In *prayer,* they committed themselves to God's mission.
3. *Fasting* helped tune their spirits to the Spirit of God.
B. We too should seek the guidance of the Holy Spirit.
   1. It is not good to do anything related to missions without first seeking the guidance of the Holy Spirit through praying and fasting.
   2. Many churches today fail in this area.
   3. We must never make this mistake; we must diligently seek revival through fasting and prayer.

III. THE CHURCH MUST SEND MISSIONARIES WHO ARE EMPOWERED BY THE HOLY SPIRIT

A. The two missionaries sent out by the church in Antioch were Spirit-empowered men.
   1. They were among the "prophets and teachers" in the church.
      a. Spiritual gifts, like prophecy and teaching, are manifested through those who are Spirit filled.
   2. Saul (Paul) was Spirit-filled. (Read Ac 9:17-18; 13:9-11.)
   3. Barnabas was Spirit-filled. (Read Ac 11:22-24.)
B. Missionaries cannot serve the Lord properly without the power of Holy Spirit.
   1. Jesus: "But you will receive power when the Holy Spirit comes on you; and you will be my witnesses in Jerusalem, and in all Judea and Samaria, and to the ends of the earth" (Ac 1:8).
   2. We must wait in prayer until we are empowered by the Spirit (Lk 24:47-49; Ac 1:4-5).
   3. Then we must go in the power of the Spirit.

Conclusion and Altar Call
1. As God's missionary people, let us cultivate the habit of praying and fasting.
2. Let us seek the guidance of the Holy Spirit, especially in times of choosing workers.
3. Come now, be filled with the Holy Spirit, and commit yourself to a lifestyle of prayer and fasting.

[CK]

54 From Groaning to Glory

Sermon in a Sentence: The Holy Spirit will help us pray for our broken world.
Sermon Purpose: That Christians will allow the Spirit to "groan" through them for a hurting world.
Text: Romans 8:18-27
Introduction
1. This passage reveals a wonderful secret that can turn our difficulties and disappointments into wonderful opportunities for intercessory prayer.
2. The entire passage is built around a tension between things as they are now and things as they will be when Jesus comes.
    a. Now: we suffer... we groan... we struggle...
    b. Then: we will rule and reign with Christ.
3. Like us, these first-century Roman believers did not live in isolation from what was going on in their world.
    a. The destructive impact of sin affected them deeply.
    b. Like us, they wanted to reach the people of their culture with the liberating gospel of Christ.
4. Let's look more closely at the strategy Paul gives them—and us—for dealing with our fallen world.

I. PAUL FIRST TALKS ABOUT OUR WONDERFUL HOPE
A. Because of the gospel, we look forward to a glorious future:
   1. Paul speaks of "the glory that will be revealed in us" (v.18).
B. Look at what Paul says about our glorious future:
   1. We will be revealed as "sons (children) of God" (v.19).
   2. Creation will be liberated from its bondage (v.21).
   3. All our hopes will be fully realized! (vv.24-25).

II. YET, PAUL POINTS OUT THAT, FOR NOW, WE MUST DEAL WITH OUR PRESENT REALITY
A. Paul described this reality as "our present sufferings" (v.18).
B. Listen to what Paul says about this present reality:
   1. It is a time when "creation groans" (v.22a).
   2. This is because creation is in bondage to decay (v.21).
      a. It bears the shock of sin's curse (Ge 3:17-18).
      b. Picture it! This globe we live on is quivering, trembling, and groaning in shock.
   3. Paul also speaks in hopeful terms (vv.19, 22).

  a. He describes the earths groaning as "birth pangs."
  b. Birth pangs speak of coming joy!
 4. We look with hope to Christ's soon coming (vv.24-25).

III. DURING THIS TIME OF "GROANING," WE HAVE THE AWESOME PRIVILEGE AND RESPONSIBILITY OF SPIRIT-PROMPTED INTERCESSORY PRAYER (vv.26-27)
 A. When we see the suffering of those around us, we groan (v.23).
  1. We identify with their helplessness and hopelessness and are moved to weep for them—and with them.
  2. Illus: We are to be like Jesus: He saw how the people were "harassed and helpless, like sheep without a shepherd" and was moved with compassion for them (Mt 9:36).
  3. However, we must do more than just feel pity; we must offer hope (vv. 24-25).
  4. We must intercede for our hurting world.
 B. The Spirit will help us to intercede effectively.
  1. Paul says we "have the firstfruits of the Spirit" (vs. 23).
  2. The Spirit who indwells and empowers us will help our weakness in prayer (vv.26-27).
   a. We do not know how or what to pray for (v.26).
   b. The Spirit will intercede through us "with groans that words cannot express" (v.26).
   c. This includes—but is not limited to—tongues.
   d. The Holy Spirit prays in accordance with God's will.
  3. Note the progression of Paul's thought: first, creation groans (v.22); then, we groan with creation (v.23), finally, the Spirit groans through us (v.24).
  4. The Spirit takes our groaning over this world's needs and—if we will allow Him—turns them into prayers!
  5. This can happen anytime, anywhere!

Conclusion and Altar Call
 1. Our world is groaning today—and we must groan with it.
 2. Let him turn our groans into intercessory prayers.
 3. Come to be filled with the Spirit and to commit yourself to Spirit-prompted intercessory prayer.

[LB]

55 The Spirit Helps Us Pray

Sermon in a Sentence: To be filled with the Spirit we must pray, and to pray as we should, we must be filled with the Spirit.

Sermon Purpose: That the hearers will be filled with the Spirit and begin to practice prayer in the Spirit.

Text: Luke 11:9-13; Romans 8:26-27

Introduction
1. If someone were to ask you, "Do you know how to pray?" how would you answer?
    a. Most of us would answer, "Yes I do, but I need to learn how to pray better."
    b. This must have been how the disciples felt when they asked Jesus, "Lord, teach us to pray" (Lk 11:1).
2. Jesus responded to His disciples' request in two ways:
    a. He gave them a model prayer—the "Lord's Prayer" (vv.2-4).
    b. He then taught them how to be filled with the Spirit (vv.9-13).
    c. He was, in effect saying, "If you want to pray like Me, then like Me, you must be filled with the Holy Spirit."
3. This message will examine the intimate relationship between prayer and the Holy Spirit.
    a. We will discover two important spiritual truths:
    b. First, to be filled with the Holy Spirit, we must pray.
    c. Second, to pray, we must be filled with the Holy Spirit.
4. Let's look at each of these parallel spiritual truths.

I. TO BE FILLED, WE MUST PRAY
A. The Bible closely connects being filled with the Spirit with believing prayer.
   1. Luke especially emphasizes this relationship.
   2. Throughout his gospel and Acts, he consistently associates prayer with the coming of the Spirit.
   3. For instance, see Lk 3:21-22; Ac 1:14; 4:31.
   4. Jesus made this same connection in Luke 11:13.
   5. In other words, God bestows His Holy Spirit on His children in answer to believing prayer.
B. From this, we learn two important lessons:
   1. First, to be filled with the Holy Spirit we must pray.
   2. Second, to remain full of the Holy Spirit, we must in the words of Jesus, "Keep on asking... keep on seeking, and... keep on knocking" (Lk 11:9, literal translation).

II. TO PRAY (AS WE SHOULD), WE MUST BE FILLED
A. In Ro 8:26-27 Paul explained how the Spirit enables our prayer.
B. Such prayer in the Spirit can occur in two ways.
   1. Generally speaking, any prayer that is prompted and directed by the Spirit of God is prayer in the Spirit.
      a. It is a "team effort" between a Spirit-filled intercessor and the Spirit Himself.
   2. More specifically, prayer in the Spirit is prayer in tongues.
      a. It is, "groans that words cannot express" (Ro 8:26).
      b. Paul explained, "If I pray in a tongue, my spirit prays" (1Co 14:14).
      c. As we yield ourselves to the Spirit, He prays through us in words that He gives.
C. A closer look at Romans 8:26-27 reveals four powerful ways the Spirit helps us in prayer.
   1. First, the Spirit *"makes intercession for us."*
      a. The Spirit prays through us directing our prayers.
   2. Second, the Spirit prays through us *"with groans which words cannot express."*
      a. He prays through us in expressions of His own creation.
   3. Third, the Spirit *searches our hearts."*
      a. As we yield to His sanctifying power, our hearts are purified (Ps 51:10-12).
      b. We are thus placed in a position where God can answer our prayers (Is 59:1).
   4. Finally, Paul tells us that the Spirit of God *"knows the mind of the Spirit."*
      a. And because He knows the mind and will of God, He *"intercedes for the saints according to the will of God."*
      b. As we allow the Holy Spirit to pray through us, we pray according to God's perfect will.
      c. Such prayers have great spiritual power (1John 5:14-15).

Conclusion and Altar Call
1. How foolish we would be to neglect prayer in the Spirit.
2. Come and be filled with the Spirit now and commit yourself to daily prayer in the Holy Spirit.

[DRM]

56 Eight Compelling Reasons You Should Be Praying in Tongues

Sermon in a Sentence: There are many positive reasons believers should pray in tongues every day.
Sermon Purpose: That believers will be baptized in the Spirit and utilize the gift of tongues in private devotion and public worship.
Text: 1 Corinthians 14:18
Introduction
1. Pentecostals are distinguished by many things (zeal, worship, preaching). One of those things is speaking in tongues.
2. Some have asked, "Why do Pentecostals emphasize speaking in tongues? What good is it?"
3. Here are eight reasons you should pray in tongues daily:

I. **BECAUSE SPEAKING IN TONGUES IS THE BIBLICAL SIGN OF BEING BAPTIZED IN THE HOLY SPIRIT**
   A. It is the recurring sign in Acts (Ac 2:4; 10:46; 19:6).
   B. When you are baptized in the Holy Spirit, you will know.
      1. Don't be cheated out of the real thing!
      2. Illus: Someone asked, "Do I *have* to speak in tongues to be filled with the Spirit?" The preacher answered, "You are asking the wrong question. The right question is, 'Do I *get* to speak in tongues?' Speaking in tongues is a privilege.

II. **BECAUSE PRAYING IN TONGUES BUILDS YOU UP SPIRITUALLY** (1Co 14:4)
   A. Like our physical bodies, our spirits need exercise.
   B. One form of spiritual exercise is praying in tongues.

III. **BECAUSE SPEAKING IN TONGUES IS A POWERFUL, GOD-GIVEN MEANS OF INTERCESSORY PRAYER**
   A. Ro 8:26-27 text tells us four things about our prayer lives:
      1. We don't know how to pray as we should.
      2. The Spirit will help us to pray.
      3. He will pray through us with words He inspires.
      4. He will pray through us "according to the will of God."
   B. Here is how it works:
      1. Sometimes. there are needs you don't know about.
      2. Other needs that you know about, but you don't know how to pray for them.

3. At such times, allow Him pray through you!

IV. BECAUSE PRAYING IN TONGUES CREATES AN AWARENESS OF GOD'S INDWELLING PRESENCE
   A. The Bible gives us wonderful promises of God's presence:
      1. Read: Mt 28:20; Ac 17:27-28; and He 13:5.
      2. And yet, sometimes God seems so distant.
   B. Praying in tongues is a wonderful remedy for this problem.

V. BECAUSE PRAYING IN TONGUES WILL BUILD YOUR FAITH
   A. The Bible speaks of ways we can build up our faith:
      1. Through reading and practicing the Word of God.
      2. By exercising the faith that we have.
   B. One oft-neglected way is praying in tongues (Jude 20).

VI. BECAUSE PRAYING IN TONGUES IS A WAY TO WRAP YOURSELF IN THE LOVE OF GOD (Jude 20-21; Ro 5:5)
   A. We sing, "Jesus loves me this I know, for the Bible tells me so."
      1. And it is true—whether we feel God's love or not!
      2. But oh, how wonderful to experience the love of God.
   B. Prayer in the Spirit helps us keep ourselves in God's love.

VII. BECAUSE, TOGETHER WITH THE GIFT OF INTERPRETATION, TONGUES IS ONE WAY GOD COMMUNICATES A PROPHETIC WORD TO HIS CHURCH (1Co 14:5)
   A. Sometimes God wants to speak directly to a congregation through the gifts of tongues and interpretation.
   B. At such times the church is edified and built up.

VIII. BECAUSE PRAYING IN TONGUES PROVIDES A PERFECT CHANNEL FOR JOYOUS PRAISE (Jn 4:24)
   A. Have you ever been so filled with joy and gratitude that you could find no words to express that joy?
   B. Prayer and praise in tongues is a perfect means to express that joy and gratitude.

Conclusion and Altar Call
   1. Is it any wonder why Paul said, "I thank my God that I speak in tongues more than you all" (1Co 14:18).
   2. Come now to be filled with the Spirit.   [DRM]

57 Prayer and the Baptism in the Holy Spirit

Sermon in a Sentence: If we will pray, God will powerfully baptize us in the Holy Spirit.

Sermon Purpose: That believers will pray to God and be empowered by the Holy Spirit as Christ's witnesses.

Text: Luke 11:1-13

Introduction
1. In our text, Jesus connects prayer with receiving the Holy Spirit.
2. This message will look at the relationship between prayer and the baptism in the Holy Spirit.
3. If we will ask in faith, God will powerfully baptize us in the Holy Spirit.

I. THE BOOK OF ACTS REPEATEDLY CONNECTS PRAYER TO THE BAPTISM IN THE HOLY SPIRIT:

A. The believers were praying before the *Day of Pentecost.*
   1. They worshiped and prayed (Luke 24:52-53; Acts 1:14).
   2. Then God poured out His Spirit (Acts 2:1-4).
B. The believers were praying before *the Second Jerusalem Outpouring* (4:23-31).
   1. The believers prayed (Acts 4:23-30).
   2. God again answered and poured out His Spirit (v. 31).
C. The apostles prayed with the believers to receive the Spirit at *Samaria.*
   1. They prayed with the believers there (Acts 8:14-17).
   2. The believers were filled with the Spirit (Acts 8:18).
D. Both *Paul and Ananias* were praying when Paul was filled with the Spirit.
   1. Paul prayed (Acts 9:5, 11); Ananias prayed (vv. 10-15).
   2. God filled Paul with the Holy Spirit (vv. 17-18).
E. Both Cornelius and Peter were praying before the outpouring of the Spirit in *Caesarea* (10:2, 9, 19).
   1. Cornelius prayed (Acts 10:2); Peter prayed (vv. 9, 19).
   2. God powerfully poured out His Spirit (Acts 10:44-46).
F. Paul prayed for the believers in *Ephesus* to receive the Spirit.
   1. Laying his hands on them, Paul prayed for them (implied) (Acts 19:6a).
   2. They were all filled with the Spirit (v. 6b).

II. TODAY, IF WE WILL PRAY AS THEY DID, GOD WILL FILL US WITH THE HOLY SPIRIT
A. If you are not born again, pray to God repenting of your sins and receiving Christ as your Lord and Savior (Acts 2:38-39).
B. Next, prepare yourself to receive the Spirit by...
 1. ...opening your heart to God and His working in your life.
 2. ...humbling yourself before God.
 3. ...committing yourself to God's mission.

III. RECEIVE THE HOLY SPIRIT BY ASKING IN FAITH
A. Believe Jesus' promise:
 1. Lk 11:13: "Your Father in heaven [will] give the Holy Spirit to those who ask him!"
 2. Mk 11:24: "Whatever you ask for in prayer, believe that you have received it, and it will be yours."
B Now take these three steps of faith:
 1. *Ask in faith.*
  a. Jesus said, *"Ask* and it will be given to you" (Lk 11:9).
  b. Pray, "Jesus, I ask You now, give me the Holy Spirit."
  c. Sense the Holy Spirit coming upon you!
 2. *Receive by faith.*
  a. Jesus promised, "Everyone who asks *receives*" (v.10).
  b. Jesus is talking about an active receiving.
  c. In faith, pray, "In Jesus name I receive the Holy Spirit."
  d. Sense the Holy Spirit coming inside you!
 3. *Speak in faith.*
  a. On the Day of Pentecost, "All of them were filled with the Holy Spirit and *began to speak* in other tongues as the Spirit enabled them" (Ac 2:4).
  b. Speak out in faith from where you sense the Holy Spirit inside.
  c. You will begin to speak in a God-given language.
  d. This is God's sign that He has empowered you to be Christ's witness (Ac 1:8).
  e. Now, go out and tell someone about Jesus!

Conclusion and Altar Call
 1. Come now to be baptized in the Holy Spirit.
 2. When you come we will *ask* in faith, *receive* by faith, and *speak* in faith. [DRM]

58 Acts 1:8 Praying

Sermon in a Sentence: We must pray "Acts 1:8 Prayers," that is, we must often ask the Spirit to empower us as Christ's witnesses.

Sermon Purpose: That God's people will be filled with the Spirit and regularly pray for the Spirit to empower them as witnesses.

Text: Acts 1:8

Introduction
1. Acts 1:8 is the "interpretative key" to the book of Acts.
    a. That is, it is the key to understanding the entire book.
2. These final words of Jesus emphasize two missional concepts:
    a. *Empowerment:* "You will receive power when…"
    b. *Witness:* "You will be my witnesses…"
3. In Acts, the early Christians based their ministry on Acts 1:8.
    a. They often prayed "Acts 1:8 Prayers."
    b. In other words, they prayed that the Spirit would empower them to fulfill the Great Commission.
    c. This is a practice we should copy today.
4. Three examples of "Acts 1:8 Praying" in the book of Acts:

I. BEFORE PENTECOST, THE DISCIPLES PRAYED ACCORDING TO ACTS 1:8
   • *Read their prayer in Ac 1:14, noting the following:*
   A. They prayed in *obedience* to Christ's final command:
      1. Read Ac 1:4: "Do not leave Jerusalem but wait…"
   B. They prayed in *anticipation* of Christ's final promise:
      1. Read Ac 1:5 and 8: "In a few days you will be baptized in the Holy Spirit… But you will receive power when…"
   C. On the Day of Pentecost, God answered their prayer.
      1. Read Acts 2:1-4.
      2. The church immediately began to fulfill Acts 1:8:
         a. Peter preached w/ power and 3,000 were saved (2:41).
      3. A Spirit-empowered missionary church was born (vv.43-47).

II. WHEN BEING PERSECUTED, THE EARLY CHRISTIANS PRAYED AN "ACTS 1:8 PRAYER"
   A. Their prayer is found in Acts 4:21-23; 29-31. (Read)
   B. In accordance with Acts 1:8, the church asked the Spirit to empower them and embolden them for continued witness:
      1. In verse 29, they made two requests:
         a. "Lord, consider their threats…"

  b. "Enable your servants to speak…"
2. In v.30, they made another request: "Stretch out your hand"
  a. This is a prayer for the Spirit to move in power.
  b. Note: the hand of the Lord = the power of the Spirit (cf. Eze 37:1; Mt 12:28 w/ Lk 11:20; Ac 11:21).
3. They prayed an "Acts 1:8 Prayer."
C. God answered their prayer
 1. Read v.31a: "After they prayed…shaken…filled…"
 2. The infilling resulted in bold witness: They "spoke the word of God boldly" (v.31b, 33).
 3. This was all a clear fulfillment of Acts 1:8.

III. WHEN SENDING OUT MISSIONARIES, THE CHURCH IN ANTIOCH ACTED IN ACCORDANCE WITH ACTS 1:8
▪ *Read Acts 13:3, and then note the following:*
A. The church in Antioch was an Acts 1:8 church.
 1. The church is described in Acts 11:19-21.
 2. Read v.21, noting the following:
  a.. "The Lord's hand (the Spirit's power) was with them."
  b. "A great number of people turned to the Lord"
  c. This mirrors Acts 1:8: *Empowerment=witness*
B. As the Antioch church prayed, the Spirit moved and directed them to send out missionaries (Ac 13:2).
 1. They chose Spirit-empowered men as missionaries.
  a. Paul (Ac 13:9) and Barnabas (Ac 11:24).
 2. This was all done in accordance with Acts 1:8.

IV. HOW WE CAN PRAY ACTS 1:8 PRAYERS TODAY
▪ *Four recommendations:*
A. We must commit to God's mission. (Like Paul in Ac 22.10)
B. We must ask for the Spirit's empowering (Lk 11:9, 13).
C. We must by faith receive the Holy Spirit (Lk 11:10; Mk 11:24).
D. We must in faith speak as the Spirit empowers us (Ac 2:4, 14).

Conclusion and Altar Call
1. Come now; let's pray an Acts 1:8 prayer together.
2. Let's ask the Lord to send His Spirit to empower us as Christ's witnesses.

[DRM]

59 The Overlooked Piece of Armor

Sermon in a Sentence: We must put on the overlooked piece of armor—the armor of prayer in the Spirit.
Sermon Purpose: That Christians be filled with the Spirit and begin to faithfully practice intercessory prayer in the Spirit.
Text: Ephesians 6:10-18
Introduction
1. In our text, Paul is closing his letter to the Ephesians.
   a. In the letter, He has vividly described the purpose, nature, and function of Christ's church.
   b. He now exhorts them to "put on the full armor of God."
2. It is normally taught that the armor consists of 6 pieces; 5 of which are defensive and 1 of which is offensive (vv.14-17).
   a. The sword of the Spirit being the only offensive weapon.
   b. However, there is another offensive piece of armor.
   c. We could call this the "overlooked piece of armor."
3. That piece of armor is prayer in the Spirit. (Read v.18).
4. Let's look at 5 things Paul teaches about this piece of armor:

I. NOTE THE NATURE OF THIS KIND OF PRAYER
A. What special kind of prayer is Paul talking about?
   1. He is talking about prayer "in the Spirit" (v.18)
   2. In 5:18, he told the Ephesian Christians to "be filled with the Spirit." Now he tells them to "pray in the Spirit."
B. Prayer in the Spirit is prayer that is filled with the Spirit, empowered by the Spirit, and dominated by the Spirit.
   1. Paul describes such prayer in 1Co 14:14 and Ro 8:26-27.
   2. Without this piece of armor, the Christian's armament is not "full" (complete).
   4. This piece of armor fits over and energizes all the other pieces of armor.
   5. We must pray in the Spirit!

II. NOTE THE TIMING OF THIS KIND OF PRAYER
A. When are we to pray in the Spirit?
   1. We are to pray in the Spirit "on all occasions" (v.18).
   2. The Greek word translated "occasions" is *kairos*.
      a. It means a special moment of kingdom opportunity.
   3. Paul has just exhorted the Ephesians to "make the most of every opportunity" (5:16; cf. Col 4:5).

      4. Now, he says that they can do this by praying in the Spirit.
- B. We in Africa are living in a *"kairos* moment."
  1. It is God's special time for Africa (Ps 68:31).
  2. We must seize the moment by praying in the Spirit.

III. NOTE THE EXTENT OF THIS KIND OF PRAYER
- A. We are to pray "with all kinds of prayers and requests" (v.18).
  1. That is, with thanksgiving, with praise, with petition, with supplication, with song, with shouting, with cries of joy, and with tears of sorrow.
  2. We are to pray in the Spirit while sitting, standing, kneeling, lying down, walking, running, and riding.
- B. We are to blanket he earth with Spirit-empowered prayer.

IV. NOTE THE POSTURE OF THIS KIND OF PRAYER
- A. As we pray, we must "be alert" (v.18).
  1. This is last-days language—It means we are to stay awake, understanding the days we are living in.
  2. Illus: We are to be like the men of Issachar (1Ch 12:32).
- B. A battle is raging for the soul of Africa.
  1. It is a spiritual battle (Ep 6:12).
  2. We must remain alert in prayer.

V. NOTE THE DURATION OF OUR PRAYER
- A. We must *"always keep on praying* for all the saints" (v.18).
  1. We must stay in prayer until God answers from heaven.
  2. Paul exhorts us to "never stop praying (1Th 5:17 NLT).
- B. The church is engaged in the battle of all battles
  1. We must remain alert and never stop praying for one another.

Conclusion and Altar Call
1. This is Africa's *kairos* moment. History's greatest missionary movement is right now being birthed in Africa.
2. However, like Ephesus, Africa must put on the full armor of God—including the armament of prayer in the Spirit.
3. Come now, be filled with the Spirit, and commit yourself to "pray in the Spirit on all occasions with all kinds of prayers and requests."

[SP]

60 Lord, Stretch Out Your Hand!
~ Praying for God's Intervention ~

Sermon in a Sentence: We can confidently ask God to stretch out His hand and intervene in our situation.
Sermon Purpose: That God's people pray with greater confidence.
Texts: Acts 4:29-31
Introduction
1. Tell the story of the outpouring of the Spirit in Acts 4.
   a. The disciples were persecuted and threatened (vv.1-21).
   b. They went back to the church and prayed (vv.23-30).
2. They ended their prayer with the petition, "Stretch out your hand to heal and perform miraculous signs and wonders..."
3. Let's look more closely at the phrase "stretch out your hand."

I WHAT DOES IT MEAN TO PRAY, "LORD, STRETCH OUT YOUR HAND"?
   A. In Scripture, the "hand (arm or finger) of God" symbolizes the active working of the Holy Spirit.
      1. Ezekiel linked the "hand of the Lord" to the "Spirit of the Lord" (Ez 37:1).
      2. The angels said of John the Baptist: "He will be great in the sight of the Lord...and he will be filled with the Holy Spirit even from birth" (Lk 1:15). Then, when he was born, the Bible says, "The Lord's hand was with him" (v.66).
   B. Three biblical examples of God stretching out His hand:
      1. God created the world with His "outstretched arm" (that is by the power of the Spirit) (Je 32:17; cf. Ge 1:2)
      2. God parted the Red Sea "by a mighty hand and an outstretched arm" (Je 32:21).
      3. Jesus cast out demons by "the finger of God," that is, "by the Spirit of God" (Lk 11:20 w/ Mt 12:28).
   C. So, when the disciples prayed, "Stretch out your hand," they are asking God to pour out His Spirit (Ac 4:30-31).
      1. They were calling on God's Spirit to fill them and powerfully intervene in their situation.
      2. Illus: Full of the Spirit, Paul told Elymas, "The hand of the Lord is against you..." (Ac 13:9-12).

II. WHEN SHOULD PRAY, "LORD, STRETCH OUT YOUR HAND"? (Four situations from Scripture:)

A. When we are being *persecuted* for preaching the gospel.
   1. Illus: The church in Jerusalem was being persecuted (Ac 4)
   2. They cried out to God, "Stretch out your hand" (Ac 4:30).
B. When we want God's kingdom to *advance* and people come to the Lord (Ac 11:21).
   1. Illus: In Antioch, "the Lord's hand was with them..."
   2. As a result, "...a great number of people came to the Lord"
C. When the way forward is *blocked*.
   1. Illus: When the children of Israel were fleeing from Pharaoh's army, the Red Sea blocked the way (Ex 14:10).
   2. The cried unto God, and He "brought [them] out with His mighty hand" (Ex 13:16; Je 32:21).
D. When we are *discouraged* in doing God's work.
   1. Illus: When trying to lead the people of Israel back to Palestine to rebuild the temple, Ezra became discouraged.
   2. But, he testified, "Because the hand of the Lord my God was on me, I took courage and gathered leading men from Israel to go up with me (Ezr 7:28).

III. HOW CAN WE EFFECTIVELY ASK GOD TO STRETCH OUT HIS HAND?
A. We must pray out of a pure heart.
   1. Read and expound Isaiah 59:1-2
   2. Repent—then pray!
B. We must pray with bold faith.
   1. When being persecuted, the church in Jerusalem "raised their voices together in prayer" (Ac 4:23-24).
   2. They boldly prayed, "Lord... enable your servants to speak your word with great boldness" (v.29).
C. We must pray in accordance with God's will (1Jn 5:14-15).
D. We must pray as the Spirit anoints and directs (Ro 8:26-27).

Conclusion and Altar Call
1. The early Christians prayed, "Stretch out your hand" (Ac 4:30).
2. Then, "after they prayed, the place where they were meeting was shaken. And they were all filled with the Holy Spirit and spoke the word of God boldly" (v.31).
3. God will do the same for us today. Let's come and pray.

[DRM]

61 Spirit-Anointed Prayer

Sermon in a Sentence: Spirit-anointed prayer enables us to effectively advance God's mission.
Sermon Purpose: That Christians will be filled with the Spirit and commit themselves to Spirit-anointed missional prayer.
Text: Acts 4:8-12, 22-31
Introduction
1. In our text, the early church prayed both *in* the Spirit and *for* the Spirit.
   a. *In* the Spirit: They were full of the Spirit (Ac 4:8).
   b. *For* the Spirit: They asked for the Spirit: "Now Lord… Stretch out your hand…" (v.30).
2. They prayed both *with* boldness and *for* boldness.
   a. *With* boldness: "They raised their voices…" (v.24).
   b. *For* boldness: "Now, Lord…enable your servants to speak your word with great boldness" (v.29).
3. Such bold, Spirit-anointed prayer is a foundational for the Christian life and ministry.
4. Let's look at four ways prayer in the Spirit emboldens us to effectively carry out the Great Commission.

I. SPIRIT-ANOINTED PRAYER ENABLED THE EARLY DISCIPLES TO BOLDLY SPEAK THE WORD OF GOD
A. The disciples asked for boldness. (Read Ac 4:29).
   1. When they asked for boldness, God gave them the Spirit: "After they prayed, the place…was shaken. And they were all filled with the Holy Spirit" (v.31a).
   2. When the disciples were again filled with the Spirit, they received boldness to speak for Christ (v.31b).
   3. This is a clear fulfillment of Acts 1:8.
B. If we will pray, the Holy Spirit will come and fill us, and give us boldness to share the gospel with others.

II. SPIRIT-ANOINTED PRAYER ENABLED THE EARLY DISCIPLES TO FACE THREATS AND PERSECUTION
A. When threatened, the early believers prayed.
   1. Peter and John were threatened for healing the lame man and preaching the gospel. (Read Ac 4:7-8, 18)
   2. They returned to the church and prayed, "Lord, *consider their threats* and enable your servants to speak…" (v.29).

  B. God answered their prayer by filling them with the Spirit and giving the courage to continue preaching.
    1. "With great power the apostles continued to testify to the resurrection of the Lord Jesus…" (v.33).
  C. God will do the same for us today.

III. SPIRIT-ANOINTED PRAYER HELPED BREAK THE STRONGHOLDS OF THE ENEMY (Acts 4:23, 31)
  A. The early disciples understood that they were involved in spiritual warfare.
    1. Paul describes that warfare. (Read Ep 6:12)
    2. We must fight with spiritual weapons. (Read 2Co 10:4)
    3. One weapon is prayer in the Spirit (Ep 6:18-20).
  B. In Acts 4, the church used prayer as a spiritual weapon to oppose the work of the enemy.
    1. They understood that the devil was behind their persecution and only God's Spirit could defeat him.
    2. Illus: Like Paul and Silas knew that a demon was using the slave girl in Acts 16:16-18.
  C. We too can demolish the devil's strongholds through Spirit-anointed prayer.

IV. SPIRIT-ANOINTED PRAYER CAUSED THE CHURCH TO GROW AND EXPAND
  A. As a result of their prayer (and God's response to their prayer), the early church grew and expanded.
    1. Following the strategy of Acts 1:8, multiplication continued throughout the book of Acts:
      a. They were empowered by the Holy Spirit then began to witness with boldness.
      b. Read: Acts 5:12-16; 6:1, 7; 9:31; 11:21
    2. The evangelistic pattern in Acts: Prayer→ outpouring→ proclamation→ confirming signs→ growth.
  B. We can experience the same results today—if we will pray.

Conclusion and Altar Call
Come to be filled with the Spirit and to allow the Spirit to anoint and empower your prayers.

[NS]

Section 6
Praying for the Church and Revival

62 Revival Praying: A Book of Acts Model

Sermon in a Sentence: We must pray for revival as they did in the book of Acts.

Sermon Purpose: That God's people will persevere in prayer until the answer comes.

Text: Acts 1:14; 4:24, 31

Introduction
1. The word of *revival* is not found in the New Testament.
    a. It is, however, found in the OT (Ps 85:6; Hab 3:2).
2. The book of Acts pictures revival as outpourings of the Holy Spirit that results in the mobilization of the church to evangelize the lost.
3. Revival comes as a result of committed prayer:
    a. Reread texts: Ac 1:14; 4:24, 31.
4. This message: "Revival Praying"
5. Let's look at four ways we can intercede for a true revival:

I. PRAY THAT GOD WILL POUR OUT HIS SPIRIT ON THE CHURCH AS HE DID IN THE BOOK OF ACTS

A. In Acts, prayer always preceded an outpouring of the Spirit: (For instance...)
   1. They prayed before Pentecost (Lk 24:53; Ac 1:14).
   2. The prayed before a Second Jerusalem Outpouring (4:31).
   3. Paul prayed before he was filled with the Spirit (9:11).
B. We too must pray that God will pour out His Spirit.
   1. Isaiah's prayer: "Oh, that you would rend the heavens and come down" (Is 64:1).
C. We must know what revival will look like when it comes.
   1. It will look like it did in the book of Acts.
   2. People will be filled with the Holy Spirit (Ac 2:4).
   3. The gospel will be preached with power (vv.14-39).
   4. People will be saved (v.41).
   5. The church will prosper and grow (v.42-47).

II. PERSONALLY RECEIVE THE EMPOWERING OF THE HOLY SPIRIT

A. Peter and the apostles were among the first filled with the Spirit.
   1. They had been used by God in the past; (Lk 9:6).
   2. However, they still needed wait in Jerusalem to be empowered by the Holy Spirit (Lk 24:49).

3. Don't exclude yourself.
4. Rather pray, "Let the revival begin in me, Lord!"
B. You can then be the example for others.
1. As was Jesus (Lk 3:21-22; 4:1, 17-19).
2. As were the apostles who waited for the Spirit at Pentecost.

III. PRAY WITH OTHERS TO RECEIVE THE SPIRIT
A. Every Christian has been commanded to be filled with the Spirit (Ac 1:4-5; Ep 5:18).
1. And, every Spirit-filled Christian should know how to pray with other Christians to be filled with the Spirit.
2. Illus: Like Peter (Ac 8:14-18) and Paul (Ac 19:1-6).
B. Here is what you can do:
1. Pray for an outpouring of the Spirit: "Ask ye of the Lord rain in the time of the latter rain" (Zec 10:1, KJV)
2. Teach and preach often on the Spirit-empowered life.
3. Ensure that the candidates understand the primary purpose of their being filled is to empower them for witness (Ac 1:8).
C. Pray with those who want to be filled.

IV. PRAYERFULLY MOVE OUT IN EVANGELISM, CHURCH PLANTING, AND MISSIONS
A. True New Testament revival is not complete without Spirit-empowered evangelism, church planting, and missions.
1. That's pattern we have in the book of Acts.
2. The primary purpose of revival is not to bless the saints but to empower the church to reach the lost.
B. Then, when the Spirit does come, don't stop praying:
1. Continue to pray for the outpouring of the Spirit.
2. Continue to pray for the Spirit's guidance.
3. Continue to pray for new believers to be empowered.
4. And continue to take the gospel to the lost.

Conclusion and Altar Call
Come, let us commit together to pray until God pours out His Spirit on us enabling us to reach the lost and plant churches in the power of the Holy Spirit.

[DRM]

63 Praying Your Church to Its Full Potential

Sermon in a Sentence: Through prayer, you can help move your church into its full potential in Christ.

Sermon Purpose: That God's people will commit to praying for their church.

Text: John 17:9-24

Introduction
1. Our church has the power to ignite the dynamite of the gospel and powerfully shake our community and our world.
   a. Prayer is the "detonator" of that potential.
2. We have just read part of Jesus' "High Priestly Prayer."
   a. He prayed this prayer the night of His capture.
   b. He prayed specifically for His church (v.17).
   c. His prayer reveals His desire for the church.
3. It can serve as a model for us to pray for our church today.

I. WHAT JESUS WANTS FOR THE CHURCH
A. That people would *sense the glory* of God.
   1. "I have given them the glory that you gave me…" (v.22)
   2. Jesus' desire is that His people continually sense God's splendor, power, and radiance in their midst.
B. That we would *follow the word* of God.
   1. "For I gave them the words you gave me…" (v.8)
   2. Jesus wants His church to find its meaning, motivation, and mission in His words.
C. That we would be *united* in the love of God.
   1. "[I pray] that all of them may be one" and "that the love you have for me may be in them" (vv.20, 26).
   2. Spirit-filled Christians united in love and guided by a purpose they truly believe in, *can do anything.*
D. That we would *go forth* in the mission of God.
   1. "As you sent me into the world, I have sent them…into the world" (v.18).
   2. Jesus' prayed that they would be "sanctified" (or set apart and equipped) for His mission (v.17).
E. That we would *experience the joy* of God.
   1. "…that they may have the full measure of my joy within them" (v.13).
   2. "The joy of the Lord is [our] strength" (Ne 8:10).

II. HOW CAN I PRAY FOR MY CHURCH?
A. Here are four ways to get you started praying for your church:
1. *Pray continually* (1Th 5:17-18).
2. *Pray strategically.*
   a. Pray for the anointing of the pastor, for people to come to Christ each service, for newcomers to be drawn to special events, and for relationships to grow.
3. *Pray geographically* (Ac 1:8).
   a. Pray for the Spirit to move in various places in the church building where ministry occurs.
   b. Pray for the community, the nation, and the world.
   c. Pray for unreached peoples and places.
4. *Pray powerfully.* (Two ways we can do this:)
   a. By being filled with the Spirit (Ep 6:18).
   b. By praying according to God's Word.

B. Use Jesus' prayer in John 17 as a model to pray for the following:
1. Pray for believers to experience *true worship.*
   a. Pray for an outpouring of God's glory in the church.
   b. Pray that God's people will respond to God's Spirit.
2. Pray that believers will know and *obey the word of God.*
   a. Pray for a clear proclamation of the gospel.
   b. Pray that sinners will understand and obey the gospel.
3. Pray for *unity* in the church.
   a. Pray for a spirit of humility among the people.
   a. Ask God to break down all tribal and cultural walls.
4. Pray for *souls* to be won to Christ.
   a. Ask God to give the church a vision for the lost.
   b. Pray for workers in the harvest.
5. Pray for *joy* in the hearts and lives of believers.
   a. Ask God to bring joy to the leaders and people of the church.

Conclusion and Altar Call

Come. Let's commit ourselves to praying for our church to reach its potential in Christ.

[JM]

Adapted from John Maxwell's book, *Partners in Prayer,*
Thomas Nelson Publishers, 1996, 93-107

64 Praying for Spiritual Leaders

Sermon in a Sentence: You should pray for your spiritual leaders.
Sermon Purpose: That God's people will commit to praying for their pastors and other spiritual leaders.
Text: Exodus 17:8-13
Introduction
1. Tell the story of how Aaron and Hur held up Moses hands (Ex 17:8-13).
2. The battle was won because Aaron and Hur helped Moses do what he could not do alone.
3. Our pastors and other spiritual leaders need our help.
   a. They face loneliness, stress, feelings of inadequacy, depresssion, personal spiritual warfare, and other challenges.
   b. They need us to come alongside them and hold up their hands in prayer.
4. Four ways we must pray for our spiritual leaders:

I. **WE MUST PRAY FOR THEIR PERSONAL NEEDS**
   A. Pray for *humility*.
      1. Ask God to give your leader true humility.
      2. Pray that he or she will rely of God.
   B. Pray that they will receive *wisdom* to know God's agenda.
      1. That they will be sensitive to God's leading.
      2. That they will live according to God's priorities.
   C. Pray for positive *relationships*.
      1. That they will be patient with themselves and others.
      2. That they will be able to deal with difficult people.
   D. Pray for *fruit of the Spirit*.
      1. That they will possess and exhibit the fruit of love, joy, peace, patience, kindness, goodness, faithfulness, gentleness, and self-control (Ga 5:22-23).

II. **WE MUST PRAY FOR THEIR FAMILY NEEDS**
   A. Pray for the *priority* of the family.
      1. That they will make their families their top priority— second only to their relationship with God.
      2. That they will spend quality time with their families.
   B. Pray for *provision* for the family
      1. That "God will meet all [their] needs according to his glorious riches in Christ Jesus" (Phi 4:19).

2. This includes financial, emotional, and spiritual needs.

III. WE MUST PRAY FOR THEIR SPIRITUAL NEEDS
  A. Pray that the will spend *time alone with God*.
     1. That they will make personal prayer, Scripture reading, and worship daily priorities.
  B. Pray for *anointing* on the lives and ministries.
     1. That they will be empowered by the Spirit (Ac 1:8).
     2. That they will walk and minister in the Spirit (Ga 5:25).
  C. Pray for their *integrity*.
     1. That God will give them power over temptation.
     2. That they will walk in moral integrity.
  D. Pray for *protection* from satanic attacks.
     1. That they will put on the full armor of God (Ep 6:10-18).
     2. That God will protect them from the lust of the flesh, the lust of the eyes, and the pride of live (1Jn 2:16).
  E. Pray for their *accountability*.
     1. That God will bring other spiritual leaders to them who can help keep accountable.

IV. WE MUST PRAY FOR THEIR CONGRATATIONAL NEEDS
  A. Pray for *evangelism*.
     1. That your spiritual leader will have a heart for the lost.
     2. That they will make winning the lost a church priority.
  B. Pray for your leader's *personal growth*.
     1. That he or she will grow in their spiritual life.
     2. That they will grow in their ability to lead the church.
  C. Pray for *mobilization* of the laity.
     1. That the leader will be an effective motivator and equipper.
  D. Pray for *intercession*.
     1. That your leader will be a powerful intercessor.
     2. They he or she will lead the church in intercession.

Conclusion and Altar Call
Come. Let's commit ourselves to holding up the hands of our pastor and other spiritual leaders in prayer.

[JM]

Adapted from John Maxwell's book, *Partners in Prayer,*
Thomas Nelson Publishers, 1996, 86-89

65 Prayer That Makes the Mission of God Unstoppable

Sermon in a Sentence: Our prayers can help make the mission of God unstoppable.

Sermon Purpose: That the church will begin to pray like the early church in Acts 4.

Text: Acts 4:23-31

Introduction:
1. The early church was unstoppable! (Read Ac 5:12-14).
2. In spite of persecution, death threats, and even executions, they continued to advance both numerically and geographically.
3. A chief factor causing such success was prayer.
4. The church today can do the same—if we will learn to pray as the early Christians prayed.
   a. Our text is an example of how the early church prayed.
   b. Let's examine the kind of prayer that makes the mission of God unstoppable. (Five traits:)

I. UNIFIED PRAYER *makes the mission of God unstoppable.*
   A. The early believers prayed in unity: "…they raised their voices *together* in prayer" (vv.23-24).
      1. When the apostles were threatened, they remained committed to God's mission (Ac 4:18-20).
      2. They returned to the church and prayed in accordance with Jesus' promise (Mt 18:19).
      3. God powerfully answered their prayer (Ac 4:31).
   B. We too must unite in prayer for God's mission.

II. PRAYER THE RECOGNIZES THE SOVEREIGNTY GOD *makes the mission of God unstoppable* (v. 24).
   A. They began their prayer by focusing on God: "Sovereign Lord…you made the heaven and the earth…" (v.24).
      1. They focused on God's greatness.
      2. As they prayed like this, their faith increased (Jude 20).
   B. We must learn to pray such God-exalting prayers.
      1. Such prayer will inspire us to fulfill God's mission.

III. SCRIPTURE-BASED PRAYER *makes the mission of God unstoppable* (v.25-28).

    A. Listen to how they based their prayer on what is written in God's word: (Read vv.25-26)
        1. They quoted Ps 2:1-4 where God laughs at His enemies.
        2. They knew they were praying in God's will (1Jn 5:14-15).
    B. We must do the same.
        1. Quoting God's word helps to focus our prayers.
        2. It also builds our faith (Ro 10:17).
        3. And God answers our prayers prayed in faith (Mt 21:22).

IV. SPIRIT-EMPOWERED, SPIRIT-DIRECTED PRAYER *makes the mission of God unstoppable.*
    A. Their prayer was empowered and directed by the Spirit.
        1. They had been filled with the Spirit at Pentecost (Ac 2:4).
        2. Now, they prayed in the power of the Spirit.
        3. God answered by refilling them with the Spirit (v.31a).
        4. They then began to witness with power (vv.31b, 33).
    B. God wants to empower and direct or prayers.

V. SPECIFIC PRAYER *makes the mission of God unstoppable.*
    A. They made a specific request from God:
        1. They asked Him, "Stretch out Your hand" and perform miracles (vv.29-30).
        2. The "hand of the Lord" represents the power of the Holy Spirit (cf. Eze 31:1; Mt 12:28).
    B. We too must ask the Lord to stretch our His hand and empower us as Christ's witnesses (Ac 1:8).

Conclusion and Altar Call
1. Such praying will help make the church unstoppable as it moves to advance God's mission.
2. We must learn to pray as the early disciples did.
3. Come, let's ask God to "stretch out His hand," empower us, and make His mission unstoppable.

[DM]

66 Jesus' Missional Prayer for Believers

Sermon in a Sentence: We must learn to pray powerful missional prayers like the one Jesus prayed in John 17.
Sermon Purpose: That God's people will use Jesus' example in John 17 to begin to pray more effectively for God's mission.
Text: John 17:1-26
Introduction
1. This prayer has been called Jesus' "High Priestly Prayer."
2. He prayed this prayer just before His arrest in Gethsemane.
3. By examining this prayer, we can learn how to pray more effectively for the completion of God's mission.
4. From this prayer, we learn three important prayer strategies:

I. LIKE JESUS, LET US PRAY THAT WE MAY GLORIFY GOD IN THE RESPONSIBILITIES HE GIVES US (Jn 17:1-5)
A. We can begin by reminding ourselves that God is in *heaven*.
   1. Jesus "looked toward heaven and prayed" (v.1; Mt 6:9).
   2. Remember, He is the Creator and Ruler over us all.
B. We must also remember that God is our heavenly *Father*.
   1. Jesus began His prayer by addressing God as "Father."
   2. As our Father, God loves and cares for us all.
C. Our prayers must reflect our desire to glorify God by fulfilling the mission He has given us.
   1. Jesus' mission was to glorify God by bringing eternal life to lost humanity (vv.2-3).
      a. Jesus asked for strength to complete His mission.
   2. Our mission is to glorify God by declaring eternal life in Christ to all nations (Mt 24:14).
      a. We too we must pray for strength to fulfil our mission.
      b. We can ask the Father and He will give us the Holy Spirit to empower us to fulfill our God-given mission (Lk 11:15; Ac 1:8).

II. LIKE JESUS, LET US PRAY FOR GOD TO PROTECT BELIEVERS FROM THE EVIL ONE
A. Jesus now begins to pray for His disciples (Jn. 17:6-19).
   1. They had believed in Him and obeyed His word (vv.6-8).
   2. He would soon entrust His redemptive mission to them.
   3. The destiny of the world would be on their shoulders.
   4. So, Jesus prays for them with all of His heart (vv.9-12).

5. We too must pray for those Christ's puts under our charge.
B. Like Jesus, we must pray that God will keep them from "the evil one," that is, Satan (vv.14-15).
   1. While we are *in* the world, we are not to be *of* the world.
   2. The "world" here speaks of society in rebellion against God. It includes society's unbelief, values, lusts, immorality, philosophies, and evil entertainments.
   3. Satan uses the world to enslave lost people and to keep the church from fulfilling God's mission (2Co 4:4; Lk 22:31).
   4. Jesus thus prayed, "Protect them from the evil one" (v.15).
C. Like Jesus, we must pray for disciple's sanctification (Jn 17:18-19).
   1. To be sanctified is to be set apart *from* sin and *to* God and His mission.
   2. We must therefore pray that the God's people will remain true to His holy nature and faithful to His redemptive mission.

III. LIKE JESUS, LET US PRAY FOR THE UNITY OF BELIEVERS (Jn 17:11, 20-26).
A. Jesus prayed that His disciples "may be one" as He and the Father were one (v.11)
   1. This is a oneness like oneness that He and the Father share.
   2. It is a oneness the world can see—a oneness that will influence them to believe in Jesus (17:21, 23).
   3. It is a oneness of commission and commitment to follow Jesus and make disciples in His name (Jn 17:18; 20:21).
   4. Where Satan is able to destroy this oneness, the church is crippled and the mission is hindered.
B. Like Jesus, we must pray for the unity of God's people.
   1. That the church will be unified like the early church after the outpouring of the Spirit at Pentecost (Ac 2:42-46).
   2. This unity resulted in powerful evangelism (Ac 2:47).

Conclusion and Altar Call
1. Come now, and be filled with God's Spirit.
2. Come and commit yourself to praying like Jesus prayed in John 17

[QMc]

Adapted from the *Faith & Action Series: Gospel of John*

67 Praying for New Believers (Part 1)
~ Paul's First Prayer for the Ephesians ~

Sermon in a Sentence: We must pray for new believers, that they will come to understand all they possess in Christ.

Sermon Purpose: That Christians will commit to praying for new believers in churches being planted throughout Africa.

Text: Ephesians 1:15-23

Introduction
1. As we go out to plant churches in formerly unreached places and among formerly unreached peoples, how should we pray for the new believers in those places?
2. Paul faced a similar situation in Ephesians.
    a. He planted the church in Ephesus (Acts 19:1-10).
    b. Now, he explains to them how he is praying for them.
3. His prayer can serve as a model of how we can pray for new believers today.
4. Let's look at three ways we should pray for new believers:

I. WE SHOULD PRAY THAT THEY WILL COME TO KNOW GOD BETTER (Read Eph 1:15-17)
A. Note *why* Paul prayed for these Ephesian believers:
   1. He begins by saying, *"For this reason...*I have not stopped...remembering you in my prayers" (v.15-16).
   2. Paul's reason is found in the preceding verses:
      a. Paul prayed for them because they had heard the truth, and had believed on Christ (vv.13-14).
   3. We must not stop praying for people when they become Christians; rather, we must increase our prayers for them.
B. Note *what* Paul prayed for...
   1. He prayed that they would come to know God better (v.17).
   2. Becoming a Christian is not the end. New believers must grow in God and learn to serve Him more perfectly.
C. Pray that new believers will come to know God intimately.
   1. Ask God to give them "the Spirit of wisdom and revelation, so that [they] may know him better" (v.17).
   2. Such knowledge will transform their lives, shaping their attitudes and behavior.
   3. The better they know God, the more they will love Him, and the more they will want to share His love with others.

II. WE SHOULD PRAY THAT THEY WILL COME TO KNOW THE HOPE GOD HAS CALLED THEM TO (Read Eph 1:18)

A. Paul told the Ephesians, "I pray also that the eyes of your heart may be enlightened in order that you may know the hope to which he has called you" (v.18).
   1. Our hope in Christ is an assurance of a bright eternity.
   2. This hope is the work of God's Spirit in us (1Co 2:9-10).
   3. Jesus purchased this hope for us through His death on the cross and His resurrection from the dead (Ro 8:32).
B. We should pray that new believers will come to understand these things.
   1. Pray that the Holy Spirit will "open the eyes of [their] heart" so that they can see the hope they have in Christ (v.18).
   2. Pray that they will acquire a deep, spiritual knowledge of their hope and inheritance.
   3. This hope will help the new believers to stand firm.

III. WE SHOULD PRAY THAT THEY WILL KNOW GOD'S GREAT POWER (Ep 1:18-23)

A. Paul prayed that the Ephesians my know and experience God's "imcomparably great power" (vv.19-20).
   1. He is talking about the power of the Holy Spirit.
   2. This same power raised Jesus from the dead (v.20).
   3. Paul had experienced this power many times in his life:
      a. It had transformed him on the Damascus Road.
      b. He was then empowered to preach the gospel.
      c. It had worked through him to heal the sick, cast out demons, and pray for believers to receive the Spirit.
      d. It had had sustained him in his missionary work.
   4. Paul knew the Ephesians needed that same power.
B. We must pray that new Christians experience the Spirit's power.
   1. Pray that God's Spirit will transform their lives.
   2. Pray that God's Spirit will empower them as witnesses.
   3. Pray that God's Spirit will work powerfully through them.
   4. Pray that God's Spirit will sustain them in the work.

Conclusion and Altar Call

Come and commit yourself to faithfully pray for new Christians.

[QMc]

68 Praying for New Believers (Part 2)
~ Paul's Second Prayer for the Ephesians ~

Sermon in a Sentence: We must pray for new Christians that they will be filled with God's power and love.

Sermon Purpose: That believers will commit themselves to praying for New Christians at home and on the mission field.

Text: Ephesians 3:14-21

Introduction
1. This is Paul's second prayer in his letter to the Ephesians.
2. As Paul did in His first prayer (1:15-23), he begins this one with the phrase, *"For this reason..."*
    a. He prays for them in light of God's abundant blessings in Christ he described in chapters 1-3.
3. In the first prayer, Paul prayed three things for the believers in Ephesus.
    a. That they would know God better.
    b. That they would know all they have in Christ.
    c. That they would experience God's great power.
4. Now, Paul adds three more ways we should pray for new Christians.
    a. Like the first prayer, this one can serve as a model for how we can pray new Christians.
    b. Let's look at those three more ways we should pray for new Christians:

I. WE SHOULD PRAY THAT GOD'S SPIRIT WILL STRENGTHEN THEM IN THEIR INNER BEING
A. Paul knew that the new Christians in Ephesus were in a great struggle with the world, the flesh, and the devil.
   1. He knew this because this fact is true for all Christians.
   2. He described some of these challenges in this letter.
      a. For instance, Paul warns about the "cunning and craftiness of men in their deceitful scheming" (4:14).
      b. He further warns them in Eph 5:3-10. (Read)
B. Paul knew that being filled with the Spirit is God's solution for overcoming the challenges of the world, flesh, and devil.
   1. He thus told the Ephesians "Be filled with the Spirit" (6:18).
   2. He prayed for them to be empowered by the Spirit: "I pray that out of his glorious riches he may strengthen you with power through his Spirit in your inner being" (v.16).

    C. We too must pray for all Christians to be strengthen in their inner being by being empowered by the Holy Spirit.

II. WE SHOULD PRAY THAT THEY WILL BE ROOTED AND GROUNDED IN GOD'S LOVE
    A. Paul also knew that the new Christians in Ephesus would struggle to follow Jesus' teaching.
        1. They must know that serving God is more than trying to keep rules, and that it impossible to live for Him in our own strength.
            a. Illus: Paul's struggle: Ro 7:18-24.
        2. Paul also knew the solution: being filled with the love of God empowers us to follow the teachings of Jesus.
        3. Paul thus prays for the Ephesian believers, that they may "grasp how wide and long and high and deep is the love of Christ that surpasses knowledge" and that they may be "filled to the measure of all the fullness of God" (Eph 3:18-19).
        4. We experience God's love through His Spirit (Ro 5:5).
    B. Like Paul, we must pray that new believers will be filled with the Spirit and thus able to grasp God's great love.

III. WE MUST PRAISE GOD FOR WHAT HE HAS DONE IN THEIR LIVES (Eph 3:20-21)
    A. Paul ends his prayer for the Ephesians with a doxology.
        1. A doxology is formal expression of praise.
        2. Paul exulted, "Now to him who is able to do immeasurably more than all we ask or imagine, according to his power that is at work within us, to him be glory in the church and in Christ Jesus throughout all generations, forever and ever! Amen" (3:20-21).
    B. As we pray for new Christians, let us not forget to praise God.
        1. Praise Him because of His powerful, immeasurable, unimaginable work in their lives.
        2. Ask Him to continue to work for them in this way.

Conclusion and Altar Call
    1. We must pray diligently for new Christians.
    2. Come and commit yourself to such praying.

[QMc]

69 Overcoming Threats in Mission

Sermon in a Sentence: Unified prayer can help us overcome the enemy's threats and fulfill God's mission.

Sermon Purpose: That God's people will commit to unified prayer for missions.

Text: Acts 4:29-33

Introduction:
1. Tell the story of the church's persecution and prayer in Acts 4.
2. As we move forward in missions, we too can expect opposition and threats.
3. At such times, we must unify in faith and prayer as did the early disciples in our text.
4. If we will do this, we too can triumph in face of opposition.
5. Let us look at what this narrative teaches about what we should do when threatened for advancing God's kingdom:

I. PRAYER HAS THE POWER TO UNITE AND EMPOWER THE CHURCH IN MISSION
   A. Our text is a great example of the unifying power of prayer.
   B. Note the two things that the disciples prayed for:
      1. They prayed for *boldness* to preach the word (v.29).
      2. They prayed for the *outpouring* of the Spirit (v.30).
         a. Note: The prayer, "Lord, stretch out your hand" is a prayer for the outpouring of the Holy Spirit.
         b. It is a plea for Jesus to fulfill His promise of Acts 1:8.
   C. We must pray in the same way today.
      1. We must pray that God will give us boldness to proclaim the gospel in the face of threats.
      2. We must ask God to confirm His word through the manifestation of signs, wonders, and miracles.
      3. Such praying will help unify the church and empower us to fulfill God's mission.

II. NOTE THE RESULTS OF THE CHURCH'S PRAYER
   A. God powerfully poured out His Spirit on them.
      1. "The place where they were meeting was shaken" (v.31).
      2. "They were all filled with the Spirit" (v.31).
      3. This reminds us of what happened on the Day of Pentecost (cf. Acts 2:1-4).
   B. The forces of darkness were overcome.

    1. "They spoke the word of God with boldness" (v.31).
    2. The enemy's threats did not stop them from fulfilling God's mission.
  C. They proclaimed Christ with great power and effectiveness.
    1. They "spoke the word of God boldly" (v.31).
    2. "With great power the apostles continued to testify to the resurrection of the Lord Jesus" (v.33).
    3. This echoes what happened on the Day of Pentecost.
    4. It is another direct fulfillment of Jesus' promise in Ac 1:8.
  D. They were unified "in heart and mind" (v.32).
    1. "In heart"—They cared for one another (vv.32, 34)
    2, "In mind"—They were all committed to the same mission.
  E. They freely gave to the work of God.
    1. They cared for one another.
    2. They funded the mission.

Conclusion and Altar Call
  1. If we will pray, we can expect the same today.
  2. We can become an irresistible force for the dynamic advance of God's kingdom.
  3. Come; let's ask God to "stretch out His hand" and pour out His Spirit on our church today.

[JMT]

Section 7
Praying for Missionaries and Missions

70 A House of Prayer for All Nations

Sermon in a Sentence: Our church must become a "house of prayer for all nations."

Sermon Purpose: That God's people will commit themselves to praying for lost people around the world.

Text: Mark 11:15-17

Introduction
1. Tell the story of Jesus cleansing the temple (Mk 11:15-17).
2. Jesus explained why He did it: "Is it not written: 'My house will be called a house of prayer for all nations'? But you have made it a den of robbers" (v.17)
3. From this story, we learn three important lessons:

I. JESUS IS AFFRONTED WHEN WE TURN HIS HOUSE INTO A MARKETPLACE
   A. The religious leaders were merchandizing in the temple.
      1. The temple was built as a place where God would dwell.
         a. The people could come there and encounter Him.
         b. They would worship and make sacrifice to Him.
      2. They had set up tables in the temple in order to exchange money and sell sacrificial animals.
      3. They had turned the temple into a place of merchandizing.
   B. Such merchandizing is happening in many churches today.
      1. False prophets are selling prayers, and they are offering God's blessings for personal profit.
      2. This was the sin of Simon the Sorcerer (Ac 8:18-24).
         a. He wanted to buy the power of the Holy Spirit so he could then sell God's blessings for a profit.
         b. Peter rebuked him for His sin (vv.20-23).
   C. Jesus is angry at such false prophets and merchandizers.
      1. He sees their greediness (Jude 4).
      2. He will drive them from His presence forever (Lk 13:27).
      3. If you are doing this, repent!

II. JESUS WANTS HIS PEOPLE TO HAVE A LOVING CONCERN FOR THE NATIONS
   A. It's important to note that the moneychangers were buying and selling in the Court of the Gentiles.
      1. This was the only place in the temple where Gentiles could come and worship God.

2. The Jews were showing that they cared more about personal gain than for the nations for whom Jesus was soon to die on the cross.
   3. This so angered Jesus that he drove them from the temple.
 B. The Jewish leaders had forgotten why God had chosen Israel.
   1. He chose them to be a "kingdom of priests" (Ex 19:6), a "light to the Gentiles" (Is 42:6; 49:6), and a "blessing to the nations" (Ge 22:18).
   2. They, however, saw themselves as special, as the only ones deserving God's blessings.
   4. This so angered Jesus that He drove them from the temple.
 C. We must never forget why God has called us.
   1. The churches exists to bless the nations,
   2. We must commit ourselves to this all-important task of preaching the gospel to all nations before Jesus returns (Mt 24:14).

III. JESUS WANTS HIS CHURCH TO BE A HOUSE OF PRAYER FOR ALL NATIONS

 A. When Jesus cleansed the temple, He cited Isaiah 56:7: "My house will be called *a house of prayer for all nations.*"
   1. Two things Jesus wants His church to be:
 B. First, He wants it to be a *"house of prayer."*
   1. We must drive out the "moneychangers" of greed and self-centeredness.
   2. We must commit ourselves to prayer.
 C. Second, the church is to be a house of prayer *"for all nations."*
   1. We must turn our prayers from our own needs and blessings.
   2. We must turn our prayers to the need of lost people:
      a. We must pray for those around us.
      b. We must pray for the unreached peoples of Africa.
      c. We must pray for the nations of the world.

Conclusion and Altar Call
   1. Let's come now, and repent of our selfishness.
   2. Let's come and commit to make this church "a house of prayer for all nations."

[DRM]

71 Ask the Lord of the Harvest

Sermon in a Sentence: Like Jesus, we must respond in compassion to the harvest of souls around us.

Sermon Purpose: That God's people will begin to look at lost people differently and begin to pray for them.

Text: Matthew 9:35-38

Introduction
1. Our text takes us to a day during Jesus' ministry in Galilee.
2. Verse 35 tells what Jesus did: He went from town to town teaching, preaching, and healing the sick.
3. Verse 36 reveals His loving heart: "When he saw the crowds, he had compassion on them…"
   a. He is the compassionate Savior—the One who cares deeply for hurting humanity.
4. His great compassion moved Him to action.
   a. Note the three phrases: (1) "He saw the crowds…" (2) "He had compassion…" (3) "He said to His disciples…"
   b. In other words, He looked… He felt… He acted…
5. From this passage, we discover three ways we must respond to the world around us:

Like Jesus, we must…

I. LIFT UP OUR EYES AND LOOK
A. It all began when Jesus "saw the crowds" (v.36).
   1. Many times, the gospels tell us that Jesus *saw* people (Four of many examples: Mt 4:18, 21; 8:14, 18).
   2. However, He saw more than their physical bodies, He saw into their hearts and needs (e.g. Mt 9:2, 9, 22; 14:14).
   3. He saw their need for a Savior.
B. We too must lift up our eyes and see the people around us.
   1. Jesus once told His disciples: "Lift up your eyes and look at the fields! They are ripe for harvest" (Jn 4:35).
   2. We must see people's pain and brokenness.
      a. They have been beaten and battered by Satan.
   3. We must see their need for a Savior.
      a. They cannot save themselves.
      b. Only Jesus can save them (Ac 4:12).
      c. Illus: Like the disciples in the storm (Mt 8:23-25).
C. Many of us need a "second touch" from Jesus.

1. He has saved and delivered us; now we need Him to fill our hearts with compassion for others.
2. Illus: We're like the blind man whom Jesus healed. We are no longer blind, yet we still other people as "trees." We don't see them as they really are. We need Jesus to touch us again so we can "see everything clearly" (Mk 8:22-25).

Like Jesus, we must...
II. LIFT UP OUR HEARTS AND FEEL
A. When Jesus saw the crowds, *"he had compassion on them..."*
   1. First Jesus saw...then He felt...
   2. He saw their hurts, needs, and hopes—and He was moved.
B. Once we have seen people with our eyes, we must feel for them with our hearts.
   1. Ask God to fill you with His compassion for the lost.
   2. God pours His love into our hearts by the Holy Spirit. (Read: Ro 5:5b; Ga 5:22a)

Like Jesus, we must...
III. WE MUST LIFT UP OUR VOICES AND PRAY
A. After explaining to His disciples, "The harvest is plentiful but the workers are few," Jesus directed them to pray.
   1. He said, "Ask the Lord of the harvest...to send out workers into his harvest field" (Mt 9:38).
   2. Someone has called this "Jesus' only prayer request."
   3. He knew that the worldwide harvest of souls is so great that it will take millions of workers.
B. We must commit ourselves to prayer for the harvest.
   1. We must pray for hurting people.
   2. We must pray for lost souls.
   3. We must pray for workers for the harvest.
   4. We must pray for an outpouring of the Spirit.
   5. And as we pray, we must offer ourselves: "Here am I, Lord, use me!"

Conclusion and Altar Call
1. We must see the lostness of people; we must feel compassion for them; and then we must pray for workers.
2. Come now, and commit yourself to intercessory prayer for the nations.

[DRM]

72 Foundations for Missional Prayer

Sermon in a Sentence: To effectively intercede for missions we must follow the pattern revealed in Scripture.
Sermon Purpose: That God's people will understand how to effectively pray for missions and that they will commit themselves to such prayer.
Text: Matthew 28:18-20
Introduction
1. We have just read the Great Commission of Jesus.
2. In it, Jesus mandates that every church—and every Christian in the church—be involved in the *mission Dei,* that is, the mission of God.
3. Although not every Christian will go as a missionary, every believer must be involved in missions through intercessory prayer.
4. This message: three biblical foundations for effective missional prayer:

Biblical foundation 1:
I. **THE LORD JESUS URGES US TO ASK THE LORD OF THE HARVEST FOR MORE MISSIONARIES**
   A. Read Matthew 9:37-38: "Then [Jesus] said to his disciples, 'The harvest is plentiful but the workers are few. Ask the Lord of the harvest, therefore, to send out workers into his harvest field.'"
   B. When Jesus saw the crowds, He was moved with compassion for them (vv.35-36).
      1. Because "they were harassed and helpless."
      2. Because they were "like sheep without a shepherd."
      3. We too must be moved by the plight of lost people.
   C. Jesus noticed two disturbing things about the harvest:
      1. The harvest is very great.
      2. The workers are very few.
   D. This understanding prompted Him to cry out, "Ask the Lord of the harvest to send out workers into his harvest field."
      1. Like Jesus, we must be moved to pray for the harvest.
      2. Let's pause now and pray for the harvest.

Biblical foundation 2:
II. THE APOSTLE PAUL URGES US TO PRAY FOR MISSIONAL ENABLEMENT
   A. Read Ephesians 6:19-20: "Pray also for me, that whenever I open my mouth, words may be given me so that I will fearlessly make known the mystery of the gospel, for which I am an ambassador in chains. Pray that I may declare it fearlessly, as I should."
   B. Paul wrote Ephesians from prison in Rome.
      1. He referred to himself as an "ambassador in chains" (v.20).
      2. He was an ambassador of Christ's kingdom (2Co 5:20).
      3. As Christ's missionary, he was bound to preach the gospel (1Co 9:16).
   C. He requested prayer from the Ephesian believers…
      1. …that he would fearlessly proclaim the gospel (Ep 6:20).
      2. …that God would give him the words to say (v.19).
   D. Let's take a moment now and pray for our missionaries:
      1. That they will be empowered by the Spirit to fearlessly proclaim the gospel (cf. Ac 4:31).
      2. That the Spirit will give them the words to say (1Co 2:13).

Biblical foundation 3:
III. JESUS SETS AN EXAMPLE BY PRAYING FOR THE UNITY OF THOSE WHO WILL BELIEVE THE GOSPEL
   A. John 17:23: "I in them and you in me. May they be brought to complete unity to let the world know that you sent me and have loved them even as you have loved me."
      1. This is part of Jesus' "High Priestly Prayer" in John 17.
      2. He is praying for His disciples (v.9).
      3. He prays that they "be brought into complete unity" (v.23).
   B. For missions to be successful, the Church must be unified.
      1. This includes unity of heart, purpose, and mission.
      2. Unity enables the church to mobilize effectively.
      3. Unity attracts the lost to the church (v.23).
   C. Let's take a moment to pray for unity.

Conclusion and Altar Call
   1. We can all join God's mission through our prayers.
   2. Come now and commit to being one of God's "prayer missionaries."

[EC]

73 A Soulwinner's Prayer

Sermon in a Sentence: David's prayer of repentance can serve as a guideline for soulwinners.

Sermon Purpose: That soulwinners will use David's prayer to prepare their hearts to reach the lost.

Text: Psalm 51:10-13

Introduction:
1. God calls us to win souls. *(Note these Scriptures:)*
    a. "Go into all the world and preach the good news to all creation" (Mk 16:15).
    b. "Go out to the roads and country lanes and make them come in, so that my house will be full" (Lk 14:23).
    c. "You did not choose me, but I chose you and appointed you to go and bear fruit…" (Jn 15:16).
    d. "He who wins souls is wise" (Pr 11:30).
2. However, we must prepare ourselves for soul winning.
3. David's prayer in Psalm 51 can help guide our preparation.

I. DAVID'S PRAYER REMINDS US OF THE WORK OF SOULWINNERS (Read v.13)
   A. The soulwinner's work is to teach transgressors God's ways.
      1. To teach them about sin (Ro 3:23; 6:23).
      2. To teach them about the Savior (Ro 5:8).
      3. To teach them the way of salvation (Ro 10:13, 9-10).
   B. The goal of the soulwinner is that "sinners will be converted."
      1. This suggests two goals:
         a. That the unsaved will turn to God.
         b. That backsliders will return to God.
   C. We must never forget that soul winning is our top job.

II. DAVID'S PRAYER HIGHLIGHTS THE SPIRITUAL PREPARATION OF SOULWINNERS (Read vv.10-13)
   • *Five "heart-preparing" prayers we must pray:*
   A. Pray for a *pure heart*.
      1. v.10: "Create in me a pure heart, O God."
      2. Our hearts are cleansed through confession and repentance. (Read and explain: 1Jn 1:7-9).
      3. Confess your sins to God and ask Him for a clean heart.
   B. Pray for a *steadfast spirit*.
      1. v. 10: "…and renew a steadfast spirit within me."

2. A steadfast spirit is a loyal spirit—a faithful heart.
   3. Ask God to give you a faithful heart.
 C. Pray to be *filled with the Spirit.*
   1. v.11: "Do not cast me from your presence or take your Holy Spirit from me."
   2. Being filled with God's Spirit will enable us to witness with power. (Read: Ac 1:8)
   3. Ask God to fill you with His Spirit (Lk 11:9-10, 13).
 D. Ask God for His *joy.*
   1. v.12: "Restore to me the joy of your salvation."
   2. Salvation brings joy—joy brings strength (Ne 8:10).
   3. Joy is a fruit of the Spirit-filled life (Ga 5:22).
 E. Ask God for a *willing spirit.*
   1. v.12: "Grant me a willing spirit to sustain me."
   2. We must willingly obey God and do His will.
   3. Such a spirit will sustain us in the work of soul winning.

III. DAVIDS PRAYER MAKES US THINK ABOUT THE MESSAGE OF SOULWINNERS
 A. Note two phrases in verse 13: "Then" and "your ways."
   1. The word *then* speaks of the result of our getting our hearts right before God:
     a. *Then*...we will be ready to win souls to Christ.
   2. The phrase *your ways* reminds us of God's way of salvation—faith in Christ.
     a. Jesus: "I am the way..." (Jn 14:6).
     b. Paul: "Believe in the Lord Jesus, and you will be saved" (Ac 16:31).
 B. The message of soulwinners is the message of eternal hope in Jesus Christ.
   1. To the sinner we cry out "Come to Jesus in faith and repentance, He welcomes you." (Lk 15:1-2)
   2. To the backslider we declare, "Return, faithless people; [He] will cure you of backsliding" (Je 3:22).

Conclusion and Altar Call
 1. Come now. Let's commit ourselves to God as His soulwinners.
 2. We will then pray these five prayers: (Recap point II above)

[DRM]

74 Pray the Lord of the Harvest

Sermon in a Sentence: We must follow Jesus' example and pray for workers for the harvest.

Sermon Purpose: That Christians will commit to intercessory prayer for the harvest of souls.

Text: Matthew 9:35-38

Introduction:
1. When Jesus saw people, He was moved with compassion.
    a. However, He saw more than just their physical needs, He saw their desperate need for a Savior.
    b. And He sensed the urgency of their need.
2. Jesus wanted His disciples to see people as He saw them.
    a. So, He challenged them, "Ask the Lord of the harvest, therefore, to send out workers into his harvest field."
    b. We must be like Jesus.
3. Three ways we must look more closely at the harvest:

I. WE MUST LOOK AT THE MULTITUDES
   A. Jesus sees the people in three ways:
      1. They are *weary*.
         a. Many are tired in the struggle of life.
         b. Life without God brings no rest (Is 57:20).
         c. Jesus offers rest (Mt 11:28).
      2. They are *scattered*.
         a. They are scattered in their beliefs.
         b. They have many philosophies but no Truth (Jn 14:6).
         c. They are scattered among the nations.
            1) When Jesus spoke of "other sheep," He was talking about people of all nations (Jn 10:16).
            2) We must take the gospel to them (Mt 28:19).
      3. They are like sheep with *no shepherd*.
         1. Without Christ, they are easily confused.
         2. They cannot care for themselves.
   B. We must see lost people as Jesus sees them.
      1. We must see that they are weary, scattered, and confused.
      2. We must be determined to do something about it.

II. WE MUST UNDERSTAND THE HARVEST
   A. We must understand that the harvest is *His*.
   1. Jesus is "Lord of the Harvest" (Mt 9:38).

      2. He planned for it (Mt 25:34), redeemed it (Re 5:9), and rejoices over it (Lk 15:7, 10)
  B. We must understand that the harvest is *lost people.*
      1. Jesus died for all people (2Co 5:14-15).
      2. We must reap them now before it is too late (Jn 4:35).
  C. We must let what we see move us to *compassion.*
      1. Jesus saw people's physical needs; however, He also saw their spiritual need (Mk 6:34).
         a. His disciples asked Him to send the multitude away so that they could get bread (v.36).
         b. But Jesus was committed to meeting their need.
         c. Jesus both fed them (physical need) and taught them (spiritual need). (vv.41, 34)
      2 Jesus made the way for all to be saved (Jn 3:16).
         a. He is not willing that any should perish (2Pe 3:9).
         b. Yet someone must tell them (Ro 10:14).
      3. Let the Holy Spirit move you to love the lost (Ro 5:5).

III. WE MUST PRAY FOR THE HARVEST
  A. Jesus commands us to pray. (Reread Mt 9:38).
      1. The Greek word here translated "Pray" literally means to pray earnestly—to beg.
      2. Jesus demonstrated earnest prayer (He 5:7; Lk 22:44).
  B. Like Jesus, we must fervently intercede for the harvest.
      1. We must make prayer a priority.
      2. We must pray, "Your will be done on earth" (Mt 6:10).
  C. Jesus tells us to pray for laborers for the harvest (Mt 9:38).
      1. There are so many to reach, yet so few workers to reach them.
  2. The landowner (Jesus) is still sending workers into His fields (Mt 20:1-16).
      a. He commands us to pray to that end.
      b. We must answer, "Here am I, Lord, use me!" (Is 6:8).

Conclusion and Altar Call
1. "The harvest is plentiful but the workers are few."
2. We must therefore pray today that God will send more laborers into the harvest.
3. Come, commit yourself to prayer for the harvest.

[LP]

75 Praying Effectively for God's Mission

Sermon in a Sentence: You can pray effectively for God's mission.
Sermon Purpose: That God's people will know how to, and commit themselves to praying for the fulfillment of God's mission.
Text: James 5:13-16
Introduction
1. God calls us to pray for His mission, including prayer for missionaries, church planters, training, and much more.
2. God promises to answer our prayers (Mt 7:7; Jn 16:24).
3. The question arises: How can we pray more effectively?
   a. What kind of prayers touch God's heart?
   b. What kind of prayer is He committed to answer?
4. Though there are no set formulas to "force God's hand," certain practices will increase the effectiveness of our prayers.
5. Let's consider three of those practices:

I. TO BE EFFECTIVE, PRAYER MUST BE OFFERED BY A "RIGHTEOUS" PERSON

  • *The prayer of a righteous man is powerful and effective* (Ja 5:16).
  A. The Bible places certain conditions to answered prayer:
   1. We must abide in Christ. (Read Jn 15:7).
   2. We must pray with pure motives. (Read Ja 4:3).
   3. We must pray in faith. (Read Ja 5:15).
  B. Further, the one who prays must be "righteous" (Ja 5:16).
   1. James is not talking about being perfect.
   2. We are made righteous through faith in Christ (Ro 3:22).
   3. We must now forsake our sinful practices (Is 59:1-2).
  C. However, it is not enough to be righteous—*we must pray!*
   1. For people to be saved, for churches to be planted by the power of the Holy Spirit, and for missionaries to effectively engage in God's work, we must pray.
   2. God wants every righteous person to help others find the righteousness that comes through faith in Christ.

II. TO BE EFFECTIVE, PRAYER MUST CONFORM TO GOD'S WILL

  • *This is the confidence we have in approaching God: that if we ask anything according to his will, he hears us"* (1Jn 5:14-15).
  A. Prayer is part of the divine purpose.
   1. Great men and women of God were people of prayer.

2. They all prayed according to God's eternal purposes.
      a. Illus: Jesus submitted to God's will (Mt 26:42).
      b. Illus: The apostles and prophets sought God's will.
   3. They all relied on the power of the Holy Spirit (Ac 1:8).
   B. If we want to see our prayers answered, we too must pray according to God's eternal purposes.
      1. God's purpose is that people from all nations come to know and serve Him (Re 5:9).
      2. Jesus orders us to pray for the harvest. (Read Mt 9:37-38)
      3. If we don't pray, nothing will happen.
      4. However, if we do pray, God will send out workers.
         a. He will strengthen those already in ministry.
         b. Churches will be planted, missionaries will be sent to new places, and the lost will be saved.

III. TO BE EFFECTIVE, PRAYER MUST BE OFFERED IN THE NAME OF JESUS CHRIST
   A. Jesus has given us His powerful name as a weapon to challenge and defeat the enemy. (Read Jn 14:13-14)
      1. To pray in Jesus' name we must submit to His authority.
   B. By relying on Jesus' name…
      1. …we can overcome the evil forces (Mk 16:17).
      2. …we can will fulfill God's mission on earth.
      3. …we can win souls and plant churches
      4 …we can do mighty works.
   C. Illus: Peter and John knew the power of Jesus' name.
      1. Tell the story of the healing of the lame man (Ac 3:1-10).
      2. Peter explained how the miracle occurred: "By faith in the name of Jesus, this man…was made strong" (v.16).
      3. We must always pray in Jesus' name.

Conclusion and Altar Call
   1. We want to see God's kingdom advance in our country and around the world.
   2. We must therefore live holy lives, pray according to God's will, and pray in Jesus' name.
   3. Come, be filled with the Spirit, and commit yourself to pray for missions.

[JN]

76 Praying for the Salvation of Souls and Workers in the Harvest

Sermon in a Sentence: We must persistently call on God for the salvation of souls and for workers in the harvest.
Sermon Purpose: That God's people commit themselves to praying for the harvest.
Text: Luke 18:1-7
Introduction
1. Tell the story of the Persistent Widow (Lk 18:1-8).
2. This message: We must persistently call on God for the salvation of souls and for Him to send workers into the harvest.
3. Three important lesson concerning such prayer:

I. GOD REQUIRES US TO CALL ON HIM FOR LOST SOULS
A. Listen to what the Bible says…
 1. God is "not willing that any should perish…" (2Pe 3:9b).
 2. Jesus: "Ask the Lord of the harvest…to send out workers into his harvest field" (Lk 10:2)
B. God promises to hear our prayers for the lost.
 1. He says, "Call to me and I will answer you and tell you great and unsearchable things you do not know" (Je 33:3).
 2. Paul wrote that God is "able to do immeasurably more than all we ask or imagine… (Ep 3:20).
 3. Jesus promised, "You may ask me for anything in my name, and I will do it" (Jn 14:14).
 4. Our text declares that God will "give justice to his chosen ones, who cry out to him day and night" (Lk 18:7).
C. God never tires of hearing us cry out to Him for the salvation of lost souls.

II. GOD PROMISES TO ANSWER OUR PRAYERS FOR THE LOST
A. If we will pray, God will hear our prayers and move on the hearts of sinners calling them to repentance.
 1. God does not shy away from our insistence on His calling people to salvation.
B. God can do anything by His mighty power.
 1. "Is anything too hard for the Lord?" (Ge 18:14).
 2. "Sovereign Lord…Nothing is too hard for you" (Je 32:17).
C. God can answer our prayers in various ways:

1. He can work with us being present or with us absent.
2. He can work through the witness of Christians and the preaching of the gospel (Ro 1:16).
3. He can send angels to work in the lives of lost people (He 1:14; e.g. Cornelius, Ac 10:1-3ff).
4. He can work through His Spirit to convince sinners of their need for salvation (Jn 16:8).
5. In summary, God can use whomever or whatever He wants, whenever He wants, and however He wants to save souls.

III. GOD PLACES CERTAIN REQUIREMENTS ON HOW WE SHOULD PRAY FOR THE LOST

A. We must *commit* to Jesus and to His Great Commission. (Read Mt 28:19)
B. We must abide in Christ and His words must abide in in us (Jn 15:7).
C. We must pray in *faith* (Ja 5:15).
   1. We must believe that God is hearing our prayer (He 11:6b).
   2. Let us exercise the faith we have and not be troubled by faith that we do not have—for God will help us (Mk 9:24).
D. We must pray with *humble hearts*.
   1. We should recognize that it is not we who save; it is the name of Jesus by which we pray that saves.
E. We must pray according to *God's will* (1Jn 5:14-15).
   1. When we pray for the salvation of souls and workers for the harvest, we can know that we are praying according to God's will.
F. We must *persevere* in prayer until the answer comes.
   1. Like the persistent widow in our text (Lk 18:5-7).
   2. If we will persevere in prayer for the lost, God will hear our prayers, advance His kingdom, and save the lost.

Conclusion and Altar Call

1. Psalms 40:1: "I waited patiently for the LORD; he turned to me and heard my cry."
2. Come now; let's commit ourselves to pray for the lost and for workers in the harvest.

[MO]

77 Prayer and God's Mission

Sermon in a Sentence: Prayer is essential in fulfilling God's mission.
Sermon Purpose: That God's people will commit to praying regularly for God's mission.
Text: Luke 3:21-22; 4:1-2

Introduction
1. Jesus came into the world to accomplish His Father's mission of redeeming lost humanity.
    a. Jesus: "For the Son of Man is come to…" (Lk 19:10).
    b. Again: "I have come to do your will, O God" (He 10:7).
    c. Fulfilling God's mission cost Jesus His life (Mt 26:42).
2. Prayer was at the heart of Jesus' missionary strategy.
3. Our texts are two examples of Jesus praying:
    a. Luke 3:21-22: He prayed as He began His ministry.
    b. Lk 4:1-2: He prayed before He went into the wilderness to be tempted by the devil.
4. This message: "Prayer and God's Mission"

I. JESUS SET THE EXAMPLE OF PRAYER
A. In Scripture, there are many examples of Jesus praying.
   1. Our texts are but two examples; there are many more.
   2. For example: Lk 6:12; Lk 9:18; Lk 22:39-41
B. Jesus did not begin His ministry until He had prayed.
   1. He prayed at His baptism (Lk 3:21).
   2. He prayed and fasted for 40 days and nights (Lk 4:1-2).
C. Throughout Jesus' ministry, Satan tried to block Him from completing His mission.
   1. However, because Jesus prayed, He won every battle with Satan and his demons.
      a. Our text is one example (Lk 4:1-2).
   2. Jesus overcame demons in the power of the Holy Spirit (Mt 12:28)—and He remained full of the Spirit through prayer (Lk 3:21-22).

II. WE MUST FOLLOW JESUS' EXAMPLE AND SPEND MORE TIME IN PRAYER
A. Prayer is essential…
   1. …if we seek to live successful lives.
   2. …if we want to accomplish the Great Commission.
B. Prayer is a powerful missionary tool:

    1. Thru prayer, we receive *power to overcome* the enemy.
        a. The devil does not fear our knowledge or celebrity.
        b. He rather fears those who seek God in prayer.
    2. Thru prayer, we receive *power to witness* (Ac 1:8).
    3. Thru prayer, we have the *power to open closed doors* (Col 4:3).
  C. If we really want to see ourselves effectively fulfilling the mission of God, we must kneel down and pray.

III. OUR CHURCHES MUST BECOME HOUSES OF PRAYER
  A. Jesus wants His church to be a "house of prayer for all nations" (Read Mk 11:15-17).
  B. We must lead our churches into missional prayer.
    1. We must schedule regular times of prayer.
    2. For example, daily early morning prayer meetings.
  C. When you gather to pray, intercede for the following:
    1. Pray that people will be hungry for the word of God.
    2. Pray that the Spirit will move in the church.
    3. Pray that people will commit themselves to God's mission.
    4. Pray that God will intervene in people's lives.
    5. Pray that people will be delivered from demons and from drug addictions.
    6. Pray that broken lives and broken homes will be restored.
    7. Pray that God's mission will be accomplished.
  D. If we will pray, God will answer.
    1. "This is what the Lord says, he who made the earth, the Lord who formed it and established it—the Lord is his name: 'Call to me and I will answer you and tell you great and unsearchable things you do not know'" (Je 33:2-3).

Conclusion and Altar Call
  1. Prayer a powerful tool to be used in accomplishing God's mission.
  2. Come now, be filled with the Spirit, and commit yourself to regular missional prayer.

[BALR]

78 Praying for the Lost

Sermon in a Sentence: We must reinforce the work of reaching the lost around the world with our prayers.

Sermon Purpose: That Christians will commit themselves to praying for the work of missions.

Text: Matthew 24:14

Introduction

1. In our text, Jesus tells us what must happen before the end of the age comes.
   a. The gospel must preached in the whole *world* as a witness to every *nation*. (See also Mk 13:10.)
   b. "World" refers to places; "nations" refers to peoples.
   c. This is the great task of the church.
2. This great work must be undergirded by prayer.
3. In this message we will look at three commands of Jesus in the gospel of Matthew.
4. We will then discuss how we can help fulfill those commands with our prayers.

I. PRAY THAT GOD WILL SEND OUT WORKERS

A. Read Matthew 9:35-38 and note the following:
   1. Jesus went into the towns and villages proclaiming the good news and healing the sick (v.35).
   2. He saw the people and was moved with compassion.
   3. Lost people are like sheep without a shepherd.
B. He calls on His disciples to pray for workers...
   1. ...because the need is so great (v.37).
   2. ...because laborers are so few (v.37).
   3. ...because God will answer our prayer (1Jn 5:14-15).
C. Let's pray that God will send out workers.

II. PRAY THAT THE WORKERS' MESSAGE WILL INCLUDE BOTH PROCLAMATION AND DEMONSTRATION

A. Read Matthew 10:7-8 and note the following:
   1. Jesus sent out the twelve (v.5).
   2. Like Jesus' ministry, their ministry included both proclamation and demonstration.
      a. Illus: Jesus' ministry: (Read Mt 9:35.)
      b. Illus: Their ministry: (Read Mt 10:7-8.)
B. Let's pray that workers will faithfully proclaim the gospel.

1. That they will call people to surrender to the rule of God (v.7).
2. That the people will "repent and believe the good news!" (Mk 1:15).
C. Let's pray that the workers will powerfully demonstrate the power of God's kingdom.
1. They must expect God's supernatural working (v.8).
2. Illus: This is what the workers did in the book of Acts (Ac 4:30-31; 5:12).
3. This has been a hallmark of Pentecostal missions from the beginning.

III. PRAY THAT THE NATIONS WILL BE DISCIPLED
A. Read Matthew 28:18-20 and note the following:
 1. Here, Jesus is issuing His "Great Commission."
 2. He wants disciples, not just converts.
 3. A disciple is a learner who seeks to fully follow Christ.
B. Let's pray that the nations will be discipled.
 1. First, let's pray that some will go.
   a, Pray that they will clearly understand their task.
     1) To preach the gospel to all nations (Mk 16:15).
     2) To proclaim repentance and forgiveness of sins (Lk 24:49).
     3) To baptized them and teach them to obey everything Jesus commands (Mt 28:20).
   b. Pray that the Holy Spirit will enable them (Ac 1:8).
 2. Next, let's pray that those who do not go will become faithful senders (Ro 10:15).
   a. Pray that they too will clearly understand their task.
     1) To provide financial support.
     2) To provide emotional support.
     3) To provide prayer support.
   b. Pray that the Holy Spirit will inspire and use them.

Conclusion and Altar Call
1. The whole church must participate in reaching the lost.
2. One way we participate is through prayer.
3. Let's all come and commit ourselves to pray for the lost.

[DS]

79 Advance God's Kingdom Through Prayer

Sermon in a Sentence: Prayer will open the door for Spirit-empowered proclamation of the gospel.
Sermon Purpose: That God's people will seek God for a fresh outpouring of the Spirit and commit themselves to ongoing missional prayer.
Text: Acts 10:1-2; 9
Introduction
1. Briefly tell the story of Peter and Cornelius, emphasizing the role of prayer in opening the door of faith to the Gentiles (Ac 10:1-11:18).
2. Jesus taught us to pray "your kingdom come, your will be done on earth as it is in heaven" (Mt 6:10).
    a. God's kingdom comes when men and women are moved by the Holy Spirit and respond in faith to the gospel.
    b. Praying for God's will to be done includes praying for the gospel to go forth, for people to be saved, and for laborers to be filled with the Spirit and join the harvest.
3. In this sermon, we will look at the story of Peter and Cornelius.
    a. We will see how prayer contributed to God's kingdom coming to the household of Cornelius.
    b. We will learn some valuable lessons for today.

In the story of Peter and Cornelius…
I. PRAYER PROVIDED A SETTING FOR GOD TO SPEAK
A. As Cornelius prayed, God gave him a vision (vv.1-8).
   1. He was a man who "prayed to God regularly" (Ac 10:2).
   2. While in prayer, God gave him a vision (vv.3, 30).
      a. Describe Cornelius' vision (vv.3-5).
      b. The angel said, "Send men to Joppa to fetch Peter."
B. Peter also prayed—and God also spoke to him.
   1. Describe Peter's vision (vv.9-16).
   2. At that exact moment the men arrive from Joppa (v.17).
   3. The Spirit told Peter, "Do not hesitate to go with them, for I have sent them" (v.20).
C. Prayer will do the same for us today.
   1. It will provided the setting for God to speak to us and guide us in the mission.
   2. We must commit to consistent Spirit-anointed prayer.

In the story of Peter and Cornelius…
II. PRAYER OPENED A NEW DOOR FOR THE PROCLAMATION OF THE GOSPEL
   A. As Cornelius prayed, his heart was opened to God.
      1. Because of this, he at once sent messengers to Peter (v.8).
      2. In doing this, Cornelius disregarded long-standing cultural prejudices between the Gentiles and Jews (vv.33-34).
         a. Cornelius was a Gentile; Peter was a Jew.
         b. Jews and Gentiles did not mix (10:28; 11:2-3).
      3. Cornelius' heart was prepared to receive the gospel.
         a. So, when Peter preached, Cornelius and his household readily received the message.
   B. Peter's heart was also opened through prayer.
      1. God gave him a vision and a word concerning Gentiles: "Do not call anything impure that God has made clean."
      2. Peter later testified, "The Spirit told me to have no hesitation about going…" (11:12).
   C. The Spirit thus opened a new door for the proclamation of the gospel.
      1. He will do the same for us today—if we will pray.
      2. And if we will hear and obey the Spirit's voice.

In the story of Peter and Cornelius…
III. PRAYER PREPARED THE WAY FOR AN OUTPOURING OF THE HOLY SPIRIT
   A. As Peter preached, the people believed, and the Spirit was poured out (10:44-46).
      1. Like on the Day of Pentecost (Ac 11:15; 2:1-4).
      2. This outpouring of the Spirit prepared these Gentile converts for Spirit-empowered witness (Ac 1:8).
      3. It all began with prayer.
   B. God will do the same for us today—if we will pray.
      1. He will pour out His Spirit on us.
      2. He will empower us to win the lost, plant churches, and send missionaries to the nations.

Conclusion and Altar Call
   1. Come, let's seek God for a fresh outpouring of the Spirit.
   2. Let's pray that God's Spirit will open hearts to go, proclaim, and receive the gospel.

[NS]

80 Prayer and Mission Connection

Sermon in a Sentence: Spirit-empowered prayer increases the impact of our missions work.

Sermon Purpose: That God's people will understand the relationship between prayer, missions, and the Holy Spirit, and that they will commit themselves to Spirit-empowered prayer for missions.

Texts: Acts 4:31; 13:1-3

Introduction
1. Acts is filled with examples of people praying in the power of the Spirit resulting in the rapid expansion of the gospel.
   a. Our two texts demonstrate the close relationship between prayer, missions, and the Holy Spirit.
   b. They are examples of how we should do missions today.
2. This message: "Prayer and Mission Connection"
   a. We will examine the close connection between prayer, the Holy Spirit, and missions.

I. NOTE THE CONNECTION BETWEEN PRAYER AND THE WORK OF THE SPIRIT

- *Two powerful truths about prayer and the Holy Spirit:*

A. Truth #1: *The work of the Spirit increases prayer.*
   1. When the Spirit of God moves on our spirits, He creates in us a desire to praye\ (Ro 15:30; Jude 20).
   2. The Holy Spirit also gives us power to pray.
      a. He knows no limitations.
      b. We therefore need His help in prayer (Ze 4:6).
   3. When we do not know how to pray (or what to pray for) the Holy Spirit will direct our prayers (Ro 8:26-27).
   4. The Spirit will increase and deepen the level of prevailing prayer (1Co 14:2, 12, 39-40).

B. Truth #2: *Prayer increases the work of the Spirit.*
   1. Prayer opens the door for the work of the Spirit.
      a. Note the phrase *"after they had prayed,* the place where they were meeting was shaken..." (Ac 4:31).
      b. After the apostles laid hands on the seven and prayed, the Spirit moved, and "the word of God spread...and the number of disciples increased rapidly" (Ac 6:6-7)
   2. Prayer brings revival and deepens the Spirit's move.

a. Illus: When the church in Antioch prayed the Spirit moved and said "Set apart for me Barnabas and Saul for the work to which I have called them" (Ac 13:2).

II. NOTE THE CONNECTION BETWEEN SPIRIT-EMPOWERED PRAYER AND MISSIONS

- *Two powerful truths about Spirit-empowered prayer and missions:*

A. Truth #1: *Spirit-empowered prayer increases missions.*
   1. Prayer results in the Spirit's outpouring that, in turn, results in powerful declaration of the gospel.
      a. Peter was filled with the Spirit and boldly proclaimed Christ (Ac 4:8-12).
      b. After the Church prayed, the Spirit came and gave them boldness to preach (Ac 4:23-4, 31, 33).
   2. Paul asked the church to pray for him to have boldness in preaching the gospel (Ro 15:30; 2Th 3:1).
B. Truth #2: *Missions increases the need for Spirit-empowered prayer.*
   1. Individual Christians need to pray for missions.
      a. Every believer should participate in the spread of the gospel through Spirit-empowered prayer (Mt 9:38).
      b. We must allow the Spirit to empower and guide our prayers (Ro 8:26-27).
   2. Christians need to pray together for missions.
      a. We must pray from house to house (Ac 2:42).
      b. We must gather for prayer in the church (2:46; 3:1).
      c. If we will do this, we can anticipate the same results as we read about in Acts.

Conclusion and Altar Call

1. Come, let's pray that the Spirit will fill us and gives us boldness to do God's work.
2. And let's commit ourselves to prayer for missions.

[NS]

81 How to Pray for Your Missionaries

Sermon in a Sentence: Paul tells us how to pray for missionaries.
Sermon Purpose: That God's people will commit themselves to consistent, effective prayer for their missionaries.
Text: Romans 15:30-32
Introduction
1. Paul was a missionary to unreached people and places.
2. He recognized the need for believers to join him in the mission by praying for him.
3. In this message, we will examine several New Testament passages where Paul requested prayer.
4. In these passages, Paul answered three key questions about how to effectively pray for missionaries:

I. **WHY SHOULD WE PRAY FOR MISSIONARIES?**
   A. In his letter to the Romans, Paul revealed that through prayer we can join our missionaries in their work.
      1. He wrote them to prepare them for his upcoming visit to Rome (Ro 1:10-11).
      2. His reason for coming was that they might help him to go on to Spain to preach the gospel there (15:24, 28).
      3. He asked them "to join me in my struggle by praying to God for me" (v.30).
   B. Prayer is a way that every believer can join in obediently participating in the Great Commission.
      1. God stands ready to answer our prayers for missionaries.
      2. However, we must commit ourselves to pray.

II. **WHEN WE PRAY FOR MISSIONARIES, WHAT SHOULD WE PRAY FOR?** (In his letters, Paul reveals three strategic themes that can help guide us in our prayers for missionaries:)
   A. First, we should pray that missionaries will be protected and that obstacles to the gospel will be removed.
      1. He asked the Romans, "Pray that I may be rescued from the unbelievers in Judea and that my service in Jerusalem may be acceptable to the saints there" (Ro 15:31-32).
      2. He also asked the church in Thessalonica for prayer:
         a. "Pray for us that the message of the Lord may spread rapidly and be honored..." (2Th 3:1).

        b. He added, "And pray that we may be delivered from wicked and evil men" (v.2).
   B. Second, we should pray that doors will opened for opportunities to present the gospel.
        1. Paul told the Colossians to "continue steadfastly in prayer…" (4:2 ESV).
        2. He added, "At the same time, pray also for us, that God may open to us a door for the word, to declare the mystery of Christ (vv.1, 3).
        3. He talked about open doors in other places (Read 1Co 16:9 and 2Co 2:12).
        4. We must pray for those places and peoples that are closed to the gospel. (Cite some examples.)
   C. Third, we should pray that the Holy Spirit will enable missionaries to speak with power and boldness:
        1. Paul told the Ephesians to pray "at all times in the Spirit, with all prayer and supplication…and also for me, that words may be given to me in opening my mouth boldly to proclaim the mystery of the gospel (Ep 6:18-19),
   D. From Paul's three requests, we learn the following:
        1. We should pray for personal needs of missionaries.
        2. However, we should focus our prayers on the mission they were sent to accomplish.
        3. When the mission is accomplished, any sacrifice we may have made will be worth it.
        4. We must never think that the mission will be accomplished without prayer.

III. HOW CAN WE PRAY EFFECTIVELY FOR MISSIONS?
   A. Ask God to fill you with His Spirit (Luke 11:1, 9-13).
        1. If you want to effectively pray for missionaries, seek to remain full of the Spirit.
        2. The Spirit will "help us in our weakness" (Ro 8:26a).
   B. Pray often in the Spirit.
        1. "Pray at all times in the Spirit" (Ep 6:18).
        2. Allow Him to intercede through you (Ro 8:26b-27).

Conclusion and Altar Call
Will you join in the mission of God by committing to pray for missionaries?   [MRT]

82 Opening Prayers

Sermon in a Sentence: We must pray that God will open the way for effective gospel witness.
Sermon Purpose: To encourage God's people to pray for the work of evangelism and mission.
Text: Acts 4:31
Introduction
1. In our text, the disciples offered a missionary prayer.
2. They asked God to empower them—and embolden them—to proclaim Jesus to the lost in the power of the Holy Spirit.
3. Every stage of kingdom advance is founded on prayer.
4. Only God can make the way. Therefore, as we go, we must pray "opening prayers."
5. This message: Three ways we can pray "opening prayers."

I. WE MUST PRAY FOR OPEN DOORS
A. It is better to walk through a door God has opened than to try to force our way through one that is closed and locked.
B. Satan seeks to keep doors closed.
  1. He blinds the eyes of unbelievers (2Co 4:4).
  2. He hinders us from going to the work (1Th 2:18).
C. Jesus, however, is the "Lord of the Open Door."
  1. He has all authority in heaven and earth (Mt 28:18).
  2. He opens and closes doors (Re 3:8).
  3. Illus: He opened doors for Paul (1Co 16:9; 2Co 2:12).
D. We must pray for open doors:
  1. Paul often asked for prayer that God would open doors.
  2. Once while in prison (Col 4:3).

II. WE MUST PRAY FOR OPEN MOUTHS
A. Once God opens the door, we must walk through it, open our mouths, and proclaim the good news.
  1. This is how the disciples prayed in our text (Ac 4:28-31).
B. We too must pray that we will be ready to preach the gospel when the opportunities come.
  1. Pray that God will give us words (Ep 6:19).
  2. Pray that God will fill us with the Holy Spirit and empower our words (Ac 1:8; 4:31, 33).

- C. Then, we will be able to preach with power and conviction (1Th 1:5).
    1. That is, with "words taught by the Spirit" (1Co 2:13).
    2. The Spirit will make our words effective (Ac 14:1).
    3. None of us really knows how to preach; we need our mouths to be opened by God.
- D. We must therefore pray that we may "speak the word with great boldness" (Ac 4:29).
    1. God will answer our prayer (Ac 4:31a).
    2. He will open our mouths to speak with power:
        - a. He did it with the apostles (Ac 4:31, 33).
        - b. He did it with Stephen (Ac 6:10).
        - c. He will do it for us today!

III. WE MUST PRAY FOR OPEN HEARTS
- A. As we go to preach the gospel, we must pray that God will open the hearts of those who hear.
- B. Paul asked people to pray to this end (2Th 3:1).
- C. If we will pray, the Spirit will open people's hearts to receive the good news.
    1. Jesus opened the hearts of the disciples on the Road to Emmaus (Lk 24:31).
    2. He further opened the disciples' hearts to understand the Scriptures (24:27, 45).
    3. The Spirit opened Lydia's heart to the gospel (Ac 16:14).
    4. The Spirit will open unbelievers' hearts (1Co 14:24-25).
- D. But we must pray for open hearts.

Conclusion and Altar Call
1. Come and commit yourself to pray for open doors, open mouths, and open hearts.
2. Then join me in walking through those open doors.

[PW]

83 Prayer and the Missionary Task

Sermon in a sentence: If we will seek the Lord in prayer, the Spirit will show us when and how to send missionaries.

Sermon Purpose: To challenge the church to pray and send missionaries in a truly Spirit-directed manner.

Text: Acts 13:1-4

Introduction
1. In Acts, the Holy Spirit is the Director of Missions.
2. We have an example of this in Acts 13:1-4.
3. With this event, the church in Acts prayerfully launches its mission to "the ends of the earth" (Acts 1:8).
4. From this story, we learn four important missionary lessons:

I. THE IMPETUS FOR MISSION: THE HOLY SPIRIT
A. The Holy Spirit is driving force behind all true missions.
  1. He is the one who compels us to go and tell others.
  2. Illus: In our text, after they had sought the Lord, the Holy Spirit ordered, "Set apart for me Barnabas and Saul for the work to which I have called them" (Ac 13:2).
  3 They were "sent on their way by the Holy Spirit" (v.4).
B. The Holy Spirit always disturbs the status-quo.
  1. He leads to the next phase of church growth and advance.
  2. He pushes us to missions beyond our "comfort zones."
C. In Acts, we see the Holy Spirit directing missions in 3 ree ways:
  1. The Holy Spirit *initiates mission.*
    a. After receiving the Spirit at Pentecost, Peter immediately began to declare Christ to the lost (Ac 2:4, 14, 41).
    b. In Antioch, the Spirit initiated Paul and Barnabas' first missionary journey (Ac 13:1-4).
  2. The Holy Spirit *guides mission.*
    a. Philip was guided by the Spirit to go to the Ethiopian nobleman (Ac 8:29).
    b. Step-by-step the Holy Spirit guided Paul and his missionary colleagues into Europe (Ac 16:6-10).
  3. The Holy Spirit *universalizes mission.*
    a. The Holy Spirit pushed Peter across the wide chasm between Jew and Gentile (Ac 10:1-48; 11:12).
    b. Opened the door for missions to the "ends of the earth."

II. THE PERSONNEL FOR MISSION: BARNABAS AND SAUL
   A. The Holy Spirit prepares the right people for mission.
   B. Barnabas and Saul had proved themselves through faithful service in the Antioch church (11:22-26; 13:1).
      1. They had gained the confidence of the people (11:30).
   C. The experience that Barnabas and Saul had gained prepared them for more effective missionary work.

III. THE TIMING OF MISSION: WAITING ON GOD
   A. Saul had known from the time of his conversion that he was called to go to the Gentiles (Ac 9:15-16; 22:21; 26:14-18).
      1. Years of preparation had passed since Saul's conversion.
      2. This day came as no surprise to Barnabas and Saul (v.2).
      3. It was a moment they had been anticipating.
   B. Waiting is sometimes part of preparation for missions.
      1. Jesus ordered His disciples to wait for Pentecost (Ac 1:4).
      2. While waiting, Paul and Barnabas involved themselves in prayer and local church ministry (Ac 11:26).
      3. While waiting for your moment, continue seeking God and keep busy serving Him in every way you can.

IV. THE SUPPORT OF MISSION: THE CHURCH
   A Not only were the two missionaries sent out by the Spirit, they were also sent out by the church (v.3).
   B. This is the proper way to deploy missionaries to the work:
      1. God calls, then the church recognises their calling and gifts.
      2. Then, as we continue in prayer, the Spirit chooses and reveals the right moment for them to go to the field.
      3. Then the church immediately moves into action (Mk 4:29).
   C. Guidelines and lessons learned:
      1. We should pray much, looking to God to identify those whom He has chosen for special service.
      2. We should anticipate moments when the Holy Spirit speaks to us and shows us those He has set apart for the ministry.
      3. We should encourage and support those whom God calls.

Conclusion and Altar Call
   1. Come and commit yourself to God and His mission.
   2. Commit yourself to faithful prayer for missions.

[PW]

84 The Mercy Prayer

Sermon in a Sentence: As we pray God's mercy on others, He changes us and opens doors of witness.

Sermon Purpose: That God's people will repent of their callousness and begin to pray God's mercy on others.

Texts: Luke 6:27-36

Introduction
1. Jesus has commissioned us to take the gospel into all the world (Mk 16:15-16).
    a. He sometimes sends us to those who hate us and seek to harm us (Mt 10:16).
    b. Illus: Think of a person (or a people) who hate you, who seek to harm you, and who you find hard to love.
2. In our Scripture reading, Jesus tells us what to do with such people. (Three key statements:)
    a. "Love your enemies" (vv. 27, 35).
    b. "Pray for those who mistreat you" (v.28).
    c. "Be merciful, just as your Father is merciful" (v.36).
3. Our witness must communicate Jesus' spirit of mercy (v.28).
4. This message: How we can develop such a loving spirit by praying the "Mercy Prayer."

I. WHAT IS THE "MERCY PRAYER"?
A. The Mercy Prayer is our sincere prayer to God that He will bless others—even those we consider enemies.
   1. It is not a formula, but the spirit of mercy expressed in word and action.
   2. The Mercy Prayer goes like this: *Lord, flood the one I am thinking of with your mercy; meet their every need as you see their need, and draw them close to Yourself.*
B. To truly pray this Mercy Prayer we must understand the biblical meaning of mercy.
   1. Mercy is God's supply system for every need.
   2. It is God kindness and compassion reaching out to others.
   3. It is a willingness to suffer with others and share in their pain so that they may be healed and restored.
   4. It accepts people as they, cherishing and nourishing them.
   5. It is one of the most important aspects of faith and mission.
C. When we are tempted to be angry or bitter at others, we can pray the Mercy Prayer.

1. Illus: Jesus prayed such a mercy prayer (Lk 23:34).
2. Illus: Stephen also prayed a mercy prayer (Ac 7:60).

II. WHY MUST WE LEARN TO PRAY THE "MERCY PRAYER"? (Four compelling reasons:)
A. Because Jesus demands that we pray for our enemies (v.28).
B. Because God loves all people as seeks their salvation.
   1. He is "not willing that any should perish..." (2Pe 3:9).
   2. When we pray the Mercy Prayer, we are doing the will of God by seeking His blessing on the other.
C. Because such praying will change us and help prepare us to share Christ with all.
   1. As we pray the Mercy Prayer, we overcome our fault-finding, critical spirit—casting it out.
   2. We put ourselves in a position to *be* merciful as God himself is merciful.
   3. We find our hearts being changed and warmed to the ones we seek to reach.
D. Because it will help to open the hearts of those we seek to reach.
   1. As they sense our mercy-filled hearts, their hearts are also melted and opened.

III. HOW CAN WE LEARN TO PRAY THE "MERCY PRAYER"?
A. We can begin by repenting.
   1. We must repent of our callousness toward others.
B. We can commit to obey Jesus and follow His example.
   1. We must commit ourselves to God's mission
   2. We must commit to love as He loves.
C. We must begin today.

Conclusion and Altar Call
1. Come, let's commit to God's mission.
2. Together let's pray: *Lord, flood that one with your mercies; meet their every need as you see it; draw them close to Yourself.*

[DB]

This message was inspired by Rex Andrews' teaching, "The Will of God is Mercy" in his book, *What the Bible Teaches about Mercy*.

85   A Prayer for the Nations

Sermon in a Sentence: God calls us to glorify Him by praying for the nations.
Sermon Purpose: That God's people will begin to pray, asking God to bless the nations.
Text: Psalm 67:1-7
Introduction
1. There is a proverb that says, "Dynamite comes in small packages" (yet it can cause a big explosion!)
2. Psalm 67 is much like a stick of dynamite.
   a. It is one of the shortest chapters in the Bible—7 verses.
   b. Yet, it carries an explosive message.
3. It is a powerful prayer for the nations.
   a. It is a prayer we should i.
   b. It contains three powerful insights into missional prayer:

I. IT IS GOOD TO ASK FOR GOD'S BLESSING
   A. Throughout Scripture, God invites us to ask for His blessings.
      1. He does this in our text (Read vv.1, 6-7a)
      2. In the Lord's Prayer, Jesus instructs us to ask, "Give us this day or daily bread…" (Mt 6:11; see also Jn 16:24).
      3. James: "You do not have, because you do not ask" (4:2).
   B. When we ask, we must be careful that our motives are right.
      1. James qualifies his promise: "When you ask, you do not receive, *because you ask with wrong motives,* that you may spend what you get on your pleasures" (Ja 4:3).
      2. Unfortunately, many Christians spend most of their prayer time asking only for personal blessing.
      3. Illus: Africa is filled with so-called "prophets" promising God's blessings on those who will give to their ministries.
   C. Do you have a need?
      1. You can approach God's throne with boldness "and find grace to help [you in your] time of need" (He 4:16).
      2. Let's take a few moments and present our needs to God.

II. IT IS IMPORTANT TO KNOW WHY GOD BLESSES US
   A. After asking for God's blessing, the Psalmist explains why he wants His blessing:
      1. He asks God to bless him so that God's "ways may be known on earth, [His] salvation among all nations" (v.2).

B. God is on a mission to bless the nations, and He graciously invites us to join Him in that mission.
  1. God's mission is to bless all nations through the seed of Abraham—that is, through Jesus (Ge 12:3b; cf. Ga 3:16).
  2. Jesus commands us to go to all nations (Mt 28:19-20).
  3. He also instructs us to pray for laborers (Mt 9:37-38).
  4. God blesses us *that we may bless the nations!*
C. Our text suggests four ways we should pray for the nations:
  1. Pray that His "ways may be known on earth," and His "salvation among all nations" (v.2).
  2. Pray that the nations may "be glad and sing for joy" (v.4).
  3. Pray that the land will yield a great harvest of souls (v.6).
  4. Pray that "all the ends of the earth" will fear God (v.7).
D. Let's take a moment and pray for the nations right now.

III. WE MUST DO ALL FOR GOD'S GLORY
A. Listen how the Psalmist glorifies God:
  1. v.3: "May the peoples praise you, O God; may all the peoples praise you." (Again in v.5)
  2. v.4: "…for you rule the peoples justly and guide the nations of the earth."
  3. The Psalmist wants the nations to be saved so they can glorify God.
B. God receives glory when the nations praise Him.
  1. The ultimate goal of missions is that God may be glorified among all peoples in all the earth.
  2. Illus: We will one day see the nations praising God in heaven. (Read Re 7:9-10).
B. Until that time, we must live to glorify God.
  1. We should glorify God with our lives (1Co 10:31).
  2. We should glorify God with our prayers.
  3. We must pray that His "kingdom come [and His] will be done" among all the peoples of the earth (Mt 6:10).

Conclusion and Altar Call
  1. Let's all commit ourselves to living in such a way that our lives and prayers bless the nations and glorify God.
  2. We do this by living, giving, and praying for God's glory.

[DRM]

86 How to Pray for the Lost

Sermon in a Sentence: We must intercede for the lost until the answer comes.
Sermon Purpose: That God's people will commit themselves to faithful, persistent intercession for the lost.
Text: Matthew 9:35-38
Introduction
1. Briefly tell the story of Jesus' Galilean ministry (Mt 9:1-38).
2. In our text, Jesus calls on us to intercede for the harvest.
3. This message: "How to Pray for the Lost." (Five directives:)

I. PRAY FROM A HEART OF COMPASSION
   A. As Jesus ministered to the people, He saw their need.
      1. As a result, He was moved with compassion (Mt 9:38).
      2. This motivated Him to ask for prayer on their behalf.
   B. Paul was also moved with compassion (Ro 9:1-4).
      1. He had "great sorrow" and "unceasing anguish" of heart for His people, the Jews (vv.2-3).
      2. This moved him to pray for them (Ro 10:1).
   C. We must allow the Spirit to move us with compassion to intercede for the lost (Ro 5:5).

II. PRAY WITH UNDERSTANDING
   A. We must pray with a *biblical understanding* of humanity's utter lostness without Christ:
      1. They are lost and bound for an eternal hell (2Th 1:7-9).
      2. Only Christ can save them (Jn 14:6; Ac 4:12; 1Ti 2:5).
   B. We must pray with a *practical* understanding of what must be done to reach them (Ro 10:13-15).
      1. Some must go and preach the gospel (Mk 16:15).
      2. Others must send (Ro 10:15).
      3. All must pray (Mt 9:38).
   C. We must pray with a *spiritual understanding* of the role of prayer in advancing the gospel to the nations.
      1. Prayer opens hearts (2Th 3:1).
      2. Prayer opens doors (Col 4:3).
      3. Prayer moves the hand of God (Ac 4:30-31).

III. PRAY IN FAITH
   A. Faith is the key to God's hearing and answering our prayers.

1. "Without faith it is impossible to please God" (He 11:6),
2. Prayer without faith is weak and feeble (Ja 1:6-7).
3. But, prayer with faith can move mountains (Mk 11:23-24).
B. When you pray for the lost…
1. Believe God is hearing your prayer.
2. Believe God is answering your prayer.
3. Act on your belief.

IV. PRAY IN THE SPIRIT
A. Many times, we do not know how to pray for a given situation.
B. At such times the Spirit will come to our rescue (Ro 8:26).
C. Here's how the Spirit will help us to pray for the lost:
1. He will *inspire* us to pray to pray for the lost.
2. He will pray *through us* interceding for the lost.
    a. Sometimes in our own language.
    b. Sometimes in a God-given language (v.26; 1Co 14:14).
3. He will pray *according to the will of God* (v.27).
D. Such prayer has great power (1Jn 5:14-15).

V. NEVER STOP PRAYING
A. We must persevere in prayer until the answer comes.
1. Paul exhorts us to "be persistent in prayer" (Ro 12:12), and to "never stop praying" (1Th 5:17).
2. Jesus also taught us about persistent prayer (Lk 18:1-8).
B. We must never stop praying…
1. …for an outpouring of the Spirit.
2. …for our lost family and friends.
3. …for the various peoples and tribes in our country.
4. …for unreached peoples and places throughout Africa.

Conclusion and Altar Call
1. We must learn to intercede for the lost with compassion, with understanding, in faith, and in the power of the Spirit. And we must never stop praying until the answer comes.
2. Come now, commit yourself to faithful, persistent intercession for the lost.

[DRM]

87 Pray for the Harvest

Sermon in a Sentence: It is the privilege and responsibility of every believer to pray for the harvest.

Sermon Purpose: That believers will be filled with the Spirit and commit themselves to praying for the harvest according to Jesus' instructions.

Text: Matthew 9:35-38; Luke 10:1-2

Introduction
1. Jesus' love for the lost moved Him to pray for them.
2. In our two Scripture passages, Jesus called on His disciples to join Him in prayer for the lost.
   a. Once, at the beginning of His ministry—as He was going from place to place ministering to the multitudes (Mt 9)
   b. Another time—when He was sending the seventy to do the same (Lk 10).
   c. On both occasions, He said, "The harvest is plentiful, but the laborers are few. Therefore pray earnestly to the Lord of the harvest to send out laborers into his harvest" (ESV).
4. Jesus still looks on the fields, and He still intercedes for them.
   a. He wants us to join Him in this spiritual ministry.
5. In this message, we will look closely at these two passages.
   a. We will answer three questions about prayer for the harvest:

I. WHY SHOULD WE PRAY FOR THE HARVEST?
A. Our two texts identify three reasons we must pray:
   1. We should pray because people are *"harassed and helpless,* like sheep without a shepherd."
      a. Jesus saw the multitudes and was moved,
      b. He still sees hurting people—and so must we.
   2. We should pray because *"the harvest is plentiful."*
      a. There are millions who are lost—"multitudes."
      b. They are ready to be harvested. (Read Jn 4:35)
      c. Our neighbors and the nations need the gospel.
   3. We should pray because *"the labors are few."*
      a. The task is greater than the work force.
      b. Jesus continues to call for labors (Mt 20:1-6)
      c. The Father is seeking laborers (Is 6:8)
B. Two more reasons we must pray:

1. We must pray because our affections are shaped by our prayers.
    a. That is, we come to love what we pray for.
2. We must pray because prayer for the harvest is essential for developing a missional church.

II. HOW SHOULD WE PRAY FOR THE HARVEST?
A. We must pray *earnestly* for the harvest.
   1. "Therefore pray earnestly…" (Mt 9:38 ESV)
B. We must pray *regularly* for the harvest.
   1. We should "always pray" and "never give up" (Lk 18:1)
   2. We must "devote ourselves to prayer" (Col 4:2-3).
C. We must pray *in the Spirit*.
   1. Paul: "Pray in the Spirit on all occasions with all kinds of prayers" (Ep 6:18).
   2. And we must "be alert and always keep on praying."
D. We must pray *with (and for) boldness*
   1. The early church prayed for boldness (Ac 4:29-31).
   2. Paul asked prayer for boldness (Ep 6:19-20).
   3. God will give us boldness in prayer (He 4:16).

III. WHAT SHOULD WE PRAY FOR THE HARVEST?
A. We should pray for Christians to be *responsive* to the call to missions (Mt 9:38).
B. We must pray for labors to be *empowered* by the Spirit so they can be effective in missions (Jn 20:21-22; Ac 1:8).
C. We must pray for *success* in the harvest.
   1. That "the threshing floors will be filled with grain; the vats will overflow with new wine and oil" (Jl 2:24).
   2. Illus: Like the disciples' great catch of fish (Jn 21:4-6).

Conclusion and Altar Call:
1. Let's pray that the Lord of the Harvest will send labors into His harvest.
2. Come, be filled with the Spirit so you too can be part of the harvest.

[NS]

88   Interceding for Our Hometown

Sermon in a sentence: God calls us to intercede for our hometown (city, town, village, or district).
Sermon purpose: That believers commit themselves to prayer for their hometowns.
Text: Genesis 18:20-33
Introduction
1. Our text tells the story of Abraham's intercession for the wicked cities of Sodom and Gomorrah.
2. Sodom and Gomorrah were wicked places
   a. However, Abraham still loved the people who lived there.
   b. He wanted them to know the true and living God.
3. Tell story of Abraham's intercessory prayer (Ge 18:22-33).
4. This story can serve as guide for us to intercede for our hometown (city, village, or district).
5. From this story, we can learn three important about how to best intercede for our hometown:

I. **LIKE ABRAHAM, WE MUST RECOGNIZE THE GRAVE DANGER THE PEOPLE ARE IN**
   A. Abraham was troubled by the people's rebellion against God.
      1. Describe Sodom's sinfulness (Ge 13:13; 18:20; 19:1-13).
      2. He knew the people were lost and in danger of judgment.
      3. We too must realize that our neighbors are lost.
   B. Abraham understood both God's justice and His compassion.
      1. Read vv.24-25 emphasizing the phrase, "Will not the Judge of all the earth do right?" (v.25).
      2. Illus: Moses also understood God's love and compassion and His justice. (Read Nu 14:18)
      3. God will surely forgive and save the penitent; however, He will just as surely judge the impenitent.
   C. God revealed to Abraham His plan to destroy Sodom (18:17).
      1. Abraham was like Jesus, who saw the people's need (Mt 9:38).
      2. Jesus also saw their sure judgment (Mt 23:37-38).
      2. Make no mistake; God will someday judge unrepentant sinners of our city.
   D. Like Sodom, the inhabitants of our city face God's judgment.
      1. They need us to intercede for them as did Abraham.

II. LIKE ABRAHAM, WE MUST LOVE AND IDENTIFY WITH THE CITIZENS OF OUR HOMETOWN

A. Abraham was different from the citizens of Sodom; they were wicked; he was good and righteous.
B. Though he was different from them, Abraham still identified with them.
  1. On his visits to Sodom, he had walked with them and gotten to know and love them.
  2. He saw the people as *his* people and the city as *his* city.
  3. His nephew Lot lived in the city.
C. Like Abraham, we must identify with our city.
  1. We must walk with them and learn to love them.
  2. We must see them as *our* people.
  3. Like Abraham, we have lost relatives in our place.

III. LIKE ABRAHAM INTERCEDED FOR SODOM, WE MUST INTERCEDED FOR OUR HOMETOWN

A. Abraham prayed an "identificational prayer" for the people of Sodom and Gomorrah.
  1. He became one with them and interceded on their behalf.
  2. Illus: He was like Nehemiah who identified with and interceded for rebellious Judah (Ne 1:6).
  3. Illus: Like Paul, who did the same (Ro 9:2-3).
B. Abraham was bold and persistent in his prayer.
  1. Note what the Bible says about Abraham's conversation with God: "The men turned away and went toward Sodom, but Abraham remained standing before the Lord" (v.22); "Abraham approached" God (v.23); "Abraham spoke up again…" (vv.27, 29).
  2. Jesus taught us to persist in prayer (Lk 18:1-8).
  3. God answered Abraham's prayer by delivering the few righteous people in Sodom and Gomorrah (Ge 19:12-16).
C. Like Abraham, we must intercede for our city.
  1. We must love and identify with those around us.
  2. We must persist until the answer comes.
  3. We must know that God will answer our prayer.

Conclusion and Altar Call
1. God is calling us to intercede for our hometown.
2. Come let's pray now. [DRM]

Section 8
Prayer Guides

89 Three Essential Missionary Prayers

Sermon in a Sentence: Let's pray for missionary "goers," "receivers," and "senders."

Sermon Purpose: That Christians join together in praying for three essential elements of missions.

Text: Romans 10:13-15

Introduction
1. In our Scripture reading, Paul answers the question, "What must happen before people can be saved?"
2. He leads the reader through a logical sequence of events.
3. In reverse order, the sequence looks like this: Missionaries are *sent*→ they *preach* the gospel→ the people *hear*→ they *believe*→they *call* on the name of the Lord→ and they are *saved*.
4. These verses can help direct our prayers for missions.
5. They identify three essential missionary prayer emphases:

I. LET US PRAY FOR THOSE WHO GO TO PROCLAIM THE GOSPEL (Read Romans 10:14. Based on this verse...)
A. *Pray* that God will call some to go and proclaim the gospel.
   1. Jesus told us to pray this way. (Read Mt 9:38.)
      - *Pray* that God's Spirit will move on people's hearts and call them as cross-cultural missionaries.
B. *Pray* for those who have said "yes" to God's call and are already preparing to go.
   - *Pray* that God will fill them with His Spirit (Ac 1:8).
   - *Pray* that the Spirit will direct them.
   - *Pray* that they will find faithful supporters.
C. *Pray* for those who are already on the field.
   - *Pray* for their success in ministry.
   - *Pray* for their safety.
   - *Pray* for their provision.

II. LET US PRAY FOR THOSE WHO WILL HEAR THE GOSPEL (Read Romans 10:13-14. Based on these verses...)
A. *Pray* that people will truly *hear* the gospel, believe the message, call on the name of the Lord, and be saved.
   - *Pray* for good soil (Mt 13:8, 23).
   - *Pray* for receptive hearts (Jn 1:12).
   - *Pray* that many will turn to the Lord (Ac 11:21).

B. *Pray* that those who are saved will become true disciples of Christ and grow in Him (Mt 28:19).
- *Pray* that they will faithfully serve the Lord.
- *Pray* that they will not be lead astray (1Co 11:3).
- *Pray* that they will not grow weary (Re 2:3).
- *Pray* that they will quickly become goers and senders.

III. LET US MUST PRAY FOR THOSE WHOSE RESPONSIBILITY IT IS TO SEND WORKERS TO PROCLAIM THE GOSPEL (Read Romans 10:15).
A. Missionaries must be sent—but who sends them?
 1. First, God sends them (Jn 20:21).
 2. Then, the church joins God in His sending mission.
 3. Illus: Note how both the Spirit and the church sent out Barnabas and Saul in Acts 13:1-4.
B. The church sends missionaries by *identifying* them, *commissioning* them, *deploying* them, and then *backing* them with funds, prayers, and emotional support.
C. Based on these truths…
- *Pray* that God will pour out His Spirit on the church.
- *Pray* that the church will catch a missionary vision.
- *Pray* that God will quickly raise up missional leaders.
- *Pray* that God will call from the church missionaries and church planters.
- *Pray* that the church will quickly become a sending church.

Conclusion and Altar Call

Let us commit ourselves to continue to pray for missionary "goers," "receivers," and "senders."

[DRM]

90 A Prayer Guide for Africa

Sermon in a Sentence: Let us pray that God will bless the African church and that, in turn, the African church will bless the nations.
Sermon Purpose: That God's people will spend time in prayer for Africa.
Text: Psalm 68:28, 31-35 (NASB: "Envoys will come out of Egypt; Ethiopia will quickly stretch out her hands to God.")

Introduction
1. Our text is an amazing prophecy about Africa.
2. It says, "Ethiopia (Greek) or Kush (Hebrew) shall quickly stretch out her hands to God" (v.31).
   a. In ancient times, the phrase *Ethiopia* or *Kush* meant Africa south of Egypt.
   b. Today, this region is sometimes called, "Black Africa."
   c. Ethiopia literally means "people with dark faces."
3. This passage can serve as a prayer guide for Africa.
4. Three prayer focuses:

I. PRAY THAT AFRICA WILL QUICKLY STRETCH OUT HER HANDS TO GOD (Read v.31)
   A. This prophecy prompts us to ponder Africa's destiny.
      1. When this prophecy was uttered, the continent of Africa lay in darkness, like the world Isaiah described (Is 60:2).
      2. However, God's glory has shined in Africa (Read vv.2-3).
      3. Africa is now stretching out her hands to the Savior!
   B. Let us now pray that Africa will stretch out her hands to God:
      - *Pray* that Africa will stretch out her hands to God in obedience to the gospel.
      - *Pray* that Africa will stretch out her hands to God in obedience to the Great Commission.

II. PRAY THAT GOD WILL POUR OUT HIS SPIRIT ON THE AFRICAN CHURCH
   A. v. 34: "Ascribe power to God, whose majesty is over Israel, and *whose power is in the skies."*
      1. This prayer directive makes us think about Pentecost.
      2. Ac 2:2: "Suddenly there came from heaven…"
   B. v.35: Awesome is God from his sanctuary; the God of Israel— he is the one who *gives power and strength to his people."*
      1. This declaration reminds us of the purpose of Pentecost.

2. Ac 1:8: "You will receive power… you will be my witnesses…to the ends of the earth."
C. Let us now pray that God will pour out His Spirit on Africa:
- *Pray* that God will pour out His Spirit on the cities of Africa.
- *Pray* that God will pour out His Spirit on rural Africa.
- *Pray* that God will pour out His Spirit on the unreached peoples and places of Africa.
- *Pray* that God will pour out His Spirit on the African church empowering it to preach the gospel with power.

III. PRAY THAT THE AFRICAN CHURCH WILL BLESS THE NATIONS

A. v.32 "O *kingdoms of the earth,* sing to God; sing praises to the Lord, Selah."
1. This injunction provokes us to think about God's mission.
2. It connects with both the destiny of Africa and the purpose of Pentecost.
3. God is pouring out His Spirit in Africa preparing the church to take the gospel to the unreached tribes of Africa and to the ends of the earth.
B. Let us now pray for the church of Africa:
- *Pray* to the Lord of the Harvest that He will raise up cross-cultural missionaries from the African church.
- *Pray* to the Lord of the Harvest that He will raise up church planters to go to the unreached people and places of Africa.
- *Pray* to the Lord of the Harvest that He will raise up missions agencies to recruit, send, and care for African missionaries.
- *Pray* to the Lord of the Harvest that He will raise up millions of Africans who will support missionaries and church planters.

Conclusion and Altar Call
1. Possibly God is calling you.
2. Come, commit yourself to God and His mission.

[DRM]

91 Praying for the Harvest

Sermon in a Sentence: Let's participate in the Great Commission, by praying for the harvest.
Sermon Purpose: That the people will pray together for world harvest.
Text: Matthew 9:35-38
Introduction
1. Jesus left His church with a "Great Commission."
   a. He said, "Go...make disciples of all nations" (Mt 28:18-20).
2. In our text, Jesus saw the harvest field.
   a. The people were "harassed and helpless."
   b. Jesus therefore commands His disciples to "Pray!" (v.38).
3. Today, we will pray for the harvest five ways:

I. LET US PRAY FOR THE HARVEST FORCE (Mt 9:35-38)
A. Jesus gave His disciples specific instructions on prayer:
   1. They were to pray to the "Lord of the Harvest."
   2. They were to pray for "workers to go into His harvest field."
   3. In other words, they were to pray for the Harvest Force.
B. Reaping the harvest requires resources.
   - *Pray* for human resources (people for the harvest).
   - *Pray* for financial resources (money for the harvest).
C. The Harvest Force also needs strategic placement.
   - *Pray* that the Holy Spirit will direct us in deploying harvest workers to where He wants them to go.
   - *Pray* for wisdom and guidance.

II. LET US PRAY FOR THE HARVEST FIELD (4:35-36.)
A. Jesus told His disciples to "Look at the fields."
   1. He informed them that the harvest was both "plentiful" (Mt 9:37) and "ripe" (Jn 4:35)
   2. Plentiful speaks of its magnitude—ripe of its "readiness."
B. Because the harvest is ripe, the time is urgent.
   - *Pray* for those in the field waiting to hear the gospel.
   - *Pray* for opened minds and receptive hearts.

III. LET US PRAY FOR THE HARVEST YIELD
A. John saw into the future and saw the ultimate yield of God's great end-time harvest. (Read Re 5:9).
   1. He saw great multitude of people "from every tribe and language and people and nation."

        2. God promised Abraham that his seed would number as the "stars in the sky and as the sand on the seashore" (Ge 22:17).
    B. Researchers estimate more than 6,000 unreached people groups in the world.
        1. Each one of these must be represented among the redeemed.
        2. We must move to engage these yet-to-be-reached peoples.
    - *Let us pray* that the church will mobilize itself to reach these unreached people groups.

IV. LET US PRAY AGAINST THE ENEMY OF THE HARVEST
   - *Read Matthew 13:19; 28 and 2 Corinthians 4:4.*
    A. We are in a spiritual battle (Eph 6:12).
        1. The enemy of the harvest is the devil (Mt 13:19, 28).
    B. The enemy opposes the harvest in three ways:
        1. He "snatches away" the effects of the gospel seed (v.19).
        2. He sows weeds (evil doers) among the wheat (Mt 13:25).
        3. He blinds the minds of unbelievers (2Co 4:4).
        4. We must fight spiritual battles with spiritual weapons (2Co10:4).
        5. One of those weapons is prayer (Ep 6:18).
    - *Let us pray* against the enemy of the harvest.

V. LET US PRAY FOR POWER TO REAP THE HARVEST
    A. If the missionary enterprise of the church is to be effective, it must be empowered by the Holy Spirit.
        1. Jesus promised power to witness. (Read Ac 1:8)
        2. We receive the Spirit's power when we are baptized in the Holy Spirit (Ac 2:4).
    B. The power of the Spirit is received and maintained through prayer (Lk 11:9. 13).
        - *Pray* for an outpouring of the Spirit on the church.
        - *Pray,* asking God to fill you with the Spirit and make you one of Christ's last-days harvesters.

Conclusion and Altar Call
Let us now come and be filled with the Spirit and commit ourselves to ongoing prayer for missions.

[UA]

92 Ways to Pray for Missions

Sermon in a Sentence: Let us pray for our missionaries.
Sermon Purpose: That God's people will spend time praying for their missionaries.
Texts: 1 Thessalonians 5:25; 2 Thessalonians 3:1-2
Introduction
1. In our texts, Paul asks the Philippian Christians to pray for him and his missionary companions.
2. In 1Th 5:25, he simply says, "Brothers, pray for us."
3. In 2Th 3:1-2, he makes two prayer requests:
   a. "That the message of the Lord may spread rapidly…"
   b. "That we may be delivered from…evil men"
4. Our missionaries need our financial and prayer support.
5. Today, we will pray for our missionaries in three ways:

I. PRAY THAT GOD WILL CALL LABORERS
- *Pray* for a powerful outpouring of God's Missionary Spirit on our churches, moving Christians to reach out to the lost at home, across Africa, and to the ends of the earth (Ac 1:8).
- *Pray* that the Lord of the Harvest will continue to speak to people about serving as missionaries (Mt 9:38).
- *Pray* for a growing vision and passion in churches to reach the unreached peoples and places of Africa and beyond (Mk 16:15-16; Pr 29:18, KJV).
- *Pray* for God's favor on missionaries as they raise funds to go to the mission field (Phi 4:19).
- *Pray* that Christians will accept their responsibility of supporting their missionaries with their finances and prayer (Phi 4:13-14).
- *Pray* for missions leaders at the local, district, and national levels, asking God to give them wisdom and direction in the decisions they make (Ja 1:5).

II. PRAY FOR MISSIONARY FAMILIES
- *Pray* that God will pour out His Spirit on missionaries, empowering them to minister cross-culturally in evangelism, church planting, pastoral training, and other ways (Ac 4:31).
- *Pray* for new missionaries on the field as they adjust to being away from family, friends, and things familiar.

- *Pray* for missionary children, that they will adjust well to the new culture and feel at home.
- *Pray* for missionary children who return home (or remain at home) while their parents serve on the missionary field.
- *Pray* for missionary parents who at times have to leave their children at home to go to the mission field (Mk 10:19-30).
- *Pray* for God's hand of blessing, care, and protection on the missionaries sent by your national church.

III. PRAY FOR GUIDANCE AND PROTECTION
- *Pray* for a mighty move of the Holy Spirit that will cause millions of people to come to Christ (Ac 2:16-17).
- *Pray* for wisdom and understanding as missionaries deal with unique customs and cultures (Ja 1:5).
- *Pray* for new missionaries that they will quickly learn the language of the people they serve so that they can effectively communicate the message of Christ's love and hope.
- *Pray* for strength and healing among the missionary families who often are exposed to disease (Ja 5:15).
- *Pray* for a hedge of God's protection around missionaries serving in difficult and sensitive places (Ps 34:7; Ps 46:1).
- *Pray* for favor with religious and government agencies so the gospel can be proclaimed and the Church established (1Co 16:9).
- *Pray* for a powerful anointing our missionaries as they preached Word.

Conclusion and Altar Call

We must faithfully support our missionaries with our finances and prayers.

Adapted from "Prayer Guide for Worlds Missions,"
Assemblies of God World Missions, Springfield, MO, USA

93 Praying the Nations Out of Darkness

Sermon in a Sentence: Let us kneel together and pray the nations out of darkness into the light of Christ.

Sermon Purpose: That God's people will spend time in intercessory prayer for the nations.

Text: Isaiah 9:2; 49:6

Introduction
1. Isaiah uttered these prophecies some 700 years before the birth of Christ.
    a. They pointed to a time when those living in darkness would discover the true light.
    b. The prophecies were fulfilled in Jesus (Mt 4:12-17).
    c. Jesus said, "I am the light of the world. Whoever follows me will never walk in darkness, but will have the light of life" (Jn 8:12).
2. As the church (the body of Christ), it is our job to take the light of the gospel to the nations.
3. There are three parts of the body that work together to take the light of Christ to a dark world:
    a. *Feet* that go to preach the gospel.
    b. *Hands* that work and give to support those who go.
    c. *Knees* that kneel and pray for the work of missions .
4. In this prayer session we will kneel before the Lord of the Harvest to pray the nations out of darkness.
5. Today, we will pray five ways:

I. PRAY THAT GOD WILL RAISE UP MEN AND WOMEN TO TAKE THE LIGHT OF THE GOSPEL TO THOSE IN DARKNESS
   A. This was the call of Jesus. (Read Luke 10:1-2)
   B. Let us join in prayer…
   - *Pray* that the Holy Spirit (the Spirit of Missions) will move among the people.
   - *Pray* that many will respond to the call to missions.

II. PRAY THAT THE GOSPEL WILL BE PREACHED TO THE ENDS OF THE EARTH
   A. The nations in darkness cannot save themselves—they need the gospel (Ro 10:13-15).
      1. This is God's plan for the nations (Ac 15:7; Mt 24:14)

B. Let us join in prayer…
- *Pray* that the church will mobilize itself to send missionaries and church planters to evangelize the lost.
- *Pray* for open doors among the lost (Col 4:3).

III. PRAY THAT GOD WILL DIRECT HIS HARVESTERS WHO ARE CARRYING THE LIGHT TO THOSE IN DARKNESS

A. God directed the first missionaries. (Read Acts 16:6-10)
B. Let us join in prayer…
- *Pray* that God will direct harvesters to unreached people groups.
- *Pray* that God will direct harvesters to people in hard-to-reach places.
- *Pray* that God will direct harvesters to the ends of the earth (Is 49:6; Ac 1:8).

IV. PRAY THAT THAT THE NATIONS WILL COME TO THE LIGHT AND BELIEVE IN CHRIST

A. Isaiah prophesied that "nations will come to your light and kings to the brightness of your dawn" (Is 60:3).
B. Let us join in prayer…
- *Pray* that people will gladly receive the gospel of Jesus Christ. (Like the Thessalonians: "You welcomed the message with the joy given by the Holy Spirit" (1Th 1:6b)
- *Pray* that those who receive the gospel will share it with others. (Like the Thessalonians: 1Th 1:7-8)

V. PRAY FOR YOURSELF, THAT GOD WILL USE YOU TO HELP PRAY THE NATIONS OUT OF DARKNESS

A. When Isaiah heard the need, he prayed "Here am I, Lord, send me!" (Read Isaiah 6:8)
B. Let us join in prayer…
- *Pray,* "Lord, use me to go, give, and pray."
- *Pray,* "Hear am I, Lord, send me!"

Conclusion and Altar Call
Come now; commit yourself to be a missionary prayer warrior.

[EG]

94 You Can Be a Prayer Missionary

Sermon in a Sentence: Let us become "prayer missionaries" through our intercessory prayers.

Sermon Purpose: That God's people will spend time together in missional intercessory prayer.

Text: Ephesians 6:18-20

Introduction:
1. In our text, Paul requests prayer from the Ephesian believers.
   a. He asks them to pray for him that he will be able to effectively proclaim Christ even in prison.
   b. In a sense, Paul is asking the Ephesians to join him in his missionary work—to become "prayer missionaries."
2. Without ever leaving home, you can become missionary.
   a. In prayer you can go anywhere in the world.
   b. You can stand by missionaries as they preach the gospel.
   c. You can help push back the darkness in heathen lands.

I. LET US PRAY FOR WORKERS FOR THE HARVEST
This is Jesus' prayer request. (Read Mt 9:35-38)
- *Pray* that the Spirit of Missions will move in the churches calling people to be missionaries and church planters.

II. LET US PRAY FOR OPEN DOORS
Paul asked for prayer for open doors. (Read Col 4:3; see also 1Co 16:9; 2Co 2:12)
- *Pray* that God will open people's hearts to the gospel and that political leaders will allow Christians workers in their countries.

III. LET US PRAY FOR AN OUTPOURING OF THE SPIRIT
God has promised to pour out His Spirit on all people (Ac 2:14-17, 21)
- *Pray* that God's Spirit will be poured out—opening sinners' hearts and empowering Christians as bold witnesses (Ac 1:8).

IV. LET US PRAY FOR BOLD PROCLAMATION
Jesus has commanded that the gospel be preached in all the world (Mk 16:15; Mt 24:14).
- *Pray* that believers will make the most of every opportunity to clearly and boldly proclaim the gospel (Ep 5:16).

V. LET US PRAY AGAINST POWERS AND PRINCIPALITIES
The work of missions involves spiritual warfare (Ep 6:12).
- *Pray,* calling on the Spirit of God to "bind the strong man" (strong demonic powers) holding people in spiritual captivity (Mt 12:28-29).

VI. LET US PRAY FOR A HARVEST OF SOULS
After Pentecost there was a great soul harvest (Ac 2:41).
- *Pray* that many people will come to Jesus, including entire villages, communities, and people groups.

VII. LET US PRAY FOR THE CARE AND SAFETY OF OUR MISSIONARIES
Missionaries need financial, spiritual, and emotional support (1Co 9:7).
- *Pray* for our missionaries that they will be safe, and that God will meet all of their needs (Phi 4:19).
- *Pray* for yourself, asking God to show you what you can do to help the missionaries.

VIII. LET US PRAY FOR THE EMERGING CHURCH
The goal of missions is to plant strong local and national churches (Mt 16:18).
- *Pray* that God will pour out His Spirit on the church and that it will emerge as a strong, Spirit-empowered, missionary church.

IX. LET US PRAY FOR GODLY, GIFTED LEADERS
Jesus knew the importance of developing leaders (Lk 6:12-13).
- *Pray* that God will raise up godly, spiritual, servant leaders to lead the churches.

X. LET US PRAY IN THE SPIRIT
Paul urges us to "pray in the Spirit" (Ep 6:18).
- *Allow* the Holy Spirit to pray through you for things you otherwise would have otherwise prayed for (Ro 6:26-27).

Conclusion and Altar Call
Come and commit yourself to being an Intercessory Prayer Missionary.

[DRM]

95 Praying with Jesus for Believers

Sermon in a Sentence: As leaders, let us use Jesus' "High Priestly Prayer" to guide our prayers for our people.

Sermon Purpose: That pastors and other spiritual leaders will follow Jesus' example as they pray for their people.

Text: John 17:1-26 (Read the entire chapter.)

Introduction:
1. Our text is Jesus' final prayer for believers.
2. It has been called Jesus' "High Priestly Prayer."
3. It shows our Lord's deepest longings for His followers.
4. It is also a Spirit-inspired example of how spiritual leaders should pray for their people.
5. In praying for those under our care, we would do will to imitate Jesus by praying for the following eight items:

I. PRAY THAT THEY MAY COME TO KNOW JESUS CHRIST INTIMATELY (Read vv.2-3)
A. Jesus prayed that His followers may know God (17:3).
   1. Earlier, Jesus had spoken of that intimacy (Jn 15:9-13)
   2. We know Christ by knowing His word (17:17) and by living in the Spirit (Jn 16:13-15).
- *Let us pray* that God's people will come to know Christ better by reading the Word and walking in the Spirit.

II. PRAY THAT GOD MAY KEEP THEM SAFE (vv.11-12)
A. All of God's children face at least four spiritual threats:
   1. Becoming conformed to the world (v.11; Ro 12:2).
   2. Attacks from Satan (v.15; 1Pe 5:8).
   3. Yielding to false teaching (vv.14, 17; Ac 20:29)
   4. Falling away from Christ (v.12)
- *Let us pray* that God will keep His people safe from these four spiritual threats.

III. PRAY THAT THEY MAY CONSTANTLY POSSESS THE FULL JOY OF CHRIST (v.13)
A. God wants His people to live joy-filled lives (v.13).
   1. Joy is hallmark of the Christian walk.
   2. With joy comes strength for the journey (Ne 8:19).
- *Let us pray* that God will flood His people with the joy of the Holy Spirit (Ac 13:52; Ro 14:17).

IV. PRAY THAT THEY MAY BE HOLY (v.17)
   A. We are called to walk as Jesus walked (1Jn 2:6).
      1. Jesus was holy in thought, deed, and character (1Pe:2:22).
      2. Jesus prayed that God would sanctify His people (v.17).
   - *Let us pray* that God's people will walk in holiness.

V. PRAY THAT THEY MAY BE ONE IN FELLOWSHIP AND PURPOSE
   A. Such unity of purpose is exemplified by Jesus and His relationship with the Father (vv.11, 21-22).
      1. The Father and Son walk in complete harmony.
      2. Jesus prayed for His church to be the same (vv.21-23).
      3. Such unity will enable us to accomplish God's mission.
   - *Let us pray* that the church will be unified in fellowship, purpose, and mission.

VI. PRAY THAT THEY MAY LEAD OTHERS TO CHRIST
(Read vv.21, 23 noting "that the world may believe...know")
   A. God's people are to live as witnesses (Lk 24:46-48; Ac 1:8).
      1. They are to shine as lights in a dark world (Phi 2:15).
      2. Our unity will serve as a witness to the world (v.23).
   - *Let us pray* that Christians will be witnesses for Christ and lead others to Him.

VII. PRAY THAT THEY MAY CONSTANTLY LIVE IN GOD'S LOVE AND PRESENCE (v.26)
   A. Christ has promised to be with us and in us—and to make God known to us (v.26; Mt 28:20)
   - *Let us pray* that God's people will live in God's presence.

VIII. PRAY THAT THEY MAY PERSEVERE IN THE FAITH AND FINALLY BE WITH CHRIST IN HEAVEN (v.24)
   A. God wants His people to make it all the way to heaven.
      1. Jesus prayed that we would be with Him in heaven to witness His eternal glory (v.24).
   - *Let us pray* that God people will remain faithful to the end, and will finally be with Christ in heaven (Mt 10:22).

[DCS]

Adapted from the author's notes on John 17:1 in the
Full Life Study Bible, Zondervan, 1990

96 A Prayer Guide for New Church Plants

Sermon in a Sentence: Let us use the description of the church in Acts 2:38-47 to guide us as we pray for new church plants.

Sermon Purpose: That Christians join together and pray biblically and effectively for new church plants.

Text: Acts 2:38-47

Introduction
1. Our text paints a picture of the Church that emerged after the outpouring of the Spirit at Pentecost.
2. This emerging church can serve as a model for the kind of new churches we want to plant and nurture.
3. It can also guide us in praying for these new churches.
4. Ten ways we can effectively pray for a new church plant:

I. PRAY FOR THE SPIRITUAL EXPERIENCE OF THE NEW BELIEVERS
- *Read* vv.38-39: "Repent and be baptized, every one of you... And you will receive the gift of the Holy Spirit."
- *Pray* that the people in the new church will be genuinely saved and empowered by the Holy Spirit (cf. Jn 3:3-5; Ac 1:8).

II. PRAY THAT THE NEW CHRISTIANS WILL BEGIN TO WALK IN HOLINESS OF LIFE
- *Read* v.40: "Save yourselves from this corrupt generation."
- *Pray* that believers will live God-honoring lives (1Th 4:1-7).

III. PRAY THAT THE NEW CHURCH WILL BECOME A POWERFUL WITNESS IN THEIR COMMUNITY
- *Read* v.41 "About 3,000 were added to their number..."
- *Pray* that Christians will witness with boldness (Ep 6:19).

IV. PRAY THAT THE NEW CONVERTS WILL BECOME TRUE DISCIPLES OF CHRIST
- *Read* v.42: "They devoted themselves to the apostles' teaching."
- *Pray* that new Christians will commit themselves fully to Christ and His work (Mt.16:24).

V. PRAY THAT THERE WILL BE A POWERFUL PRESENCE OF THE HOLY SPIRIT WHEN THE CHURCH GATHERS

- *Read* v.43: "Everyone was filled with awe, and many wonders and miraculous signs were done by the apostles."
- *Pray* that the new believers will experience the transforming presence of God in their church services (Ac 2:2; 4:31).

VI. PRAY THAT CHURCH MEMBERS WILL GENUINELY LOVE AND CARE FOR ONE ANOTHER
- *Read* vv.44, 46: "All the believers were together and had everything in common… They broke bread…together…"
- *Pray* that God will pour out His Spirit of love on the people in the new church (Ro 5:5).

VII. PRAY THAT THE NEW CHRISTIANS WILL BECOME GENEROUS IN THEIR GIVING TO GOD'S WORK
- *Read* v.45: "…they gave to anyone as he had need."
- *Pray* that the people will begin to tithe and give generously to the work of God and to people in need (2Co 9:6-8).

VIII. PRAY THAT THE NEW BELIEVERS WILL FAITHFULLY ATTEND CHURCH MEETINGS
- *Read* v.46: "…they continued to meet together in the temple"
- *Pray* that the people will be faithful in attendance (He 10:25).

IX. PRAY THAT THE CHURCH WILL ATTAIN A GOOD NAME IN THE COMMUNITY
- *Read* v.47a: "…enjoying the favor of all the people"
- *Pray* that the people will live in such a way that they will be spoken well of in their community (Pr 3:3-4).

X. PRAY THAT THE CHURCH WILL GROW
- *Read* v.47b: "And the Lord added to their number daily…"
- *Pray* that the church will prosper, grow, and become strong (Ac 11:21).

[DRM]

97 Acts 1:8 Conference Prayer Guide: Day 1
"Empower Us Today" and "Save the World's Least-reached"

Sermon in a Sentence: We must invite God's Spirit to empower us and send us to the world's least-reached peoples.

Sermon Purpose: To lead the church in prayer for the Spirit's empowerment and for the least-reached peoples of the world.

Introduction
1. This prayer guide has been adapted from the booklet, "Acts 1:8 Conference Prayer Guide," which has been used in conferences across Africa.
2. In this prayer session we will ask God to send His Spirit upon this conference.
3. We will also intercede for the world's least-reached peoples.

I. **PART 1: PRAYER FOR THE SPIRIT: "OH LORD, EMPOWER US TODAY"**
   A. Introducing this session:
      1. The purpose of this prayer session is to intercede to God for this conference.
      2. Our prayer is that the Holy Spirit will come upon us in power during our days together.
   B. Prayer points:
      - Lord, Send your Holy Spirit to anoint our *Prayer Sessions*.
      - Lord, Send your Holy Spirit to enlighten our *Teaching Sessions*.
      - Lord, Send your Holy Spirit to guide our *Strategy Sessions*.
      - Lord, Send your Holy Spirit to empower our evening *Holy Spirit Services*.
      - Lord, Send your Holy Spirit to bless our *Commitment and Covenant Signing Service*.
      - Lord, Send your Holy Spirit on the *Churches* of our city and country this coming Sunday.

II. **PART 2: PRAYER FOR THE NATIONS: "O LORD, SAVE THE WORLD'S LEAST-REACHED"**
   A. Introducing this session:
      1. In our times of prayer for the nations, we will cry out to God to save the lost, and we will offer ourselves to God to reach them.

2. According to the Joshua Project, there are 3.1 billion unreached people in the world today, comprising 7,087 people groups. (July 2018)
3. In this session, we will intercede for the world's least-reached peoples.

B. Prayer Points:
- O Lord, save the world's least-reached peoples.
- O Lord, create in our hearts an awareness of those who are least-reached with the gospel.
- O Lord, create in our hearts a deep burden for these lost ones for whom you died.
- O Lord, give us the wisdom and courage we need to reach out to these least-reached people.
- O Lord, fill us with your Spirit, and move us into action to do something about their plight.
- O Lord, send laborers from our midst to the least-reached peoples of the world.

You can download the booklet, "Acts 1:8 Conference Prayer Guide" for free at the following link: http://www.decadeofpentecost.org/wp-content/uploads/2015/08/A18-Conference-Prayer-Booklet.pdf

98 Acts 1:8 Conference Prayer Guide: Day 2
"Empower Our Churches" and "Save the Unreached Tribes of Africa"

Sermon in a Sentence: We must invite God's Spirit to empower our churches and send us to Africa's unreached tribes.

Sermon Purpose: To lead the church in prayer for the Spirit's empowerment and for Africa's unreached tribes.

Introduction
1. This prayer guide has been adapted from the booklet, "Acts 1:8 Conference Prayer Guide" which has been used in conferences across Africa.
2. In this prayer session we will ask God to empower our churches
3. We will also intercede for the unreached tribes of Africa.

I. PART 1: PRAYER FOR THE SPIRIT: "OH, LORD, EMPOWER OUR CHURCHES"

A. Introducing this session:
   1. There is a great need for our churches to be truly Pentecostal.
   2. And yet, our records tell us that only a small percentage of our people are Spirit-baptized. Of our more than 22 million Africa Assemblies of God adherents, only about 5 million have been baptized in the Holy Spirit.
   3. We must have a new Pentecostal outpouring in our churches with millions of our members being baptized in the Holy Spirit.
   4. The purpose of this session is to intercede for such an outpouring on our churches.

B. Prayer Points:
   - Lord, pour out your Spirit on the Assemblies of God churches of in Africa.
   - Lord, pour out your Spirit on my national church.
   - Lord, pour out your Spirit on the church(es) under my leadership.
   - Lord, pour out your Spirit on my local church.
   - Lord, pour out your Spirit on me, so that I may help lead the church into Pentecostal revival.

II. PART 2: PRAYER FOR THE NATIONS: "O LORD, SAVE THE UNREACHED TRIBES OF AFRICA"
A. Introducing this session:
   1. According to the Joshua Project, there remain 853 tribes in Sub-Saharan Africa that do not have an adequate witness of the gospel. (July 2018)
   2. Of that number…
      a. 350 are located in East and Southern Africa, amounting to 83 million people.
      b. 503 are located in West and Central Africa, amounting to 168 million people.
   3. Many live in our own country.
   4. In this session, we will intercede for these unreached tribes.
B. Prayer points:
   - O Lord, save the unreached tribes of Africa.
   - O Lord, open our eyes to the lost tribes of Africa that are in our own country and region.
   - O Lord, help us to realize our responsibility to reach out to these neglected tribes with the gospel of Jesus Christ.
   - O Lord, create in our hearts a burden to reach these lost peoples.
   - O Lord, give us the wisdom to know what we must do to reach them.
   - O Lord, fill us again with your Spirit, and move us into action to reach these lost tribes.

You can download the booklet, "Acts 1:8 Conference Prayer Guide" for free at the following link: http://www.decadeofpentecost.org/wp-content/uploads/2015/08/A18-Conference-Prayer-Booklet.pdf

99 Acts 1:8 Conference Prayer Guide: Day 3
"Empower Our Pastors" and "Save the World of Islam"

Sermon in a Sentence: We must call on God's Spirit to empower our pastors and lay leaders and to save the world of Islam.

Sermon Purpose: To lead the church in prayer for their pastors and leaders and for the world of Islam.

Introduction
1. This prayer guide has been adapted from the booklet, "Acts 1:8 Conference Prayer Guide" which has been used in conferences across Africa.
2. In this prayer session we will ask God to empower our pastors and lay leaders.
3. We will also intercede for the world of Islam.

I. PART 1: PRAYER FOR THE SPIRIT: "OH LORD, EMPOWER OUR PASTORS AND LAY LEADERS"

A. Introducing this session:
 1. Our pastors and lay leaders are the key to seeing our people filled with the Spirit and the church mobilized for effective evangelism and missions.
 2. The purpose of this session is to intercede for these men and women that they will themselves be filled and refilled with the Spirit, and that they will become powerful proclaimers of Pentecost.

B. Prayer points:
- Lord, empower the pastors in my area of responsibility.
    a. Fill them again with Your Holy Spirit.
    b. Empower them to preach Your gospel to the lost.
    c. Empower them to lead their churches in to Pentecostal experience and practice.
    d. Empower them to lead their churches into powerful missions involvement.
    e. Lord, fill me and use me to lead in this effort.
- Lord, empower the pastors in my area of responsibility.
    a. Fill them again with Your Holy Spirit.
    b. Empower them to preach Your gospel to the lost.
    c. Empower them to lead their churches into Pentecostal experience and practice.
    d Empower them to lead their churches into powerful missions involvement.

e. Lord, fill me and use me to lead in this effort.
- Lord, empower the lay leaders in our churches.
  a. Fill them again with Your Holy Spirit.
  b. Empower them to preach Your gospel to the lost.
  c. Empower them to lead their churches in to Pentecostal experience and practice.
  d. Empower them to lead their churches into powerful missions involvement.

II. PART 2: PRAYER FOR THE NATIONS: "O LORD, SAVE THE WORLD OF ISLAM"

A. Introducing this session:
  1. The world of Islam is perhaps the church's greatest missionary challenge.
  2. Today, there are about 1.8 billion Muslims in the world who desperately need the gospel of Jesus Christ.
  3. In this session, we will intercede for the world of Islam.

B. Prayer points:
- O Lord, save the world of Islam.
- O Lord, give us wisdom and understanding as to how we may best reach them.
- O Lord, fill us with your Spirit and move us into action to Islam.
- O Lord, help us to realize our responsibility before God to reach out to Muslims with the gospel.
- O Lord, put a burden in our heart for these Muslims in our midst.
- O Lord, fill us with your Spirit and move us into action to reach Muslims with the gospel.
- O Lord, send out labors from our midst to the world of Islam.

You can download the booklet, "Acts 1:8 Conference Prayer Guide" for free at the following link: http://www.decadeofpentecost.org/wp-content/uploads/2015/08/A18-Conference-Prayer-Booklet.pdf

100 Acts 1:8 Conference Prayer Guide: Day 4
"Empower Our Bible Schools" and "Empower Our Young People"

Sermon in a Sentence: We must call on God's Spirit to empower our Bible schools and our young people. We must also offer ourselves as missionaries to the nations.

Sermon Purpose: To lead the church in prayer for our Bible schools and our youth, and to commit ourselves to reach the nations.

Introduction
1. This prayer guide has been adapted from the booklet, "Acts 1:8 Conference Prayer Guide" which has been used in conferences across Africa.
2. In this prayer session we will pray for our Bible schools and young people. We will also commit ourselves to reaching the unreached peoples of Africa and beyond.

I. **PART 1: PRAYER FOR THE SPIRIT: "EMPOWER OUR BIBLE SCHOOLS AND OUR YOUNG PEOPLES"**
   A. Introducing this session:
      1. Our Bible schools hold the key to the future of our movement.
         a. In order to produce truly Spirit-empowered missional leaders they must each experience Pentecostal revival.
      2. Also, should Jesus tarry His coming, our youth will soon lead our churches.
         a. They will be our pastors and church leaders.
         b. If they are not filled with the Spirit now, the future of our church is in peril.
         c. However, if they are powerfully filled with the Spirit, and properly discipled, our future is bright.
      3. The purpose of this session is to intercede for our Bible schools that God will powerfully pour out if His Spirit on each one of them
      4. We will also pray that a powerful Pentecostal revival will sweep across the children and youth of our Assemblies of God churches in Africa.
   B. Prayer points:
      • Pray for out Bible schools:
         a. Lord, pour out your Spirit on our Bible Schools.

-
    - b. Lord, fill and empower our Bible School administrators and teachers. (Mention as many administrators and teachers as you know by name.)
    - c. Lord, fill and empower our Bible School students. (Mention those students you know by name.)
    - d. Lord, pour out your Spirit in our schools' chapel services and spiritual emphases.
  - Pray for our young people:
    - a. Lord, send Pentecostal revival to the children and youth of Africa.
    - b. Lord, pour out your Spirit and empower the children and youth of our Assemblies of God churches. (Mention by name as many children and youth as you can remember.)
    - c. Lord, empower and direct the children's and youth leaders of our churches. (Mention by name those youth leaders whom you know.)

II. PART 2: PRAYER FOR THE NATIONS: "O LORD, SEND US!"

A. Introducing this session:
1. In previous sessions we have interceded for the unreached peoples of the world, including the unreached tribes of Africa and the world of Islam.
2. In this session we will offer ourselves to God as His ambassadors to these peoples.
3. And we will ask Him to empower us for the task.

b. Prayer Points:
- O Lord, send us to preach the gospel to the nations!
- O Lord, burden our churches and church leaders for missions.
- O Lord, give us the wisdom and grace we need to lead our churches into missions involvement.
- O Lord, empower me by your Spirit and send me!

You can download the booklet, "Acts 1:8 Conference Prayer Guide" for free at the following link: http://www.decadeofpentecost.org/wp-content/uploads/2015/08/A18-Conference-Prayer-Booklet.pdf

Scripture Text Index

Scripture Text	Sermon Number
Genesis 18:20-33	88
Exodus 3:1-4	15
Exodus 4:1-4	15
Exodus 17:8-13	18, 64, 95
Nehemiah 1:1-4	18
Nehemiah 1:3-4	34
1 Samuel 1:1-28	21
1 Samuel 12:23	6
1Kings 18:20-40	41
2 Chronicles 7:14	7, 8, 14
Psalm 51:10-13	73
Psalm 67:1-7	85
Psalm 68:28	90
Psalm 68:31-35	90
Isaiah 9:2	93
Isaiah 49:6	93
Isaiah 59:16	34
Isaiah 62:6-7	18, 34
Jeremiah 32:17	19
Ezekiel 22:29-31	18, 34, 40
Daniel 9:1-7; 16-19	10
Matthew 6:5-15	2
Matthew 6:9-13	1, 9

Matthew 6:10	5, 13
Matthew 6:16-18	3
Matthew 9:35-38	71, 74. 86, 87, 91
Matthew 24:14	78
Matthew 28:18-20	72
Mark 10:46-52	26
Mark 11:15-17	70
Mark 11:22-24	20
Luke 1:37	19
Luke 3:21-22	77
Luke 4:1-2	77
Luke 5:15-16	33
Luke 6:27-36	84
Luke 10:1-2	87
Luke 11:1-13	4, 36, 57
Luke 11:9-13	50, 51, 55
Luke 18:1-8	32, 76
Luke 24:53	51
John 15:4-5	11
John 17:1-26	66
John 17:9-24	63
Acts 1:8	58
Acts 1:12-14	51
Acts 1:14	37, 62
Acts 2:38-47	96
Acts 2:42	30, 37
Acts 4:8-12	61
Acts 4:23-33	17, 23, 25, 31, 52, 61, 65
Acts 4:24	62
Acts 4:29-31	60
Acts 4:29-33	69

Acts 4:31	62, 80, 82
Acts 6:1-4	33
Acts 6:1-7	44
Acts 6:4	37
Acts 10:1-2	79
Acts 10:9	79
Acts 12:1-5	27
Acts 12:4-17	24
Acts 13:1-4	44, 53, 80, 83
Acts 16:6-10	44
Romans 1:9-10	45
Romans 8:18-27	54
Romans 8:26-27	42, 55
Romans 10:13-15	89
Romans 15:30-32	81
1 Corinthians 14:14	42
1 Corinthians 14:18	56
Galatians 3:14	50
Ephesians 1:15-16	45
Ephesians 1:15-23	67
Ephesians 3:14-21	68
Ephesians 6:10-20	48, 49, 59
Ephesians 6:18-20	43, 94
Colossians 4:12	39
1 Thessalonians 5:25	92
2 Thessalonians 3:1-2	92
1 Timothy 2:1-3	47
1 Timothy 2:1-7	29
1 Timothy 2:8	12, 47

Hebrews 11:32-35	35
James 1:6-7	38
James 4:3	38
James 5:13-16	38, 75
James 5:17-18	28, 41
Jude 20-21	42
Revelation 22:17-20	16

Other Decade of Pentecost Books
~ Available from the Acts in Africa Initiative ~

Other Sermon Outline Books

Proclaiming Pentecost: 100 Sermon Outlines on the Power of the Holy Spirit (2011) (Available in French, Spanish, Portuguese, Swahili, Mooré, Kirundi, Chichewa, and Amharic)

Proclaiming Christ to the Nations: 100 Sermon Outlines of Spirit-Empowered Mission (2017)

Power Ministry: How to Minister in the Spirit's Power (2004) (also available in French, Portuguese, Malagasy, Kinyarwanda, and Chichewa)

Empowered for Global Mission: A Missionary Look at the Book of Acts (2005)

From Azusa to Africa to the Nations (2005) (also available in French, Spanish, and Portuguese)

Acts: The Spirit of God in Mission (2007)

In Step with the Spirit: Studies in the Spirit-filled Walk (2008)

The Kingdom and the Power: The Kingdom of God: A Pentecostal Interpretation (2009)

Experiencing the Spirit: A Study of the Work of the Spirit in the Life of the Believer (2009)

Teaching in the Spirit (2009)

Power Encounter: Ministering in the Power and Anointing of the Holy Spirit: Revised (2009) (also available in Kiswahili)

You Can Minister in God's Power: A Guide for Spirit-filled Disciples (2009)

The Spirit of God in Mission: A Vocational Commentary on the Book of Acts (2011)

Globalizing Pentecostal Missions in Africa (2011)

The 1:8 Promise of Jesus: The Secret of World Harvest (2012)

Walking with the Apostles: Forty-five Days in the Book of Acts (2016)

Walking with the Holy Spirit: Thirty Days of Spiritual Discovery (2017)

How to Live for God: A Guide for New Christians (2018)

All of the above books are available from AIA Publications
580A Central Street, Springfield, MO, 65802, USA
E-mail: ActsinAfrica@agmd.org

www.ingramcontent.com/pod-product-compliance
Lightning Source LLC
Chambersburg PA
CBHW061637040426
42446CB00010B/1459